Functional Kotlin

Extend your OOP skills and implement Functional
techniques in Kotlin and Arrow

Mario Arias
Rivu Chakraborty

BIRMINGHAM - MUMBAI

Functional Kotlin

Commissioning Editor: Aaron Lazar
Acquisition Editor: Sandeep Mishra
Content Development Editor: Zeeyan Pinheiro
Technical Editor: Ruvika Rao
Copy Editor: Safis Editing
Project Coordinator: Vaidehi Sawant
Proofreader: Safis Editing
Indexer: Tejas Daruwale Soni
Graphics: Jason Monteiro
Production Coordinator: Arvindkumar Gupta

First published: February 2018

Production reference: 1220218

Published by Packt Publishing Ltd.
Livery Place
35 Livery Street
Birmingham
B3 2PB, UK.

ISBN 978-1-78847-648-5

www.packtpub.com

To my parents; my wife, Esha; and our newborn son, Rishaan.

– Rivu Chakraborty

To Ari, see you soon, and to my Dad, see you in heaven.

– Mario Arias

`mapt.io`

Mapt is an online digital library that gives you full access to over 5,000 books and videos, as well as industry leading tools to help you plan your personal development and advance your career. For more information, please visit our website.

Why subscribe?

- Spend less time learning and more time coding with practical eBooks and Videos from over 4,000 industry professionals

- Improve your learning with Skill Plans built especially for you

- Get a free eBook or video every month

- Mapt is fully searchable

- Copy and paste, print, and bookmark content

PacktPub.com

Did you know that Packt offers eBook versions of every book published, with PDF and ePub files available? You can upgrade to the eBook version at `www.PacktPub.com` and as a print book customer, you are entitled to a discount on the eBook copy. Get in touch with us at `service@packtpub.com` for more details.

At `www.PacktPub.com`, you can also read a collection of free technical articles, sign up for a range of free newsletters, and receive exclusive discounts and offers on Packt books and eBooks.

Contributors

About the authors

Mario Arias is a software engineer and Spring certified instructor with more than 12 years of experience in software development and design, databases, training material design, and training delivery. He currently works as a software engineer in Manchester, UK, for Cake Solutions Ltd., a BAMTECH media company.

Mario is well-known member of the Kotlin community and is part of the Arrow team, the group that developed and maintains the Arrow functional library. In his free time, he rides his bicycle and trains Brazilian Jiu-Jitsu.

My first and the most important acknowledgement is to my Lord and Saviour, Jesus Christ.

Thanks to my soon-to-be wife, Ari, for her continuous support and patience. To my family and friends. Thanks to the JetBrains team for creating a fantastic language, my teammates at Arrow, to my co-author, Rivu Chakraborty, and the entire team at Packt.

Rivu Chakraborty is a Caster.io instructor, Google Certified Android Developer, and senior tech member of Institute of Engineers (India). With more than 5 years of experience, he is currently working as a senior software engineer (Android) at Indus Net Technologies Pvt. Ltd.

Rivu is a Kotlin and Android enthusiast and a Kotlin evangelist. He has been using Kotlin for more than 2 years. Rivu is the founder organizer of Kotlin Kolkata UG. He is also a core organizing team member of GDG Kolkata. Rivu has previously authored, *Reactive Programming in Kotlin*, and is working on two more books on Kotlin.

Thanks to my parents; my wife, Esha; and my son, Rishaan; for having my back and trusting me. Thanks to the Kotlin Kolkata community for inspiring me to write books and sharing my knowledge. Thanks to the reviewers of this book for their valuable feedback and inputs.

Thanks a lot to my co-author, Mario Arias, for writing this book with me. I've learned a lot from him.

About the reviewer

Ganesh Samarthyam is a co-founder of CodeOps Technologies, a software technology, consultancy, and training company based in Bangalore. He has 16 years of experience in the IT industry, and his latest book, *Refactoring for Software Design Smells: Managing Technical Debt* by Morgan Kaufmann/Elsevier, has been translated to languages like Korean and Chinese. Ganesh loves exploring anything and everything about technology in his free time.

Packt is searching for authors like you

If you're interested in becoming an author for Packt, please visit `authors.packtpub.com` and apply today. We have worked with thousands of developers and tech professionals, just like you, to help them share their insight with the global tech community. You can make a general application, apply for a specific hot topic that we are recruiting an author for, or submit your own idea.

Table of Contents

Preface

With Google's announcement at the I/O Conference in 2017 to make Kotlin an official language for Android, Kotlin has been gaining popularity among developers around the world.

However, Kotlin's use and popularity aren't limited to the Android community. Many other communities, such as the desktop, web, and backend community are embracing Kotlin too. Many new libraries and frameworks are being created and existing ones are providing support for Kotlin.

With more developers coming to the Kotlin community and with its natural flexibility, more programming styles are being tried. The purpose of this book is to introduce the functional programming style to the wide Kotlin community, leading and guiding on the first steps, and giving the basic tools to progress further to more advanced concepts.

Who this book is for

This book is for Kotlin users (programmers, engineers, library authors, and architects) who have a basic understanding of Kotlin and want to understand the basics ideas behind functional programming and how to use it in a practical way (if you're entirely new to Kotlin, our Appendix, *Kotlin's Quick Start* will give you a quick start with the language).

What this book covers

Chapter 1, *Kotlin - Data Types, Objects, and Classes*, introduces you to object-oriented programming in Kotlin. Kotlin is primary object-oriented programming, and we'll use these features to introduce a functional programming style.

Chapter 2, *Getting Started with Functional Programming*, covers the basic principles of functional programming using Kotlin's object-oriented programming features.

Chapter 3, *Immutability - It's Important*, emphasizes on immutability as one of the most important concepts in functional programming. This chapter will give you an in-depth understanding of immutability.

Chapter 4, *Functions, Function Types, and Side Effects*, introduces you to the basic functional programming concepts around functions, pure functions, and various function types and side effects.

Chapter 5, *More on Functions*, talks about Kotlin's features for functional programming such as extension functions, operator overloading, DSLs, and corecursion.

Chapter 6, *Delegates in Kotlin*, covers how Kotlin has language-level support for delegates. Though delegates are a object-oriented programming concept, they can be helpful in making your code more modular.

Chapter 7, *Asynchronous Programming with Coroutines*, gives you an introduction to asynchronous programming in Kotlin, comparing different styles against coroutines.

Chapter 8, *Collections and Data Operations in Kotlin*, covers the enhanced collections API by Kotlin and the functional interfaces that Kotlin's collections framework has to offer.

Chapter 9, *Functional Programming and Reactive Programming*, shows how functional programming can be combined with other programming paradigms to get the best out of them. This chapter discusses how you can combine functional programming with object-oriented programming and reactive programming.

Chapter 10, *Functors, Applicatives and Monads*, gives you an introduction to typed functional programming and its basic concepts. It also talks about how to implement it in Kotlin.

Chapter 11, *Working with Streams in Kotlin*, gets you introduced to the Streams API in Kotlin.

Chapter 12, *Getting Started with Arrow*, covers how to use Arrow and its extensions for functional programming, function composition, currying, partial application, memoization, and optics.

Chapter 13, *Arrow Types*, helps you understand Arrow data types such as Option, Either, Try, and State and its type classes, functors, and monads.

Appendix, *Kotlin's Quick Start*, it provides everything that you need to start writing a Kotlin code, such as tools, basic syntax constructs and other resources to help you progress in your Kotlin journey.

To get the most out of this book

The only recommended software to run and write Kotlin programs is IntelliJ IDEA (there are other ways to do it, and we cover them in the `Appendix`, *Kotlin's Quick Start*).

You can download IntelliJ IDEA from `https://www.jetbrains.com/idea/download/`.

You can install IntelliJ IDEA on Windows, Mac, and Linux:

- **For Windows**: You can use any Windows version from XP to 10. To install it on Windows, run the installer executable and follow the instructions.
- **For Mac**: You can use any macOS version starting from 10.8. To install it on macOS, mount the disk image file and copy *IntelliJ IDEA.app60* to your *Application* folder.
- **For Linux**: You can use any GNOME or KDE desktop. To install it Linux unpack the *tar.gz* file using the *tar -xzf idea-*.tar.gz* command and run the *idea.sh* from the *bin* subdirectory.

Download the example code files

You can download the example code files for this book from your account at `www.packtpub.com`. If you purchased this book elsewhere, you can visit `www.packtpub.com/support` and register to have the files emailed directly to you.

You can download the code files by following these steps:

1. Log in or register at `www.packtpub.com`.
2. Select the **SUPPORT** tab.
3. Click on **Code Downloads & Errata**.
4. Enter the name of the book in the **Search** box and follow the onscreen instructions.

Once the file is downloaded, please make sure that you unzip or extract the folder using the latest version of:

- WinRAR/7-Zip for Windows
- Zipeg/iZip/UnRarX for Mac
- 7-Zip/PeaZip for Linux

The code bundle for the book is also hosted on GitHub at `https://github.com/PacktPublishing/Functional-Kotlin`. In case there's an update to the code, it will be updated on the existing GitHub repository.

We also have other code bundles from our rich catalog of books and videos available at `https://github.com/PacktPublishing/`. Check them out!

Download the color images

We also provide a PDF file that has color images of the screenshots/diagrams used in this book. You can download it here: `https://www.packtpub.com/sites/default/files/downloads/FunctionalKotlin_ColorImages.pdf` .

Conventions used

There are a number of text conventions used throughout this book.

`CodeInText`: Indicates code words in text, database table names, folder names, filenames, file extensions, pathnames, dummy URLs, user input, and Twitter handles. Here is an example: "We introduced a new `BakeryGood` class, with the shared behavior and state of both `Cupcake` and `Biscuit` classes and we made both classes extend `BakeryGood`."

A block of code is set as follows:

```
open class BakeryGood(val flavour: String) {
  fun eat(): String {
    return "nom, nom, nom... delicious $flavour bakery good"
  }
}

class Cupcake(flavour: String): BakeryGood(flavour)
class Biscuit(flavour: String): BakeryGood(flavour)
```

When we wish to draw your attention to a particular part of a code block, the relevant lines or items are set in bold:

```
fun main(args: Array<String>) {
    val emptyList1 = listOf<Any>()
    val emptyList2 = emptyList<Any>()
    println("emptyList1.size = ${emptyList1.size}")
    println("emptyList2.size = ${emptyList2.size}")
}
```

Any command-line input or output is written as follows:

```
$ kotlin HelloKt
```

Bold: Indicates a new term, an important word, or words that you see onscreen. For example, words in menus or dialog boxes appear in the text like this. Here is an example: "A dialog will appear that will ask whether you want to open it as a file or as a project. Click on **Open As Project**"

Warnings or important notes appear like this.

Tips and tricks appear like this.

Get in touch

Feedback from our readers is always welcome.

General feedback: Email `feedback@packtpub.com` and mention the book title in the subject of your message. If you have questions about any aspect of this book, please email us at `questions@packtpub.com`.

Errata: Although we have taken every care to ensure the accuracy of our content, mistakes do happen. If you have found a mistake in this book, we would be grateful if you would report this to us. Please visit `www.packtpub.com/submit-errata`, selecting your book, clicking on the Errata Submission Form link, and entering the details.

Piracy: If you come across any illegal copies of our works in any form on the Internet, we would be grateful if you would provide us with the location address or website name. Please contact us at `copyright@packtpub.com` with a link to the material.

If you are interested in becoming an author: If there is a topic that you have expertise in and you are interested in either writing or contributing to a book, please visit `authors.packtpub.com`.

Reviews

Please leave a review. Once you have read and used this book, why not leave a review on the site that you purchased it from? Potential readers can then see and use your unbiased opinion to make purchase decisions, we at Packt can understand what you think about our products, and our authors can see your feedback on their book. Thank you!

For more information about Packt, please visit packtpub.com

1
Kotlin – Data Types, Objects, and Classes

In this chapter, we'll cover Kotlin's type system, **object-oriented programming** (**OOP**) with Kotlin, modifiers, destructuring declarations, and more.

Kotlin is, primarily, an OOP language with some functional features. When we use OOP languages to resolve problems, we try to model the objects that are a part of our problem in an abstract way with the information that is relevant to the problem.

If we're designing an HR module for our company, we'll model employees with state or data (name, date of birth, social security number, and others) and behavior (pay salary, transfer to another division, and others). Because a person can be very complex, there is information that isn't relevant for our problem or domain. For example, the employee's favorite style of bicycle isn't relevant for our HR system, but it is very relevant for an online cycling shop.

Once we identify the objects (with data and behavior) and the relationship with other objects of our domain, we can start developing and writing the code that we'll make a part of our software solution. We'll use language constructs (construct is a fancy way to say allowed syntax) to write the objects, categories, relationships, and so on.

Kotlin has many constructs that we can use to write our programs and, in this chapter, we'll cover many of those constructs, such as:

- Classes
- Inheritance
- Abstract classes

- Interfaces
- Objects
- Generics
- Type alias
- Null types
- Kotlin's type system
- Other types

Classes

Classes are the foundational type in Kotlin. In Kotlin, a class is a template that provides a state, a behavior, and a type to instances (more on that later).

To define a class, only a name is required:

```
class VeryBasic
```

VeryBasic is not very useful, but is still a valid Kotlin syntax.

The VeryBasic class doesn't have any state or behavior; nonetheless, you can declare values of type VeryBasic, as shown in the following code:

```
fun main(args: Array<String>) {
    val basic: VeryBasic = VeryBasic()
}
```

As you can see, the basic value has a VeryBasic type. To express it differently, basic is an instance of VeryBasic.

In Kotlin, types can be inferred; so, the previous example is equivalent to the following code:

```
fun main(args: Array<String>) {
    val basic = VeryBasic()
}
```

By being a VeryBasic instance, basic has a copy of the VeryBasic type's state and behavior, namely, none. So sad.

Properties

As discussed previously, classes can have a state. In Kotlin, a class's state is represented by **properties**. Let's have a look at the blueberry cupcake example:

```
class BlueberryCupcake {
  var flavour = "Blueberry"
}
```

The `BlueberryCupcake` class has an *has-a* property `flavour` of type `String`.

Of course, we can have instances of the `BlueberryCupcake` class:

```
fun main(args: Array<String>) {
    val myCupcake = BlueberryCupcake()
    println("My cupcake has ${myCupcake.flavour}")
}
```

Now, because we declare the `flavour` property as a variable, its internal value can be changed at runtime:

```
fun main(args: Array<String>) {
    val myCupcake = BlueberryCupcake()
    myCupcake.flavour = "Almond"
    println("My cupcake has ${myCupcake.flavour}")
}
```

That is impossible in real life. Cupcakes do not change their flavor (unless they become stale). If we change the `flavour` property to a value, it cannot be modified:

```
class BlueberryCupcake {
    val flavour = "Blueberry"
}

fun main(args: Array<String>) {
    val myCupcake = BlueberryCupcake()
    myCupcake.flavour = "Almond" //Compilation error: Val cannot be
reassigned
    println("My cupcake has ${myCupcake.flavour}")
}
```

Let's declare a new class for almond cupcakes:

```
class AlmondCupcake {
    val flavour = "Almond"
}
```

```
fun main(args: Array<String>) {
    val mySecondCupcake = AlmondCupcake()
    println("My second cupcake has ${mySecondCupcake.flavour} flavour")
}
```

There is something fishy here. `BlueberryCupcake` and `AlmondCupcake` are identical in structure; only an internal value is changed.

In real life, you don't have different baking tins for different cupcake flavors. The same good quality baking tin can be used for various flavors. In the same way, a well-designed `Cupcake` class can be used for different instances:

```
class Cupcake(flavour: String) {
  val flavour = flavour
}
```

The `Cupcake` class has a constructor with a parameter, `flavour`, that is assigned to a `flavour` value.

Because this is a very common idiom, Kotlin has a little syntactic sugar to define it more succinctly:

```
class Cupcake(val flavour: String)
```

Now, we can define several instances with different flavors:

```
fun main(args: Array<String>) {
    val myBlueberryCupcake = Cupcake("Blueberry")
    val myAlmondCupcake = Cupcake("Almond")
    val myCheeseCupcake = Cupcake("Cheese")
    val myCaramelCupcake = Cupcake("Caramel")
}
```

Methods

In Kotlin, a class's behavior is defined by methods. Technically, a **method** is a member function, so, anything that we learn about functions in the following chapters also applies to the methods:

```
class Cupcake(val flavour: String) {
  fun eat(): String {
    return "nom, nom, nom... delicious $flavour cupcake"
  }
}
```

The `eat()` method returns a `String` value. Now, let's call the `eat()` method, as shown in the following code:

```
fun main(args: Array<String>) {
    val myBlueberryCupcake = Cupcake("Blueberry")
    println(myBlueberryCupcake.eat())
}
```

The following expression is the output of the preceding code:

```
nom, nom, nom... delicious Blueberry cupcake
```

Nothing mind-blowing, but this is our first method. Later on, we'll do more interesting stuff.

Inheritance

As we continue modelling our domain in Kotlin, we realize that specific objects are quite similar. If we go back to our HR example, an employee and a contractor are quite similar; both have a name, a date of birth, and so on; they also have some differences. For example, a contractor has a daily rate, while an employee has a monthly salary. It is obvious that they are similar—both of them are people; people is a superset where both contractor and employee belong. As such, both have their own specific features that make them different enough to be classified into different subsets.

This is what inheritance is all about, there are groups and subgroups and there are relationships between them. In an inheritance hierarchy, if you go up in the hierarchy, you will see more general features and behaviors, and if you go down, you will see more specific ones. A burrito and a microprocessor are both objects, but they have very different purposes and uses.

Let's introduce a new `Biscuit` class:

```
class Biscuit(val flavour: String) {
    fun eat(): String {
        return "nom, nom, nom... delicious $flavour biscuit"
    }
}
```

Again, this class looks almost exactly same as `Cupcake`. We could refactor these classes to reduce code duplication:

```
open class BakeryGood(val flavour: String) {
  fun eat(): String {
    return "nom, nom, nom... delicious $flavour bakery good"
  }
}

class Cupcake(flavour: String): BakeryGood(flavour)
class Biscuit(flavour: String): BakeryGood(flavour)
```

We introduced a new `BakeryGood` class, with the shared behavior and state of both `Cupcake` and `Biscuit` classes and we made both classes extend `BakeryGood`. By doing so, `Cupcake` (and `Biscuit`) has an *is-a* relationship with `BakeryGood` now; on the other hand, `BakeryGood` is the `Cupcake` class's super or parent class.

Note that `BakeryGood` is marked as `open`. This means that we specifically design this class to be extended. In Kotlin, you can't extend a class that isn't `open`.

The process of moving common behaviors and states to a parent class is called **generalisation**. Let's have a look at the following code:

```
fun main(args: Array<String>) {
    val myBlueberryCupcake: BakeryGood = Cupcake("Blueberry")
    println(myBlueberryCupcake.eat())
}
```

Let's try out our new code:

```
nom, nom, nom... delicious Blueberry bakery good
```

Bummer, not what we were expecting. We need to refract it more:

```
open class BakeryGood(val flavour: String) {
  fun eat(): String {
    return "nom, nom, nom... delicious $flavour ${name()}"
  }

  open fun name(): String {
    return "bakery good"
  }
}

class Cupcake(flavour: String): BakeryGood(flavour) {
```

```
    override fun name(): String {
      return "cupcake"
    }
  }

  class Biscuit(flavour: String): BakeryGood(flavour) {
    override fun name(): String {
      return "biscuit"
    }
  }
```

It works! Let's have a look at the output:

```
nom, nom, nom... delicious Blueberry cupcake
```

We declared a new method, name(); it should be marked as open, because we designed it to be optionally altered in its subclasses.

Modifying a method's definition on a subclass is called **override** and that is why the name() method in both subclasses is marked as override.

The process of extending classes and overriding behavior in a hierarchy is called **specialisation**.

Rule of thumb

Put general states and behaviors at the top of the hierarchy (generalisation), and specific states and behaviors in subclasses (specialisation).

Now, we can have more bakery goods! Let's have a look at the following code:

```
open class Roll(flavour: String): BakeryGood(flavour) {
  override fun name(): String {
    return "roll"
  }
}

class CinnamonRoll: Roll("Cinnamon")
```

Subclasses can be extended too. They just need to be marked as open:

```kotlin
open class Donut(flavour: String, val topping: String) :
BakeryGood(flavour)
{
    override fun name(): String {
        return "donut with $topping topping"
    }
}

fun main(args: Array<String>) {
    val myDonut = Donut("Custard", "Powdered sugar")
    println(myDonut.eat())
}
```

We can also create classes with more properties and methods.

Abstract classes

So far, so good. Our bakery looks good. However, we have a problem with our current model. Let's look at the following code:

```kotlin
fun main(args: Array<String>) {
    val anyGood = BakeryGood("Generic flavour")
}
```

We can instantiate the BakeryGood class directly, which is too generic. To correct this situation, we can mark BakeryGood as abstract:

```kotlin
abstract class BakeryGood(val flavour: String) {
  fun eat(): String {
    return "nom, nom, nom... delicious $flavour ${name()}"
  }

  open fun name(): String {
    return "bakery good"
  }
}
```

An **abstract class** is a class designed solely to be extended. An abstract class can't be instantiated, which fixes our problem.

What makes `abstract` different from `open`?

Both modifiers let us extend a class, but `open` lets us instantiate while `abstract` does not.

Now that we can't instantiate, our `name()` method in the `BakeryGood` class isn't that useful anymore, and all our subclasses, except for `CinnamonRoll`, override it anyway (`CinnamonRoll` relays on the `Roll` implementation):

```
abstract class BakeryGood(val flavour: String) {
  fun eat(): String {
    return "nom, nom, nom... delicious $flavour ${name()}"
  }
  abstract fun name(): String
}
```

A method marked as `abstract` doesn't have a body, just the signature declaration (a method signature is a way to identify a method). In Kotlin, a signature is composed of the method's name, its number, the type of parameters, and the return type.

Any class that extends `BakeryGood` directly must override the `name()` method. The technical term for overriding an abstract method is **implement** and, from now on, we will use it. So, the `Cupcake` class implements the `name()` method (Kotlin doesn't have a keyword for method implementation; both cases, method implementation, and method overriding, use the keyword `override`).

Let's introduce a new class, `Customer`; a bakery needs customers anyway:

```
class Customer(val name: String) {
  fun eats(food: BakeryGood) {
    println("$name is eating... ${food.eat()}")
  }
}

fun main(args: Array<String>) {
    val myDonut = Donut("Custard", "Powdered sugar")
    val mario = Customer("Mario")
    mario.eats(myDonut)
}
```

The `eats(food: BakeryGood)` method takes a `BakeryGood` parameter, so any instance of any class that extends the `BakeryGood` parameter, it doesn't matter how many hierarchy levels. Just remember that we can instantiate `BakeryGood` directly.

What happens if we want a simple `BakeryGood`? For example, testing.

There is an alternative, an anonymous subclass:

```
fun main(args: Array<String>) {
    val mario = Customer("Mario")

    mario.eats(object : BakeryGood("TEST_1") {
        override fun name(): String {
            return "TEST_2"
        }
    })
}
```

A new keyword is introduced here, `object`. Later on, we'll cover `object` in more detail, but for now, it is enough to know that this is an **object expression**. An object expression defines an instance of an anonymous class that extends a type.

In our example, the object expression (technically, the **anonymous class**) must override the `name()` method and pass a value as the parameter for the `BakeryGood` constructor, exactly as a standard class would do.

Remember that an `object` expression is an instance, so it can be used to declare values:

```
val food: BakeryGood = object : BakeryGood("TEST_1") {
  override fun name(): String {
    return "TEST_2"
  }
}

mario.eats(food)
```

Interfaces

The open and abstract classes are great for creating hierarchies, but sometimes they aren't enough. Some subsets can span between apparently unrelated hierarchies, for example, birds and great apes are bipedal, and both are animals and vertebrates, but they not directly related. That is why we need a different construct and Kotlin gives us interfaces (other languages deal with this problem differently).

Our bakery goods are great, but we need to cook them first:

```
abstract class BakeryGood(val flavour: String) {
  fun eat(): String {
    return "nom, nom, nom... delicious $flavour ${name()}"
  }

  fun bake(): String {
    return "is hot here, isn't??"
  }

  abstract fun name(): String
}
```

With our new `bake()` method , it will cook all our amazing products, but wait, donuts aren't baked, but fried.

What if we could move the `bake()` method to a second abstract class, `Bakeable`? Let's try it in the following code:

```
abstract class Bakeable {
  fun bake(): String {
    return "is hot here, isn't??"
  }
}

class Cupcake(flavour: String) : BakeryGood(flavour), Bakeable() {
//Compilation error: Only one class may appear in a supertype list
  override fun name(): String {
    return "cupcake"
  }
}
```

Wrong! In Kotlin, a class can't extend two classes at the same time. Let's have a look at the following code:

```
interface Bakeable {
  fun bake(): String {
    return "is hot here, isn't??"
  }
}

class Cupcake(flavour: String) : BakeryGood(flavour), Bakeable {
  override fun name(): String {
    return "cupcake"
  }
}
```

However, it can extend many interfaces. An **interface** is a type that defines a behavior; in the `Bakeable` interface's case, that is the `bake()` method.

So, what are the differences between an open/abstract class and an interface?

Let's start with the following similarities:

- Both are types. In our example, `Cupcake` has an *is-a* relationship with `BakeryGood` and has an *is-a* relationship with `Bakeable`.
- Both define behaviors as methods.
- Although open classes can be instantiated directly, neither abstract classes nor interfaces can.

Now, let's look at the following differences:

- A class can extend just one class (open or abstract), but can extend many interfaces.
- An open/abstract class can have constructors.
- An open/abstract class can initialize its own values. An interface's values must be initialized in the classes that extend the interface.
- An open class must declare the methods that can be overridden as open. An abstract class could have both open and abstract methods.

In an interface, all methods are open and a method with no implementation doesn't need an abstract modifier:

```kotlin
interface Fried {
  fun fry(): String
}

open class Donut(flavour: String, val topping: String) :
BakeryGood(flavour), Fried {
  override fun fry(): String {
    return "*swimming on oil*"
  }

  override fun name(): String {
    return "donut with $topping topping"
  }
}
```

When should you use one or the other?:

- Use open class when:
  - The class should be extended and instantiated
- Use abstract class when:
  - The class can't be instantiated
  - A constructor is needed it
  - There is initialization logic (using `init` blocks)

Let's have a look at the following code:

```
abstract class BakeryGood(val flavour: String) {
  init {
    println("Preparing a new bakery good")
  }

  fun eat(): String {
    return "nom, nom, nom... delicious $flavour ${name()}"
  }

  abstract fun name(): String
}
```

- Use interface when:
  - Multiple inheritances must be applied
  - No initialized logic is needed

 My recommendation is that you should always start with an interface. Interfaces are more straightforward and cleaner; they also allow a more modular design. In the case that data initialization/constructors are needed, move to abstract/open.

As with abstract classes, object expressions can be used with interfaces:

```
val somethingFried = object : Fried {
  override fun fry(): String {
    return "TEST_3"
  }
}
```

Objects

We already covered object expressions, but there is more on objects. **Objects** are natural singletons (by natural, I mean to come as language features and not as behavior pattern implementations, as in other languages). A **singleton** is a type that has just one and only one instance and every object in Kotlin is a singleton. That opens a lot of interesting patterns (and also some bad practices). Objects as singletons are useful for coordinating actions across the system, but can also be dangerous if they are used to keep global state.

Object expressions don't need to extend any type:

```kotlin
fun main(args: Array<String>) {
    val expression = object {
        val property = ""

        fun method(): Int {
            println("from an object expressions")
            return 42
        }
    }

    val i = "${expression.method()} ${expression.property}"
    println(i)
}
```

In this case, the `expression` value is an object that doesn't have any specific type. We can access its properties and functions.

There is one restriction—object expressions without type can be used only locally, inside a method, or privately, inside a class:

```kotlin
class Outer {
    val internal = object {
        val property = ""
    }
}

fun main(args: Array<String>) {
    val outer = Outer()

    println(outer.internal.property) // Compilation error: Unresolved
reference: property
}
```

In this case, the `property` value can't be accessed.

Object declarations

An object can also have a name. This kind of object is called an **object declaration**:

```
object Oven {
  fun process(product: Bakeable) {
    println(product.bake())
  }
}

fun main(args: Array<String>) {
    val myAlmondCupcake = Cupcake("Almond")
    Oven.process(myAlmondCupcake)
}
```

Objects are singletons; you don't need to instantiate Oven to use it. Objects also can extend other types:

```
interface Oven {
  fun process(product: Bakeable)
}

object ElectricOven: Oven {
  override fun process(product: Bakeable) {
    println(product.bake())
  }
}

fun main(args: Array<String>) {
    val myAlmondCupcake = Cupcake("Almond")
    ElectricOven.process(myAlmondCupcake)
}
```

Companion objects

Objects declared inside a class/interface can be marked as companion objects. Observe the use of companion objects in the following code:

```
class Cupcake(flavour: String) : BakeryGood(flavour), Bakeable {
  override fun name(): String {
    return "cupcake"
  }
  companion object {
    fun almond(): Cupcake {
      return Cupcake("almond")
```

```
    }

    fun cheese(): Cupcake {
      return Cupcake("cheese")
    }
  }
}
```

Now, methods inside the companion object can be used directly, using the class name without instantiating it:

```
fun main(args: Array<String>) {
    val myBlueberryCupcake: BakeryGood = Cupcake("Blueberry")
    val myAlmondCupcake = Cupcake.almond()
    val myCheeseCupcake = Cupcake.cheese()
    val myCaramelCupcake = Cupcake("Caramel")
}
```

Companion object's methods can't be used from instances:

```
fun main(args: Array<String>) {
    val myAlmondCupcake = Cupcake.almond()
    val myCheeseCupcake = myAlmondCupcake.cheese() //Compilation error:
Unresolved reference: cheese
}
```

Companion objects can be used outside the class as values with the name `Companion`:

```
fun main(args: Array<String>) {
    val factory: Cupcake.Companion = Cupcake.Companion
}
```

Alternatively, a `Companion` object can have a name:

```
class Cupcake(flavour: String) : BakeryGood(flavour), Bakeable {
    override fun name(): String {
        return "cupcake"
    }

    companion object Factory {
        fun almond(): Cupcake {
            return Cupcake("almond")
        }

        fun cheese(): Cupcake {
            return Cupcake("cheese")
        }
    }
}
```

```
    }
fun main(args: Array<String>) {
    val factory: Cupcake.Factory = Cupcake.Factory
}
```

They can also be used without a name, as shown in the following code:

```
fun main(args: Array<String>) {
    val factory: Cupcake.Factory = Cupcake
}
```

Don't be confused by this syntax. The `Cupcake` value without parenthesis is the companion object; `Cupcake()` is an instance.

Generics

This section is just a short introduction to generics; later, we'll cover it in detail.

Generic programming is a style programming that focuses on creating algorithms (and collaterally, data structures) that work on general problems.

The Kotlin way to support generic programming is using type parameters. In a few words, we wrote our code with type parameters and, later on, we pass those types as parameters when we use them.

Let's take, for example, our `Oven` interface:

```
interface Oven {
  fun process(product: Bakeable)
}
```

An oven is a machine, so we could generalize it more:

```
interface Machine<T> {
  fun process(product: T)
}
```

The `Machine<T>` interface defines a type parameter `T` and a method `process(T)`.

Now, we can extend it with `Oven`:

```
interface Oven: Machine<Bakeable>
```

Now, `Oven` is extending `Machine` with the `Bakeable` type parameter, so the `process` method now takes `Bakeable` as a parameter.

Type alias

Type alias provides a way to define names of types that already exist. Type alias can help to make complex types easier to read, and can also provide other hints.

The `Oven` interface is, in some sense, just a name, for a `Machine<Bakeable>`:

```
typealias Oven = Machine<Bakeable>
```

Our new type alias, `Oven`, is exactly like our good old `Oven` interface. It can be extended and have the values of the type `Oven`.

Types alias also can be used to enhance information on types, providing meaningful names related to your domain:

```
typealias Flavour = String

abstract class BakeryGood(val flavour: Flavour) {
```

It can also be used on collections:

```
typealias OvenTray = List<Bakeable>
```

It can also be used with objects:

```
typealias CupcakeFactory = Cupcake.Companion
```

Nullable types

One of the main features of Kotlin is nullable types. **Nullable types** allow us to define if a value can contain or being null explicitly:

```
fun main(args: Array<String>) {
    val myBlueberryCupcake: Cupcake = null //Compilation error: Null can
not be a value of a non-null type Cupcake
}
```

This isn't valid in Kotlin; the `Cupcake` type doesn't allow null values. To allow null values, `myBlueberryCupcake` must have a different type:

```
fun main(args: Array<String>) {
    val myBlueberryCupcake: Cupcake? = null
}
```

In essence, `Cupcake` is a non-null type and `Cupcake?` is a nullable type.

In the hierarchical structure, `Cupcake` is a subtype of `Cupcake?`. So, in any situation where `Cupcake?` is defined, `Cupcake` can be used, but not the other way around:

```
fun eat(cupcake: Cupcake?){
//    something happens here
}

fun main(args: Array<String>) {
    val myAlmondCupcake = Cupcake.almond()
    eat(myAlmondCupcake)
    eat(null)
}
```

Kotlin's compiler makes a distinction between instances of nullable and non-null types.

Let's take these values, for example:

```
fun main(args: Array<String>) {
    val cupcake: Cupcake = Cupcake.almond()
    val nullabeCupcake: Cupcake? = Cupcake.almond()
}
```

Next, we will invoke the `eat()` method on both nullable and non-null types:

```
fun main(args: Array<String>) {
    val cupcake: Cupcake = Cupcake.almond()
    val nullableCupcake: Cupcake? = Cupcake.almond()

    cupcake.eat() // Happy days
    nullableCupcake.eat() //Only safe (?.) or non-null asserted (!!.) calls
are allowed on a nullable receiver of type Cupcake?
}
```

Calling the `eat()` method on `cupcake` is easy as pie; calling `eat()` on `nullableCupcake` is a compilation error.

Why? For Kotlin, calling a method from a nullable value is dangerous, a potential `NullPointerException` (**NPE** from now on) could be thrown. So, to be safe, Kotlin marks this as a compilation error.

What happens if we really want to invoke a method or access a property from a nullable value?

Well, Kotlin provides you options to deal with nullable values, with a catch—all are explicit. In some sense, Kotlin is telling you, *Show me that you know what you are doing*.

Let's review some options (there are more options that we'll cover in the following chapters).

Checking for null

Check for null as a condition in the `if` block:

```
fun main(args: Array<String>) {
    val nullableCupcake: Cupcake? = Cupcake.almond()

    if (nullableCupcake != null) {
      nullableCupcake.eat()
    }
}
```

Kotlin will do a smart cast. Inside the `if` block, `nullableCupcake` is a `Cupcake`, not a `Cupcake?`; so, any method or property can be accessed.

Checking for non-null types

This is similar to the previous one, but it checks directly for the type:

```
if (nullableCupcake is Cupcake) {
  nullableCupcake.eat()
}
```

It also works with `when`:

```
when (nullableCupcake) {
  is Cupcake -> nullableCupcake.eat()
}
```

Both options, checking for null and non-null types, are a little bit verbose. Let's check other options.

Safe calls

Safe calls let you access methods and properties of nullable values if the value isn't null (under the hood, at the bytecode level, a safe call is transformed into `if(x != null)`):

```
nullableCupcake?.eat()
```

But, what if you use it in an expression?

```
val result: String? = nullableCupcake?.eat()
```

It will return null if our value is null, so `result` must have a `String?` type.

That opens up the chance to use safe calls on a chain, as follows:

```
val length: Int? = nullableCupcake?.eat()?.length
```

The Elvis (?:) operator

The Elvis operator (`?:`) returns an alternative value if a null value is used in an expression:

```
val result2: String = nullableCupcake?.eat() ?: ""
```

If `nullabluCupcake?.eat()` is `null`, the `?:` operator will return the alternative value `""`.

Obviously, the Elvis operator can be used with a chain of safe calls:

```
val length2: Int = nullableCupcake?.eat()?.length ?: 0
```

The (!!) operator

Instead of a `null` value, the `!!` operator will throw an NPE:

```
val result: String = nullableCupcake!!.eat()
```

If you can deal with an NPE, the `!!` operator gives you a pretty convenient feature, a free smart cast:

```
val result: String = nullableCupcake!!.eat()

val length: Int = nullableCupcake.eat().length
```

If `nullableCupcake!!.eat()` doesn't throw an NPE, Kotlin will change its type from `Cupcake?` to `Cupcake` from the next line and onwards.

Kotlin's type system

Type systems are a set of rules that determine the type of a language construct.

A (good) type system will help you with:

- Making sure that the constituent parts of your program are connected in a consistent way
- Understanding your program (by reducing your cognitive load)
- Expressing business rules
- Automatic low-level optimizations

We have already covered enough ground to understand Kotlin's type system.

The Any type

All types in Kotlin extend from the `Any` type (hold on a second, actually this isn't true but for the sake of the explanation, bear with me).

Every class and interface that we create implicitly extends `Any`. So, if we write a method that takes `Any` as a parameter, it will receive any value:

```
fun main(args: Array<String>) {
    val myAlmondCupcake = Cupcake.almond()
    val anyMachine = object : Machine<Any> {
      override fun process(product: Any) {
        println(product.toString())
      }
    }
    anyMachine.process(3)
    anyMachine.process("")
```

```
        anyMachine.process(myAlmondCupcake)
    }
```

What about a nullable value? Let's have a look at it:

```
fun main(args: Array<String>) {
    val anyMachine = object : Machine<Any> {
        override fun process(product: Any) {
            println(product.toString())
        }
    }

    val nullableCupcake: Cupcake? = Cupcake.almond()

    anyMachine.process(nullableCupcake) //Error:(32, 24) Kotlin: Type
  mismatch: inferred type is Cupcake? but Any was expected
    }
```

`Any` is the same as any other type and also has a nullable counterpart, `Any?`. `Any` extends from `Any?`. So, in the end, `Any?` is the top class of Kotlin's type system hierarchy.

Minimum common types

Due to its type inference and expression evaluation, sometimes there are expressions in Kotlin where it is not clear which type is being returned. Most languages resolve this problem by returning the minimum common type between the possible type options. Kotlin takes a different route.

Let's take a look at an example of an ambiguous expression:

```
fun main(args: Array<String>) {
    val nullableCupcake: Cupcake? = Cupcake.almond()

    val length = nullableCupcake?.eat()?.length ?: ""
}
```

What type does `length` have? `Int` or `String`? No, `length` value's type is `Any`. Pretty logical. The minimum common type between `Int` and `String` is `Any`. So far, so good. Let's look at the following code now:

```
val length = nullableCupcake?.eat()?.length ?: 0.0
```

Following that logic, in this case, `length` should have the `Number` type (the common type between `Int` and `Double`), shouldn't it?

Wrong, `length` is still `Any`. Kotlin doesn't search for the minimum common type in these situations. If you want a specific type, it must be explicitly declared:

```
val length: Number = nullableCupcake?.eat()?.length ?: 0.0
```

The Unit type

Kotlin doesn't have methods with `void` return (as Java or C do). Instead, a method (or, to be precise, an expression) could have a `Unit` type.

A `Unit` type means that the expression is called for its side effects, rather than its return. The classic example of a `Unit` expression is `println()`, a method invoked just for its side effects.

`Unit`, like any other Kotlin type, extends from `Any` and could be nullable. `Unit?` looks strange and unnecessary, but is needed to keep consistency with the type system. Having a consistent type system have several advantages, including better compilation times and tooling:

```
anyMachine.process(Unit)
```

The Nothing type

`Nothing` is the type that sits at the bottom of the entire Kotlin hierarchy. `Nothing` extends all Kotlin types, including `Nothing?`.

But, why do we need a `Nothing` and `Nothing?` types?

`Nothing` represents an expression that can't be executed (basically throwing exceptions):

```
val result: String = nullableCupcake?.eat() ?: throw RuntimeException() //
equivalent to nullableCupcake!!.eat()
```

On one hand of the Elvis operator, we have a `String`. On the other hand, we have `Nothing`. Because the common type between `String` and `Nothing` is `String` (instead of `Any`), the value `result` is a `String`.

`Nothing` also has a special meaning for the compiler. Once a `Nothing` type is returned on an expression, the lines after that are marked as unreachable.

`Nothing?` is the type of a null value:

```
val x: Nothing? = null

val nullsList: List<Nothing?> = listOf(null)
```

Other types

Classes, interfaces, and objects are a good starting point for an OOP type system, but Kotlin offers more constructs, such as data classes, annotations, and enums (there is an additional type, named sealed class, that we'll cover later).

Data classes

Creating classes whose primary purpose is to hold data is a common pattern in Kotlin (is a common pattern in other languages too, think of JSON or Protobuff).

Kotlin has a particular kind of class for this purpose:

```
data class Item(val product: BakeryGood,
    val unitPrice: Double,
    val quantity: Int)
```

To declare `data class`, there are some restrictions:

- The primary constructor should have at least one parameter
- The primary constructor's parameters must be `val` or `var`
- Data classes can't be abstract, open, sealed, or inner

With these restrictions, data classes give a lot of benefits.

Canonical methods

Canonical methods are the methods declared in `Any`. Therefore, all instances in Kotlin have them.

For data classes, Kotlin creates correct implementations of all canonical methods.

The methods are as follows:

- `equals(other: Any?): Boolean`: This method compares value equivalence, rather than reference.
- `hashCode(): Int`: A hash code is a numerical representation of an instance. When `hashCode()` is invoked several times in the same instance, it should always return the same value. Two instances that return true when they are compared with `equals` must have the same `hashCode()`.
- `toString(): String`: A `String` representation of an instance. This method will be invoked when an instance is concatenated to a `String`.

The copy() method

Sometimes, we want to reuse values from an existing instance. The `copy()` method lets us create new instances of a data class, overriding the parameters that we want:

```
val myItem = Item(myAlmondCupcake, 0.40, 5)

val mySecondItem = myItem.copy(product = myCaramelCupcake) //named
parameter
```

In this case, `mySecondItem` copies `unitPrice` and `quantity` from `myItem`, and replaces the `product` property.

Destructuring methods

By convention, any instance of a class that has a series of methods named `component1()`, `component2()` and so on can be used in a destructuring declaration.

Kotlin will generate these methods for any data class:

```
val (prod: BakeryGood, price: Double, qty: Int) = mySecondItem
```

The `prod` value is initialized with the return of `component1()`, `price` with the return of `component2()`, and so on. Although the preceding example use explicit types, those aren't needed:

```
val (prod, price, qty) = mySecondItem
```

In some circumstances, not all values are needed. All unused values can be replaced by (_):

```
val (prod, _, qty) = mySecondItem
```

Annotations

Annotations are a way to attach meta info to your code (such as documentation, configuration, and others).

Let's look at the following example code:

```
annotation class Tasty
```

An `annotation` itself can be annotated to modify its behavior:

```
@Target(AnnotationTarget.CLASS)
@Retention(AnnotationRetention.RUNTIME)
annotation class Tasty
```

In this case, the `Tasty` annotation can be set on classes, interfaces, and objects, and it can be queried at runtime.

For a complete list of options, check the Kotlin documentation.

Annotations can have parameters with one limitation, they can't be nullable:

```
@Target(AnnotationTarget.CLASS)
@Retention(AnnotationRetention.RUNTIME)
annotation class Tasty(val tasty:Boolean = true)

@Tasty(false)
object ElectricOven : Oven {
  override fun process(product: Bakeable) {
    println(product.bake())
  }
}

@Tasty
class CinnamonRoll : Roll("Cinnamon")

@Tasty
interface Fried {
  fun fry(): String
}
```

To query annotation values at runtime, we must use the reflection API (`kotlin-reflect.jar` must be in your classpath):

```
fun main(args: Array<String>) {
    val annotations: List<Annotation> = ElectricOven::class.annotations
```

```
        for (annotation in annotations) {
            when (annotation) {
                is Tasty -> println("Is it tasty? ${annotation.tasty}")
                else -> println(annotation)
            }
        }
    }
}
```

Enum

Enum in Kotlin is a way to define a set of constant values. Enums are very useful, but not limited, as configuration values:

```
enum class Flour {
    WHEAT, CORN, CASSAVA
}
```

Each element is an object that extends the `Flour` class.

Like any object, they can extend interfaces:

```
interface Exotic {
    fun isExotic(): Boolean
}

enum class Flour : Exotic {
    WHEAT {
        override fun isExotic(): Boolean {
            return false
        }
    },

    CORN {
        override fun isExotic(): Boolean {
            return false
        }
    },

    CASSAVA {
        override fun isExotic(): Boolean {
            return true
        }
    }
}
```

Enum can also have abstract methods:

```
enum class Flour: Exotic {
  WHEAT {
    override fun isGlutenFree(): Boolean {
      return false
    }

    override fun isExotic(): Boolean {
      return false
    }
  },

  CORN {
    override fun isGlutenFree(): Boolean {
      return true
    }

    override fun isExotic(): Boolean {
      return false
    }
  },

  CASSAVA {
    override fun isGlutenFree(): Boolean {
      return true
    }

    override fun isExotic(): Boolean {
      return true
    }
  };

  abstract fun isGlutenFree(): Boolean
}
```

Any method definition must be declared after the (;) separating the last element.

When enums are used with when expressions, Kotlin's compiler checks that all cases are covered (individually or with an else):

```
fun flourDescription(flour: Flour): String {
  return when(flour) { // error
    Flour.CASSAVA -> "A very exotic flavour"
  }
}
```

In this case, we're only checking for CASSAVA and not the other elements; therefore, it fails:

```kotlin
fun flourDescription(flour: Flour): String {
   return when(flour) {
      Flour.CASSAVA -> "A very exotic flavour"
      else -> "Boring"
   }
}
```

Summary

In this chapter, we covered the basics of OOP and how Kotlin supports it. We learned how to use classes, interfaces, objects, data classes, annotations, and enums. We also explored the Kotlin type system and saw how it helps us to write better and safer code.

In the next chapter, we will start with an introduction to functional programming.

2
Getting Started with Functional Programming

Functional programming has been making big waves in the software industry for the last five years, and everyone wants to jump on the bandwagon. Functional programming is a lot older, starting in the 1950s with **Lisp** being considered the first programming language (or at least, the first one to introduce functional features) which still exists as **Common Lisp,** and other dialects such as **Scheme** and **Clojure**.

In this chapter, we'll cover the following topics:

- What is functional programming?
- Basic concepts
- Functional collections
- Implementing a functional list

What is functional programming?

Functional programming is a paradigm (a style of structuring your programs). In essence, the focus is on transforming data with expressions (ideally such expressions should not have side effects). Its name, functional, is based on the concept of a mathematical function (not in sub-routines, methods, or procedures). A mathematical function defines a relation between a set of inputs and outputs. Each input has just one output. For example, given a function, $f(x) = X^2$; $f(5)$ is always 25.

The way to guarantee, in a programming language, that calling a function with a parameter always returns the same value, is to avoid accessing to mutable state:

```
fun f(x: Long) : Long {
    return x * x // no access to external state
}
```

The f function doesn't access any external state; therefore, calling *f(5)* will always return *25*:

```
fun main(args: Array<String>) {
    var i = 0

    fun g(x: Long): Long {
        return x * i // accessing mutable state
    }

    println(g(1)) //0
    i++
    println(g(1)) //1
    i++
    println(g(1)) //2
}
```

The g function, on the other hand, depends on mutable state and returns different values for the same.

Now, in a real-life program (a **Content Management System** (**CMS**), shopping cart, or chat), state changes. So, in a functional programming style, state management must be explicit and careful. The techniques to manage state change in functional programming will be covered later.

A functional programming style will provide us with the following benefits:

- **Code is easy to read and test**: Functions that don't depend on external mutable state are more accessible to reason about and to prove
- **State and side effects are carefully planned**: Limiting state management to individual and specific places in our code makes it easy to maintain and refactor
- **Concurrency gets safer and more natural**: No mutable state means that concurrency code needs less or no locks around your code

Basics concepts

Functional programming is composed of a few well-defined concepts. A short introduction of these concepts will follow and, later on, each concept will be covered in depth, in the next chapters.

First-class and higher-order functions

The most foundational concept of functional programming is **first-class functions**. A programming language with support for first-class functions will treat functions as any other type; such languages will allow you to use functions as variables, parameters, returns, generalization types, and so on. Speaking of parameters and returns, a function that uses or returns other functions is a **higher-order function**.

Kotlin has support for both concepts.

Let's try a simple function (in Kotlin's documentation this kind of function is named lambda):

```
val capitalize = { str: String -> str.capitalize() }

fun main(args: Array<String>) {
    println(capitalize("hello world!"))
}
```

The `capitalize` lambda function is of type `(String) -> String`; in other words, `capitalize` will take `String` and return another `String`—in this case, a capitalized `String`.

As a lambda function, `capitalize` can be executed using parentheses with parameters (or no parameters at all, depending on the situation).

But what does the `(String) -> String` type mean?

`(String) -> String` is a shortcut (some could call it syntactic sugar) for `Function1<String, String>`, `Function1<P1, R>` is an interface defined in the Kotlin standard library. `Function1<P1, R>` has a single method, `invoke(P1): R`, that is marked as an operator (we'll cover operators later).

Kotlin's compiler can translate the shortcut syntax into a fully fledged function object at compile time (indeed, the compiler will apply many more optimizations) as follows:

```
val capitalize = { str: String -> str.capitalize() }
```

It is equivalent to the following code:

```
val capitalize = object : Function1<String, String> {
    override fun invoke(p1: String): String {
        return p1.capitalize()
    }
}
```

As you can see, the `capitalize` value's body is located inside the `invoke` method.

In Kotlin, lambda functions can be used as parameters in other functions as well.

Let's take a look at the following example:

```
fun transform(str:String, fn: (String) -> String): String {
    return fn(str)
}
```

The `transform(String, (String) -> String)` function takes one `String` and applies a lambda function to it.

For all intents and purposes, we can generalize `transform`:

```
fun <T> transform(t: T, fn: (T) -> T): T {
    return fn(t)
}
```

Using `transform` is very simple. Take a look at the following code snippet:

```
fun main(args: Array<String>) {
    println(transform("kotlin", capitalize))
}
```

We can pass `capitalize` as a parameter directly, great stuff.

There are more ways to call the `transform` function. Let's try some more:

```
fun reverse(str: String): String {
    return str.reversed()
}

fun main(args: Array<String>) {
    println(transform("kotlin", ::reverse))
}
```

`reverse` is a function; we can pass a reference to it using a double colon (`::`) as follows:

```
object MyUtils {
    fun doNothing(str: String): String {
        return str
    }
}

fun main(args: Array<String>) {
    println(transform("kotlin", MyUtils::doNothing))
}
```

`doNothing` is an object method, and in this case, we use `::` after the `MyUtils` object name:

```
class Transformer {
    fun upperCased(str: String): String {
        return str.toUpperCase()
    }

    companion object {
        fun lowerCased(str: String): String {
            return str.toLowerCase()
        }
    }
}

fun main(args: Array<String>) {
    val transformer = Transformer()

    println(transform("kotlin", transformer::upperCased))
    println(transform("kotlin", Transformer.Companion::lowerCased))
}
```

We can also pass references to instances or companion object methods. But probably the most common case is to pass a lambda directly:

```
fun main(args: Array<String>) {
    println(transform("kotlin", { str -> str.substring(0..1) }))
}
```

There is a shorter version of this using the `it` implicit parameter as follows:

```
fun main(args: Array<String>) {
    println(transform("kotlin", { it.substring(0..1) }))
}
```

`it` is an implicit parameter (you don't declare it explicitly) that can be used in lambdas with just one parameter.

 Although it is tempting to use `it` for all cases, once you start using it with successive or nested lambdas, they can be difficult to read. Use it sparingly and when it is clear which type it is (no pun intended).

If a function receives a lambda as the last parameter, the lambda can be passed outside the parentheses:

```
fun main(args: Array<String>) {
    println(transform("kotlin") { str -> str.substring(0..1) })
}
```

This feature opens up the possibility of creating **Domain Specific Language** (**DSL**) with Kotlin.

Do you know about the `unless` flow control statement from **Ruby**? `unless` is a control statement that executes a block of code if a condition is `false`; it's kind of a negated `if` condition but without an `else` clause.

Let's create a version for Kotlin by executing the following code snippet:

```
fun unless(condition: Boolean, block: () -> Unit){
    if (!condition) block()
}

fun main(args: Array<String>) {
    val securityCheck = false // some interesting code here

    unless(securityCheck) {
        println("You can't access this website")
    }
}
```

`unless` receives a condition as a Boolean and blocks to execute as a lambda `() -> Unit` (no parameters and no return). When `unless` is executed, it looks exactly like any other Kotlin's control flow structure.

Now, type alias can be mixed with functions and used to replace simple interfaces. Let's take the following example, our Machine<T> interface from Chapter 1, *Kotlin – Data Types, Objects, and Classes*:

```
interface Machine<T> {
    fun process(product: T)
}

fun <T> useMachine(t: T, machine: Machine<T>) {
    machine.process(t)
}

class PrintMachine<T> : Machine<T> {
    override fun process(t: T) {
        println(t)
    }
}

fun main(args: Array<String>) {
    useMachine(5, PrintMachine())

    useMachine(5, object : Machine<Int> {
        override fun process(t: Int) {
            println(t)
        }
    })
}
```

It can be replaced with a type alias and used with all the function's syntactical features:

```
typealias Machine<T> = (T) -> Unit

fun <T> useMachine(t: T, machine: Machine<T>) {
    machine(t)
}

class PrintMachine<T>: Machine<T> {
    override fun invoke(p1: T) {
        println(p1)
    }
}

fun main(args: Array<String>) {
    useMachine(5, PrintMachine())

    useMachine(5, ::println)
```

```
    useMachine(5) { i ->
        println(i)
    }
}
```

Pure functions

Pure functions don't have side effects, nor memory, nor I/O. Pure functions have many properties, including referential transparency, caching (memoization), and others (we'll cover these features in the next chapters).

It is possible to write pure functions in Kotlin, but the compiler doesn't enforce it as in other languages. It is up to you to create pure functions to enjoy its benefits. Because Kotlin doesn't enforce pure functions, many programmers said that Kotlin isn't a real functional programming tool, and maybe they are right. Yes, Kotlin doesn't enforce pure functional programming, and that gives you great flexibility including the ability to write in a purely functional style, if you wish.

Recursive functions

Recursive functions are functions that invoke themselves, with some sort of condition to stop the execution. In Kotlin, a recursive function maintains a stack but can be optimized with a `tailrec` modifier.

Let's look at an example, an implementation of a `factorial` function.

First, let's take a look at a typical imperative implementation, loops, and state change in the following code snippet:

```
fun factorial(n: Long): Long {
    var result = 1L
    for (i in 1..n) {
        result *= i
    }
    return result
}
```

It's nothing fancy nor particularly elegant. Now, let's take a look at a recursive implementation, no loops, and no state change:

```
fun functionalFactorial(n: Long): Long {
    fun go(n: Long, acc: Long): Long {
        return if (n <= 0) {
            acc
        } else {
            go(n - 1, n * acc)
        }
    }

    return go(n, 1)
}
```

We use an internal recursive function; the go function calling itself until a condition is reached. As you can see, we're starting with the last n value and reducing it in each recursive iteration.

An optimized implementation is similar but with a tailrec modifier:

```
fun tailrecFactorial(n: Long): Long {
    tailrec fun go(n: Long, acc: Long): Long {
        return if (n <= 0) {
            acc
        } else {
            go(n - 1, n * acc)
        }
    }

    return go(n, 1)
}
```

To test which implementation is faster, we can write a poor's man profiler function:

```
fun executionTime(body: () -> Unit): Long {
    val startTime = System.nanoTime()
    body()
    val endTime = System.nanoTime()
    return endTime - startTime
}
```

For our purposes, the `executionTime` function is okay, but any serious production code should be profiled with a proper profiling tool, such as **Java Microbenchmark Harness (JMH)**:

```
fun main(args: Array<String>) {
    println("factorial :" + executionTime { factorial(20) })
    println("functionalFactorial :" + executionTime {
functionalFactorial(20) })
    println("tailrecFactorial :" + executionTime { tailrecFactorial(20) })
}
```

Here's the output for the preceding code:

```
factorial :966332
functionalFactorial :1730842
tailrecFactorial :798309
```

The `tailrec` optimized version is even faster than the normal imperative version. But `tailrec` isn't a magic incantation that will make your code run faster. As a general rule, the `tailrec` optimized code will run faster than the unoptimized version, but will not always beat a good old imperative code.

Let's explore a Fibonacci implementation, starting with an imperative one as follows:

```
fun fib(n: Long): Long {
    return when (n) {
        0L -> 0
        1L -> 1
        else -> {
            var a = 0L
            var b = 1L
            var c = 0L
            for (i in 2..n) {
                c = a + b
                a = b
                b = c
            }
            c
        }
    }
}
```

Now, let's take a look at a functional recursive implementation:

```
fun functionalFib(n: Long): Long {
    fun go(n: Long, prev: Long, cur: Long): Long {
        return if (n == 0L) {
            prev
        } else {
            go(n - 1, cur, prev + cur)
        }
    }

    return go(n, 0, 1)
}
```

Now let's check with its corresponding `tailrec` version, as follows:

```
fun tailrecFib(n: Long): Long {
    tailrec fun go(n: Long, prev: Long, cur: Long): Long {
        return if (n == 0L) {
            prev
        } else {
            go(n - 1, cur, prev + cur)
        }
    }

    return go(n, 0, 1)
}
```

Then again, let's see its profiling with `executionTime`:

```
fun main(args: Array<String>) {
    println("fib :" + executionTime { fib(93) })
    println("functionalFib :" + executionTime { functionalFib(93) })
    println("tailrecFib :" + executionTime { tailrecFib(93) })
}
```

The output will look something like the following:

```
fib :670550
functionalFib :1486167
tailrecFib :768623
```

The `tailrec` implementation is much faster than the recursive version, but not as fast as a normal imperative implementation.

Lazy evaluation

Some functional languages provide a `lazy` (non-strict) evaluation mode. Kotlin, by default, uses an *eager (strict) evaluation.*

Kotlin doesn't provide native support for lazy evaluation as part of the language itself, but as part of Kotlin's Standard Library and a language feature named **delegate properties** (we'll cover this in detail in future chapters):

```
fun main(args: Array<String>) {
    val i by lazy {
        println("Lazy evaluation")
        1
    }

    println("before using i")
    println(i)
}
```

The output will look something like the following screenshot:

After the `by` reserved word, the `lazy()` higher-function receives an `(() -> T)` initializer lambda function that will be executed the first time that `i` is accessed.

But also a normal lambda function can be used for some lazy use cases:

```
fun main(args: Array<String>) {
    val size = listOf(2 + 1, 3 * 2, 1 / 0, 5 - 4).size
}
```

If we try to execute this expression, it will throw an `ArithmeticException` exception, as we are dividing by zero:

```
fun main(args: Array<String>) {
    val size = listOf({ 2 + 1 }, { 3 * 2 }, { 1 / 0 }, { 5 - 4 }).size
}
```

There's no problem executing this. The offending code isn't being executed, effectively making it a `lazy` evaluation.

Functional collections

Functional collections are collections that offer a way to interact with its elements through high-order functions. Functional collections have common operations with names such as `filter`, `map`, and `fold`; these names are defined by convention (similar to a design pattern) and are being implemented in several libraries and languages.

Don't get confused with purely functional data structures—a data structure implemented in a pure functional language. A purely functional data structure is immutable and uses the `lazy` evaluation and other functional techniques.

Functional collections can but needn't necessarily be purely functional data structures. We have already covered how imperative implementations of algorithms can be faster than functional ones.

Kotlin comes with an excellent functional collection library. Let's have a look at it:

```
val numbers: List<Int> = listOf(1, 2, 3, 4)
```

Our value `numbers` as a `List<Int>` type. Now, let's print its members as follows:

```
fun main(args: Array<String>) {
    for(i in numbers) {
        println("i = $i")
    }
}
```

So far, so good, but it doesn't look very functional.

Worry no more; Kotlin collections include many functions that receive lambdas to operate on their members. We can replace this loop with a lambda as follows:

```
fun main(args: Array<String>) {
    numbers.forEach { i -> println("i = $i") }
}
```

Now, let's transform our collection in the following code:

```
val numbers: List<Int> = listOf(1, 2, 3, 4)

fun main(args: Array<String>) {
    val numbersTwice: List<Int> = listOf()

    for (i in numbers) {
        numbersTwice.add(i * 2) //Compilation error: Unresolved reference:
add
    }
}
```

This code doesn't compile; `numberTwice` doesn't have an `add(T)` method. `List<T>` is an immutable list; it can be modified once it is initialized. To add elements to a list, it must have a different type—`MutableList<T>` in our case:

```
val numbers: List<Int> = listOf(1, 2, 3, 4)

fun main(args: Array<String>) {
    val numbersTwice: MutableList<Int> = mutableListOf()

    for (i in numbers) {
        numbersTwice.add(i * 2) //Nice!
    }
}
```

`MutableList<T>` extends `List<T>`; it adds the methods to modify the collection itself, such as `add(T)`, `remove(T)`, `clear`, and others.

All major Kotlin collection types (`List<T>`, `Set<T>`, and `Map<K, V>`) have mutable subtypes (`MutableList<T>`, `MutableSet<T>`, and `MutableMap<K, V>`).

But we can replace this transformation with a single line expression as shown in the following code:

```
val numbers: List<Int> = listOf(1, 2, 3, 4)

fun main(args: Array<String>) {
    val numbersTwice: List<Int> = numbers.map { i -> i * 2 }
}
```

The `map` operation lets you transform (technically mapping a value to another). This code has many advantages and is a lot cleaner, and now the `numbersTwice` value is a `List<Int>` list, instead of a `MutableList<T>` list.

Let's have another couple of examples. We can sum all elements of numbers using a loop:

```
val numbers: List<Int> = listOf(1, 2, 3, 4)

fun main(args: Array<String>) {
    var sum = 0
    for (i in numbers) {
        sum += i
    }
    println(sum)
}
```

It could be reduced to just one line, with an immutable `sum` value as follows:

```
val numbers: List<Int> = listOf(1, 2, 3, 4)

fun main(args: Array<String>) {
    val sum = numbers.sum()
    println(sum)
}
```

Nice, but not interesting, so let's raise the stakes:

```
val numbers: List<Int> = listOf(1, 2, 3, 4)

fun main(args: Array<String>) {
    val sum = numbers.fold(0) { acc, i -> acc + i }

    println(sum)
}
```

The `fold` method iterates over a collection, keeping an accumulator value. `fold` takes a T value as the initial value; in the first iteration, this initial value will be the accumulator and subsequent iterations will use the lambda's return as the next accumulator value:

```
val numbers: List<Int> = listOf(1, 2, 3, 4)

fun main(args: Array<String>) {
    val sum = numbers.fold(0) { acc, i ->
        println("acc, i = $acc, $i")
        acc + i
    }
```

```
        println(sum)
    }
```

The output will look something like the following screenshot:

```
acc, i = 0, 1
acc, i = 1, 2 |
acc, i = 3, 3
acc, i = 6, 4
10
```

Similar to `fold`, `reduce` iterates over a collection, with an accumulator but without an initial value:

```kotlin
val numbers: List<Int> = listOf(1, 2, 3, 4)

fun main(args: Array<String>) {
    val sum = numbers.reduce { acc, i ->
        println("acc, i = $acc, $i")
        acc + i
    }

    println(sum)
}
```

The output will look something like the following screenshot:

```
acc, i = 1, 2
acc, i = 3, 3
acc, i = 6, 4
10
```

`fold` and `reduce` have counterparts in `foldRight` and `reduceRight` that start iterating from the last item to the first.

Implementing a functional list

With everything that we've learned in the first two chapters, we can implement a pure functional list:

```
sealed class FunList<out T> {
    object Nil : FunList<Nothing>()

    data class Cons<out T>(val head: T, val tail: FunList<T>) : FunList<T>()
}
```

The `FunList` class is a sealed class; just two possible subclasses exist—`Nil`, an empty list (in other books you can see this defined as `Null` or `Empty`) and `Cons` (a construct, name inherited from Lisp, that holds two values).

The `T` type is marked `out`; this is for variance, which we'll cover variance in future chapters.

`Nil` is an object (we don't need different instances of `Nil`) extending `FunList<Nothing>` (remember that `Nothing` is the bottom of Kotlin's type hierarchy).

The `Cons` value contains two values—`head`, a single `T`, and `tail`, a `FunList<T>`; therefore, it can be a `Nil` value or another `Cons`.

Let's create a list instance as follows:

```
import com.packtpub.functionalkotlin.chapter02.FunList.Cons
import com.packtpub.functionalkotlin.chapter02.FunList.Nil

fun main(args: Array<String>) {
    val numbers = Cons(1, Cons(2, Cons(3, Cons(4, Nil))))
}
```

It's functional, but not very readable. We can create a better initialization function:

```
import com.packtpub.functionalkotlin.chapter02.FunList.Cons
import com.packtpub.functionalkotlin.chapter02.FunList.Nil

fun intListOf(vararg numbers: Int): FunList<Int> {
    return if (numbers.isEmpty()) {
        Nil
    } else {
        Cons(numbers.first(),
intListOf(*numbers.drop(1).toTypedArray().toIntArray()))
    }
}
```

There are quite a few new things here. The argument numbers are marked as `vararg`, which means that we can invoke this function with as many parameters as we want. For all intents and purposes, `numbers` is an `IntArray` value (a specialized type of array). If `numbers` is empty, we can return `Nil`. If not, we can extract the first element as our `head` value and recursively invoke `intLisfOf` for the `tail` value. To extract the `tail` value, we use the `drop` method and convert its result to an `IntArray` value. But we can't directly pass any array as `vararg`; therefore, we must use the spread (`*`) operator to pass each member of an array individually.

Now, we can create our `FunList<Int>` value:

```
fun main(args: Array<String>) {
    val numbers = intListOf(1, 2, 3, 4)
}
```

Let's implement `forEach` as follows:

```
sealed class FunList<out T> {
   object Nil : FunList<Nothing>()

   data class Cons<out T>(val head: T, val tail: FunList<T>) : FunList<T>()

   fun forEach(f: (T) -> Unit) {
      tailrec fun go(list: FunList<T>, f: (T) -> Unit) {
         when (list) {
            is Cons -> {
               f(list.head)
               go(list.tail, f)
            }
            is Nil -> Unit//Do nothing
         }
      }

      go(this, f)
   }

}
```

The `forEach` implementation is similar to our examples of Factorial and Fibonacci functions in the recursion section, including `tailrec`.

FunList is, technically, an **Algebraic Data Type** (**ADT**). FunList can be either a Nil or
Cons and nothing else. Kotlin's compiler can use this information to check that both values
are evaluated when a FunList type is used as the argument in a when control structure:

```
fun main(args: Array<String>) {
    val numbers = intListOf(1, 2, 3, 4)
    numbers.forEach { i -> println("i = $i") }
}
```

Implementing fold will be similar to the following code:

```
sealed class FunList<out T> {
  /*Previous code here*/

    fun <R> fold(init: R, f: (R, T) -> R): R {
        tailrec fun go(list: FunList<T>, init: R, f: (R, T) -> R): R = when
(list) {
            is Cons -> go(list.tail, f(init, list.head), f)
            is Nil -> init
        }

        return go(this, init, f)
    }
}
```

Did you notice that these functions are very easy to implement? Let's have a look at the
following code:

```
fun main(args: Array<String>) {
    val numbers = intListOf(1, 2, 3, 4)
    val sum = numbers.fold(0) { acc, i -> acc + i}
}
```

What about a little contest between Kotlin's list and our functional list?

```
fun main(args: Array<String>) {
    val funList = intListOf(1, 2, 3, 4)
    val list = listOf(1, 2, 3, 4)

    println("fold on funList : ${executionTime { funList.fold(0) { acc, i
-> acc + i } }}")
    println("fold on list : ${executionTime { list.fold(0) { acc, i -> acc
+ i } }}")
}
```

The output will look something like the following screenshot:

```
fold on funList : 2138372
fold on list : 203832
```

Ouch! Our implementation is 10 times slower. No worries, Kotlin's implementation is a heavily optimized imperative solution and ours is just to learn and have fun (pun intended).

What about `map`? To implement `map` in a functional way we need to implement other functions first. Let's start with `reverse`.

`reverse` is a function that returns a list in reverse order:

```
sealed class FunList<out T> {

    /*previous code*/

    fun reverse(): FunList<T> = fold(Nil as FunList<T>) { acc, i -> Cons(i,
acc) }
}
```

We can reuse `fold` and build a new `Cons` value in each iteration, using the `acc` value as `tail`. This is one of the big advantages of functional programming—reusing existing functions.

Now, we can implement `foldRight`:

```
sealed class FunList<out T> {

    /*previous code*/

  fun <R> foldRight(init: R, f: (R, T) -> R): R {
   return this.reverse().fold(init, f)
  }
}
```

Again, we are reusing existing functions. It is time to implement our map function. At this point, it is not surprising that we'll reuse our existing functions:

```
sealed class FunList<out T> {

  /*previous code*

  fun <R> map(f:(T) -> R): FunList<R> {
    return foldRight(Nil as FunList<R>){ tail, head -> Cons(f(head), tail) }
  }
}
```

foldRight is all that we need. As you can see, we can implement a complete list using functions and other basic concepts as building blocks. And that is all about functional programming.

Summary

In this chapter, we covered the basics of functional programming, including high-order functions, pure functions, recursion functions, and lazy evaluation. We also covered functional collections and we implemented a functional collection, using a functional programming style.

In the next chapter, we'll cover a foundational stone of functional programming—immutability.

3
Immutability - It's Important

So, we are in the third chapter of, *Functional Kotlin*. In this chapter, we are going to discuss immutability. Immutability is probably the most important aspect of functional programming; actually, not only in functional programming, but OOP also gives some room to nurture immutability with immutable objects. So, why is it so important? What does it mean? How can we implement immutability in Kotlin? Let's answer these questions in this chapter.

The following are the points we are going to cover in this chapter:

- What is immutability?
- The advantages of immutability
- How to implement immutability in Kotlin?
- Immutability in variables
- `val` **versus** `var`
- `val` and `const val`—are they truly immutable?
- Compiler optimization
- Immutable collections
- The disadvantages of immutability

What is immutability?

Functional programming, by its nature, is thread safe; immutability has a great role in making it thread safe. If you go by the dictionary definition, **immutability** means that something is unchangeable. So, as per the dictionary, an **immutable variable** is a variable that cannot change. Now, how can that be of any help to thread safety?

The following example shows a simple class, with no extra protective measures for thread safety:

```
class MutableObject {
    var mutableProperty:Int = 1
}
```

Just think of a situation when you're calling this class from multiple threads at the same time. There is no guarantee of integrity in this, right?

Now, imagine making `mutableProperty` immutable; the problem is partly solved, right?

However, if you think of immutability as creating a class and making all its variables read-only, then such a simplified explanation would not only be wrong, but would also be horrible. Actually, immutability is not about forbidding change, but about handling change. Instead of changing the underlying value of a property directly, create a new property and copy the value with applied changes. This applies to things such as the primitive data types in Kotlin and Java (or even in C). For instance, in the following example, when we're writing `var y = x.capitalize()`, the value of x remains unchanged, instead the x value is copied to y with applied changes:

```
fun main(args: Array<String>) {
    var x:String = "abc"
    var y = x.capitalize()
    println("x = $x, y = $y")
}
```

Most of the primitive types operate in the same way; that is what is called **immutability**. Now, let's see how can we implement immutability in Kotlin and then, we will have a look at its advantages and disadvantages.

Implementing immutability in Kotlin

Unlike Clojure, Haskell, F#, and the likes, Kotlin is not a pure functional programming language, where immutability is forced; rather, we may refer to Kotlin as a perfect blend of functional programming and OOP languages. It contains the major benefits of both worlds. So, instead of forcing immutability like pure functional programming languages, Kotlin encourages immutability, giving it automatic preference wherever possible.

In other words, Kotlin has immutable variables (`val`), but no language mechanisms that would guarantee true deep immutability of the state. If a `val` variable references a mutable object, its contents can still be modified. We will have a more elaborate discussion and a deeper dive on this topic, but first let us have a look at how we can get referential immutability in Kotlin and the differences between `var`, `val`, and `const val`.

> By true deep immutability of the state, we mean a property will always return the same value whenever it is called and that the property never changes its value; we can easily avoid this if we have a `val` property that has a custom getter. You can find more details at the following link: `https://artemzin.com/blog/kotlin-val-does-not-mean-immutable-it-just-means-readonly-yeah/`

The difference between var and val

So, in order to encourage immutability but still let the developers have the choice, Kotlin introduced two types of variables. The first one is `var`, which is just a simple variable, just like in any imperative language. On the other hand, `val` brings us a bit closer to immutability; again, it doesn't guarantee immutability. So, what exactly does the `val` variable provide us? It enforces read-only, you cannot write into a `val` variable after initialization. So, if you use a `val` variable without a custom getter, you can achieve referential immutability.

Let's have a look; the following program will not compile:

```
fun main(args: Array<String>) {
    val x:String = "Kotlin"
    x+="Immutable"//(1)
}
```

As I mentioned earlier, the preceding program will not compile; it will give an error on comment (1). As we've declared variable x as `val`, x will be read-only and once we initialize x; we cannot modify it afterwards.

So, now you're probably asking why we cannot guarantee immutability with `val`? Let's inspect this with the following example:

```
object MutableVal {
    var count = 0
    val myString:String = "Mutable"
        get() {//(1)
            return "$field ${++count}"//(2)
```

```
        }
    }

fun main(args: Array<String>) {
    println("Calling 1st time ${MutableVal.myString}")
    println("Calling 2nd time ${MutableVal.myString}")
    println("Calling 3rd time ${MutableVal.myString}")//(3)
}
```

In this program, we declared `myString` as a `val` property, but implemented a custom `get` function, where we tweaked the value of `myString` before returning it. Have a look at the output first, then we will further look into the program:

```
"C:\Program Files\Java\jdk1.8.0_131\bin\java" ...
Calling 1st time Mutable 1
Calling 2nd time Mutable 2
Calling 3rd time Mutable 3


Process finished with exit code 0
```

As you can see, the `myString` property, despite being `val`, returned different values every time we accessed it. So, now, let us look into the code to understand such behavior.

On comment `(1)`, we declared a custom getter for the `val` property `myString`. On comment `(2)`, we pre-incremented the value of `count` and added it after the value of the `field` value, `myString`, and returned the same from the getter. So, whenever we requested the `myString` property, `count` got incremented and, on the next request, we got a different value. As a result, we broke the immutable behavior of a `val` property.

Compile time constants

So, how can we overcome this? How can we enforce immutability? The `const val` properties are here to help us. Just modify `val myString` with `const val myString` and you cannot implement the custom getter.

While `val` properties are read-only variables, `const val` on the other hand are compile time constants. You cannot assign the outcome (result) of a function to `const val`. Let's discuss some of the differences between `val` and `const val`:

- The `val` properties are read-only variables, while `const val` are compile time constants
- The `val` properties can have custom getters, but `const val` cannot
- We can have `val` properties anywhere in our Kotlin code, inside functions, as a class member, anywhere, but `const val` has to be a top-level member of a class/object
- You cannot write delegates for the `const val` properties
- We can have the `val` property of any type, be it our custom class or any primitive data type, but only primitive data types and `String` are allowed with a `const val` property
- We cannot have nullable data types with the `const val` properties; as a result, we cannot have null values for the `const val` properties either

As a result, the `const val` properties guarantee immutability of value, but have lesser flexibility and you are bound to use only primitive data types with `const val`, which cannot always serve our purposes.

Now, that I've used the word *referential immutability* quite a few times, let us now inspect what it means and how many types of immutability there are.

Types of immutability

There are basically the following two types of immutability:

- Referential immutability
- Immutable values

Immutable reference (referential immutability)

Referential immutability enforces that, once a reference is assigned, it can't be assigned to something else. Think of having it as a `val` property of a custom class, or even `MutableList` or `MutableMap`; after you initialize the property, you cannot reference something else from that property, except the underlying value from the object. For example, take the following program:

```
class MutableObj {
    var value = ""

    override fun toString(): String {
        return "MutableObj(value='$value')"
    }
}

fun main(args: Array<String>) {
    val mutableObj:MutableObj = MutableObj()//(1)
    println("MutableObj $mutableObj")
    mutableObj.value = "Changed"//(2)
    println("MutableObj $mutableObj")

    val list = mutableListOf("a","b","c","d","e")//(3)
    println(list)
    list.add("f")//(4)
    println(list)
}
```

Have a look at the output before we proceed with explaining the program:

```
"C:\Program Files\Java\jdk1.8.0_131\bin\java" ...
MutableObj MutableObj(value='')
MutableObj MutableObj(value='Changed')
[a, b, c, d, e]
[a, b, c, d, e, f]


Process finished with exit code 0
```

So, in this program we've two `val` properties—`list` and `mutableObj`. We initialized `mutableObj` with the default constructor of `MutableObj`, since it's a `val` property it'll always refer to that specific object; but, if you concentrate on comment `(2)`, we changed the `value` property of `mutableObj`, as the `value` property of the `MutableObj` class is mutable (`var`).

It's the same with the `list` property, we can add items to the list after initialization, changing its underlying value. Both `list` and `mutableObj` are perfect examples of immutable reference; once initialized, the properties can't be assigned to something else, but their underlying values can be changed (you can refer the output). The reason behind that is the data type we used to assign to those properties. Both the `MutableObj` class and the `MutableList<String>` data structures are mutable themselves, so we cannot restrict value changes for their instances.

Immutable values

The **immutable values**, on the other hand, enforce no change on values as well; it is really complex to maintain. In Kotlin, the `const val` properties enforces immutability of value, but they lack flexibility (we already discussed them) and you're bound to use only primitive types, which can be troublesome in real-life scenarios.

Immutable collections

Kotlin gives preference to immutability wherever possible, but leaves the choice to the developer whether or when to use it. This power of choice makes the language even more powerful. Unlike most languages, where they have either only mutable (like Java, C#, and so on) or only immutable collections (like F#, Haskell, Clojure, and so on), Kotlin has both and distinguishes between them, leaving the developer with the freedom to choose whether to use an immutable or mutable one.

Kotlin has two interfaces for collection objects—`Collection<out E>` and `MutableCollection<out E>`; all the collection classes (for example, `List`, `Set`, or `Map`) implement either of them. As the name suggests, the two interfaces are designed to serve immutable and mutable collections respectively. Let us have an example:

```
fun main(args: Array<String>) {
    val immutableList = listOf(1,2,3,4,5,6,7)//(1)
    println("Immutable List $immutableList")
    val mutableList:MutableList<Int> = immutableList.toMutableList()//(2)
    println("Mutable List $mutableList")
```

```
        mutableList.add(8)//(3)
        println("Mutable List after add $mutableList")
        println("Mutable List after add $immutableList")
    }
```

The output is as follows:

```
"C:\Program Files\Java\jdk1.8.0_131\bin\java" ...
Immutable List [1, 2, 3, 4, 5, 6, 7]
Mutable List [1, 2, 3, 4, 5, 6, 7]
Mutable List after add [1, 2, 3, 4, 5, 6, 7, 8]
Mutable List after add [1, 2, 3, 4, 5, 6, 7]


Process finished with exit code 0
```

So, in this program, we created an immutable list with the help of the `listOf` method of Kotlin, on comment `(1)`. The `listOf` method creates an immutable list with the elements (`varargs`) passed to it. This method also has a generic type parameter, which can be skipped if the elements array is not empty. The `listOf` method also has a mutable version—`mutableListOf()` which is identical except that it returns `MutableList` instead. We can convert an immutable list to a mutable one with the help of the `toMutableList()` extension function, we did the same in comment `(2)`, to add an element to it on comment `(3)`. However, if you check the output, the original `Immutable List` remains the same without any changes, the item is, however, added to the newly created `MutableList` instead.

The advantages of immutability

We've mentioned several times that immutability brings safety along with it. But that's not all; the following is a brief list of advantages that immutability brings with it, we will discuss them one by one:

- Thread safety
- Low coupling
- Referential transparency
- Failure atomicity
- Compiler optimization
- Pure functions

Let us now discuss each of the advantages to understand them better.

Thread safety

We have probably seen a thousand times that immutability brings thread safety to the table along with it. What does it actually mean and how does immutability achieve thread safety? Working with multiple threads is itself a complex job. When you are accessing a class from multiple threads, you need to ensure certain things, like locking and releasing of the object and synchronization, but none of them are required if you are accessing any immutable data from multiple threads.

Confused? Let's have an example with threads and mutable data:

```
class MyData {
    var someData:Int = 0
}

fun main(args: Array<String>) {
    val myData:MyData = MyData()

    async(CommonPool) {
        for(i in 11..20) {
            myData.someData+=i
            println("someData from 1st async ${myData.someData}")
            delay(500)
        }
    }

    async(CommonPool) {
        for(i in 1..10) {
            myData.someData++
            println("someData from 2nd async ${myData.someData}")
            delay(300)
        }
    }

    runBlocking { delay(10000) }
}
```

In this program, we've used two coroutines (we will cover coroutines in detail in `Chapter 7, Asynchronous Processing with Coroutines`) which works on the same mutable data. Let's have a look in the following output and then we will describe and discuss the problems in this program:

```
"C:\Program Files\Java\jdk1.8.0_131\bin\java" ...
someData from 1st async 11
someData from 2nd async 12
someData from 2nd async 13
someData from 1st async 25
someData from 2nd async 26
someData from 2nd async 27
someData from 1st async 40
someData from 2nd async 41
someData from 1st async 55
someData from 2nd async 56
someData from 2nd async 57
someData from 1st async 72
someData from 2nd async 73
someData from 1st async 89
someData from 2nd async 90
someData from 2nd async 91
someData from 1st async 108
someData from 1st async 126
someData from 1st async 145
someData from 1st async 165


Process finished with exit code 0
```

So, look closely at the output. As both the coroutines works simultaneously on `myData.someData`, data consistency is not ensured in either one.

The traditional solution to this problem is to use locking-releasing techniques and synchronization, but then also you'll need to write a lot of code for that and to avoid deadlock while implementing locking and releasing of data.

Functional programming provides a one-stop solution to this problem through immutability. Let's have a look how immutability and local variables can save you in multithreading:

```
class MyDataImmutable {
    val someData:Int = 0
}

fun main(args: Array<String>) {
    val myData: MyDataImmutable = MyDataImmutable()

    async(CommonPool) {
        var someDataCopy = myData.someData
        for (i in 11..20) {
            someDataCopy += i
            println("someData from 1st async $someDataCopy")
            delay(500)
        }
    }

    async(CommonPool) {
        var someDataCopy = myData.someData
        for (i in 1..10) {
            someDataCopy++
            println("someData from 2nd async $someDataCopy")
            delay(300)
        }
    }

    runBlocking { delay(10000) }
}
```

We've modified the previous program to make `someData` immutable (as we're not using custom getter with this variable, so it will remain immutable) and used local variables inside both the coroutines.

Have a look at the following output; it clearly shows that the problem is solved:

```
"C:\Program Files\Java\jdk1.8.0_131\bin\java" ...
someData from 1st async 11
someData from 2nd async 1
someData from 2nd async 2
someData from 1st async 23
someData from 2nd async 3
someData from 2nd async 4
someData from 1st async 36
someData from 2nd async 5
someData from 1st async 50
someData from 2nd async 6
someData from 2nd async 7
someData from 1st async 65
someData from 2nd async 8
someData from 2nd async 9
someData from 1st async 81
someData from 2nd async 10
someData from 1st async 98
someData from 1st async 116
someData from 1st async 135
someData from 1st async 155


Process finished with exit code 0
```

Low coupling

The code dependency between threads is referred to as coupling. We should try to keep coupling as low as possible, to avoid complexity and make the code base easy to read and maintain. Now, what does that actually mean? Refer to the program with threading where we accessed and modified the someData value from two threads simultaneously. That can be called **coupling**, as both the threads were dependent on each other. For your reference, we copied the following code-snippet:

```
async(CommonPool) {
        for(i in 11..20) {
            myData.someData+=i
            println("someData from 1st async ${myData.someData}")
            delay(500)
        }
```

```
    }

    async(CommonPool) {
        for(i in 1..10) {
            myData.someData++
            println("someData from 2nd async ${myData.someData}")
            delay(300)
        }
    }
}
```

In the next program, where we introduced immutability, the coupling is reduced. Here, both the threads were reading the same element, but one thread's operations and changes didn't affect the other one.

Referential transparency

The concept of **referential transparency** says that, an expression always evaluates to the same value, irrespective of context or any other variance. To be more specific, you can replace a function with its return value.

Immutability, with help of pure functions, can establish referential transparency. Referential transparency strongly denies the mutable state of data.

Failure atomicity

In traditional programming, failure in one thread can easily affect the other one. As immutability enforces low coupling, the internal state of the application will be consistent, even when we have exceptions on any module/thread.

The reason is simple, the immutable objects never change state. So, even if failure occurs in one part/module/thread, it stops right there and doesn't get any chance to get spread to other parts of the application.

Caching

As immutable objects are not going to change, they can be easily cached to improve performance. Thus, you can easily avoid making multiple calls to the same function/variable and, instead, cache it locally and save an ample amount of processing time. The following are some of the advantages of caching:

- It reduces the overhead from server resources
- It increases the performance of the application by serving it with the cached output
- It decreases CPU round trips for fetching data from the database by persisting data in the memory
- It increases reliability

Compiler optimization

Immutability and referential transparency help compilers to perform extensive optimizations, replacing the need of manual optimization of code and free programmers from this trade-off.

For example, this applies when you're using compile time constants (`const val`), as the compiler knows that the value of those variables will never change.

Pure functions

Probably the biggest gift we can get by using immutability are the *pure functions* (covered in the next chapter). Basically, pure functions and immutability are not only companions, but are complimentary to each other.

We cannot implement pure functions without immutability and immutability isn't complete without pure functions.

So, as we've learned a lot about immutability and its advantages, let us now focus on the other side: the disadvantages of immutability and check if they truly are disadvantages.

The disadvantages of immutability

Nothing in the world comes only with advantages.

There's a great proverb: everything comes at its own price.

The only thing you can hear against immutability is that you need to create a new object every time you want to modify it. That's true in some scenarios, especially where you're working with large sets of objects. However, when you are working with small datasets or objects, it doesn't have any effect.

Summary

In this chapter, we learned about immutability and how to implement immutability with Kotlin. We learned that Kotlin provides us with the freedom to choose between immutability or mutable objects, based on our requirements. We not only discussed the advantages of immutability, but talked about its limitations as well.

The next chapter focuses on function, function types, and side effects. We will also learn about pure functions, which are not only a companion but a complimentary part of immutability, in the next chapter.

So what are you waiting for? Turn the page right now.

4
Functions, Function Types, and Side Effects

Functional programming revolves around the concepts of immutability and functions. We learned about immutability in the last chapter; we also got a glimpse of pure functions while discussing immutability. Pure functions are basically one of the many types (but probably the most important one) that functional programming has to offer.

This chapter will revolve around functions. To go into depth on functional programming, you need a strong base in functions. To get your concepts clear, we will start with ordinary Kotlin functions and then gradually move on to discuss abstract concepts on functions that functional programming defines. We will also see their implementation in Kotlin.

In this chapter, we are going to cover the following topics:

- Functions in Kotlin
- Function types
- Lambda
- High order functions
- Understanding side effects and pure functions

So, let's get started by defining functions.

Functions in Kotlin

Functions are one of the most important parts of programming. We write tons of functions every week for our projects. Functions are also a part of the fundamentals of programming. To learn functional programming, we must have our concepts clear with regard to functions. In this section, we will cover the basics of functions, in order to get you brushed up and ready for the next sections in this chapter, where we will be discussing abstract functional concepts and their implementation in Kotlin.

So, let's start by defining functions.

 A **function** is a block of organized, reusable code that is used to perform a single, related action.

Not very clear? We will explain, but first, let's learn why we should write functions. In short, what is the functionality of a function? Have a look:

- Functions allow us to break the program into a bunch of steps and substeps
- Functions encourages code reuse
- Functions, if used properly, help us keep the code clean, organized, and easy to understand
- Functions make testing (unit testing) easy, testing each small part of the program is easier than the complete program in a single go

In Kotlin, a function generally looks like the following:

```
fun appropriateFunctionName(parameter1:DataType1,
parameter2:DataType2,...): ReturnType {
    //do your stuff here
    return returnTypeObject
}
```

In Kotlin, a function declaration starts with the `fun` keyword, followed by the function name, then braces. Inside the braces, we can specify function arguments (optional). After the braces, there would be a colon (:) and return type, which specifies the datatype of the value/object to be returned (you can skip return type if you don't plan to return anything from the function; in that case, the default return type `Unit` will be assigned to the function). After those, there would be the function body, covered in curly braces (curly braces are also optional for Single-Expression functions, covered next in `Chapter 5`, *More on Functions*).

Unit is a datatype in Kotlin. Unit is a singleton instance of itself and holds a value that is Unit itself. Unit corresponds to void in Java, but it's quite different than void. While void means nothing in Java and void cannot contain anything, we have Nothing in Kotlin for that purpose, which indicates that a function would never complete successfully (due to an exception or an infinite loop).

Now, what are those return types, parameters (arguments), and function bodies? Let's explore them.

The following is a more realistic function example than the abstract one previously shown:

```
fun add(a:int, b:Int):Int {
    val result = a+b
    return result
}
```

Now, have a look at the following explanations for each parts of a function:

- **Function arguments/parameters**: These are the data (unless lambda) for the function to work on. In our example, a and b are the function parameters.
- **Function body**: Everything we write inside the curly braces of a function is called the **function body**. It is the part of a function, where we write the logic or set of instructions to accomplish a particular task. In the preceding example, two lines inside the curly braces is the function body.
- **Return statement, datatype**: If we are willing to return some value from the function, we have to declare the datatype of the value we are willing to return; that datatype is called the return type—in this case, Int is the return type and return result is the return statement, it enables you to return a value to the calling function.

We can make the previous example shorter by removing val result = a+b and replacing the return statement with return a+b. In Kotlin, we can further shorten this example, as we will see in Chapter 5, *More on Functions*.

While writing functions is easy, Kotlin makes it easier for you.

Kotlin has bundled various features with functions that make a developer's life easier. The following is a brief list of the features bundled with Kotlin:

- Single-expression functions
- Extension functions
- Inline functions
- Infix notation and more

We will cover them in detail in the *Lambda, Generics, Recursions, Corecursion* section of `Chapter 5`, *More on Functions*.

Returning two values from a function

While, generally, a function can return only a single value, in Kotlin, by leveraging the benefits of the `Pair` type and destructuring declarations, we can return two variables from a function. Consider the following example:

```
fun getUser():Pair<Int,String> {//(1)
    return Pair(1,"Rivu")
}
fun main(args: Array<String>) {
    val (userID,userName) = getUser()//(2)
     println("User ID: $userID t User Name: $userName")
}
```

In the preceding program, on comment `(1)`, we created a function that would return a `Pair<Int,String>` value.

On comment `(2)`, we used that function in a way that seems like it returns two variables. Actually, destructuring declarations allows you to destructure a `data class`/`Pair` and get its underlying values in standalone variables. When this feature is used with functions, it seems like the function is returning multiple values, though it returns only one value that is a `Pair` value or another `data class`.

Extension functions

Kotlin provides us with extension functions. What are they? They are like an ad hoc function on top of an existing datatype/class.

For example, if we want to count the number of words in a string, the following would be a traditional function to do it:

```
fun countWords(text:String):Int {
    return text.trim()
            .split(Pattern.compile("\s+"))
            .size
}
```

We would pass a `String` to a function, have our logic count the words, and then we would return the value.

But don't you feel like it would always be better if there was a way that this function could be called on the `String` instance itself? Kotlin allows us to perform such an action.

Have a look at the following program:

```
fun String.countWords():Int {
    return trim()
            .split(Pattern.compile("\s+"))
            .size
}
```

Have a careful look at the function declaration. We declared the function as `String.countWords()`, not just `countWords` as it was previously; that means it should be called on a `String` instance now, just like the member functions of `String` class. Just like the following code:

```
fun main(args: Array<String>) {
    val counts = "This is an example StringnWith multiple
words".countWords()
    println("Count Words: $counts")
}
```

You can check out the following output:

```
"C:\Program Files\Java\jdk1.8.0_131\bin\java" ...
Count Words: 8


Process finished with exit code 0
```

Default arguments

We may have a requirement where we want to have an optional parameter for a function. Consider the following example:

```
fun Int.isGreaterThan(anotherNumber:Int):Boolean {
    return this>anotherNumber
}
```

We want to make `anotherNumber` parameter optional; we want it to be 0, if it is not passed as an argument. The traditional way is to have another overloaded function without any parameters, which would call this function with 0, like the following:

```
fun Int.isGreaterThan(anotherNumber:Int):Boolean {
    return this>anotherNumber
}
fun Int.isGreaterThan():Boolean {
    return this.isGreaterThan(0)
}
```

However, in Kotlin, things are quite easy and straightforward and they don't require us to define the function again just to make an argument optional. For making arguments optional, Kotlin provides us with default arguments, by which we can specify a default value of a function right away at the time of declaration.

The following is the modified function:

```
fun Int.isGreaterThan(anotherNumber:Int=0):Boolean {
    return this>anotherNumber
}
```

We would use the `main` function as follows:

```
fun main(args: Array<String>) {
    println("5>0: ${5.isGreaterThan()}")
    println("5>6: ${5.isGreaterThan(6)}")
}
```

For the first one, we skipped the argument and for the second one, we provided 6. So, for the first one, the output should be true (as 5 is really greater than 0), while for the second one, it should be false (as 5 isn't greater than 6).

The following screenshot output confirms the same:

```
"C:\Program Files\Java\jdk1.8.0_131\bin\java" ...
5>0: true
5>6: false


Process finished with exit code 0
```

Nested functions

Kotlin allows you to nest functions, one within another. We can declare and use a function within another function.

When you declare a function within another function, the nested functions, visibility will stay exclusively within the parent function and cannot be accessed from outside.

So, let's have an example:

```kotlin
fun main(args: Array<String>) {
    fun nested():String {
        return "String from nested function"
    }
    println("Nested Output: ${nested()}")
}
```

In the preceding program, we declared and used a function—nested()—inside the main function.

The following is the output, if you're curious:

```
"C:\Program Files\Java\jdk1.8.0_131\bin\java" ...
Nested Output: String from nested function


Process finished with exit code 0
```

So, as we've got our basics brushed up in functions, let's move forward in functional programming. In the following section, we will learn about function types.

Function types in functional programming

One of the main objectives of functional programming is to implement modular programming. Side effects (a functional term, defined later in this chapter) are often sources of bugs; functional programming wants you to avoid side effects totally.

To achieve that, functional programming has defined the following types of functions:

- Lambda functions as property
- High order functions
- Pure functions
- Partial functions

In this section, we will discuss each of these concepts in order to get a solid grip on functional programming paradigms.

So, let's get started with lambda.

Lambda

Lambda, which can also be called **anonymous functions**, has a first-class citizen support in Kotlin. While, in Java, lambda is only supported starting with Java 8, in Kotlin, you can use Kotlin with JVM 6 onwards, so there's really no barrier for lambda in Kotlin.

Now, we were talking about lambda, anonymous classes (or objects) and anonymous functions, but what are they? Let us explore.

To be generic, lambda or lambda expressions generally means **anonymous functions**, that is, functions without names, which can be assigned to variables, passed as arguments, or returned from another function. It is a kind of nested function, but is more versatile and more flexible. You can also say all the lambda expressions are functions, but not every function is a lambda expression. Being anonymous and unnamed brings a lot of benefits to lambda expressions, which we will discuss soon.

As I mentioned earlier, not all languages support lambda and Kotlin is one of rarest languages, and it provides extensive support for lambda.

So, why is it called lambda? Let us dig up a bit of history now.

Lambda, Λ, λ (uppercase Λ, lowercase λ) is the 11th letter of the Greek alphabet. Pronunciation: lám(b)da.
Source: https://en.wikipedia.org/wiki/Lambda

During the 1930s, Alonzo Church, who was at that time studying mathematics at Princeton University, used the Greek alphabet, specifically lambda, to denote what he called **functions**. The thing to note is that, at that time, there were only anonymous functions in computing; the concept of modern-day named functions were yet to come.

So, with this practice of Alonzo Church, the word lambda got attached to anonymous functions (then the only type of function) which is, to date, referred to in the same way.

Alonzo Church (June 14, 1903-August 11, 1995), was an American mathematician and logician who made major contributions to mathematical logic and the foundations of theoretical computer science. He is best known for the lambda calculus, *Church-Turing* thesis, proving the undecidability of the *Entscheidungsproblem*, *Frege-Church* ontology, and the *Church-Rosser* theorem. He also worked on philosophy of language (for example, Church, 1970).
Source: https://en.wikipedia.org/wiki/Alonzo_Church

Don't you think we have had enough of theories? Shouldn't we now focus on learning what lambda actually is, or what, exactly, it looks like? We will have a look at how lambdas look in Kotlin, but we would prefer to introduce you to lambda in Java first, and later in Kotlin, to make you fully understand how much power lambdas possess in Kotlin and what exactly is meant by first-class citizen support. You'll also learn the difference between lambda in Java and Kotlin.

Consider the following Java example. It's a simple example, where we are passing an instance of an interface to a method and, in that method, we are calling a method from the instance:

```java
public class LambdaIntroClass {
    interface SomeInterface {
        void doSomeStuff();
    }
    private static void invokeSomeStuff(SomeInterface someInterface) {
        someInterface.doSomeStuff();
    }
    public static void main(String[] args) {
        invokeSomeStuff(new SomeInterface() {
            @Override
            public void doSomeStuff() {
```

```
                    System.out.println("doSomeStuff invoked");
            }
        });
    }
}
```

So, in this program, SomeInterface is an interface (the inner interface of LambdaIntroClass) with a single method—doSomeStuff(). The static method (it's static to make it easily accessible by the main method) invokeSomeStuff takes an instance of SomeInterface and calls its method doSomeStuff().

It was a simple example; now, let's make it simpler: let's add lambda to it. Have a look at the following updated code:

```
public class LambdaIntroClass {
    interface SomeInterface {
        void doSomeStuff();
    }
    private static void invokeSomeStuff(SomeInterface someInterface) {
        someInterface.doSomeStuff();
    }
    public static void main(String[] args) {
        invokeSomeStuff(()->{
                System.out.println("doSomeStuff called");
        });
    }
}
```

So, here, the definition of SomeInterface and invokeSomeStuff() stays the same. The only difference is on passing the instance of SomeInterface. Instead of creating an instance of SomeInstance with a new SomeInstance, what we wrote is an expression (in bold) that looks pretty much like mathematical function expressions (except obviously the System.out.println()). That expression is called a **lambda expression**.

Wasn't that fantastic? You didn't need to create an instance of the interface, then override the method and all that stuff. What you did is a simple expression. That expression would be used as the method body of the doSomeStuff() method inside the interface.

The output for both the programs is identical; it is as shown in the following screenshot:

```
"C:\Program Files\Java\jdk1.8.0_131\bin\java" ...
doSomeStuff called

Process finished with exit code 0
```

Java doesn't have any types for lambda; you can only use lambda to create instances of classes and interfaces on the go. The only benefit of lambda in Java is that it makes Java programs easier to read (by humans) and reduces line counts.

We cannot actually blame Java for that. After all, Java is basically a purely object-oriented language. Kotlin, on the other hand, is a perfect blend of object-oriented and functional programming paradigms; it brings both the worlds closer together. In our words, Kotlin is the best language if you want to get started with functional programming with previous knowledge of object-oriented programming.

So, no more lectures, let us move on to the code. Let us now have a look how the same program would look in Kotlin:

```
fun invokeSomeStuff(doSomeStuff:()->Unit) {
    doSomeStuff()
}
fun main(args: Array<String>) {
    invokeSomeStuff({
        println("doSomeStuff called");
    })
}
```

Yes, that's the complete program (well, except the `import` statements and package name). I know you're a bit confused; you're asking if it is really the same program? Where is the interface definition then? Well, in Kotlin that is not actually required.

The `invokeSomeStuff()` function is actually a high-order function (covered next); we pass our lambda there and it directly calls the function.

Brilliant, isn't it? Kotlin has a bunch of features with lambda. Let us have a look at them.

Function as property

Kotlin also allows us to have functions as properties. Functions as properties means that a function can be used as a property.

For instance, take the following example:

```
fun main(args: Array<String>) {
    val sum = { x: Int, y: Int -> x + y }
    println("Sum ${sum(10,13)}")
    println("Sum ${sum(50,68)}")
}
```

In the preceding program, we created a property, sum, which will actually hold a function to add two numbers passed to it.

While sum is a val property, what it holds is a function (or lambda) and we can call that function just like the usual function we call; there are no differences there at all.

If you're curious, the following is the output:

```
"C:\Program Files\Java\jdk1.8.0_131\bin\java" ...
Sum 23
Sum 120

Process finished with exit code 0
```

Now, let us discuss the syntax of lambda.

In Kotlin, a lambda always stays embraced by the curly braces. This makes a lambda easy to identify, unlike in Java, where parameters/arguments reside outside the curly braces. In Kotlin, parameters/arguments reside inside curly braces separated by (->) from the logic of the function. The last statement in a lambda (which may just be a variable/property name or another function call) is considered as the return statement. So, whatever is the evaluation of the last statement of a lambda is the return value of a lambda.

Also, if your function is a single parameter function, you can also skip the property name. So, how can you use that parameter if you don't specify the name? Kotlin provides you with a default it property for single parameter lambdas where you don't specify the property name.

So, let's modify the previous lambda to add it. Have a look at the following code:

```
reverse = {
        var n = it
        var revNumber = 0
        while (n>0) {
            val digit = n%10
            revNumber=revNumber*10+digit
            n/=10
        }
        revNumber
}
```

We skipped the complete program and output, as they remain the same.

TIP

You must have noticed that we assigned the function parameters value to another `var` property (both when the parameter was named and when we denoted with `it`). The reason is that, in Kotlin, function parameters are immutable, but with the reverse number program, we needed a way to change the value; so, we assigned the value to a `var` property, which is mutable.

Now, you have lambda as properties, but what about their datatypes? Every property/variable has a datatype (even if the type is inferred), so what about lambdas? Let's have a look at the following example:

```kotlin
fun main(args: Array<String>) {
    val reverse:(Int)->Int//(1)
    reverse = {number ->
        var n = number
        var revNumber = 0
        while (n>0) {
            val digit = n%10
            revNumber=revNumber*10+digit
            n/=10
        }
        revNumber
    }// (2)
    println("reverse 123 ${reverse(123)}")
    println("reverse 456 ${reverse(456)}")
    println("reverse 789 ${reverse(789)}")
}
```

In the preceding program, we declared a `reverse` property as a function. In Kotlin, when you're declaring a property as a function, you should mention the datatypes of parameters/arguments inside braces, followed by an arrow and then the return type of the function; if the function is not planned to return something, you should mention `Unit`. While declaring a function as a property, you need not specify the parameter/argument name and while defining/assigning the function to the property, you can skip providing datatypes of the property.

The following is the output:

```
"C:\Program Files\Java\jdk1.8.0_131\bin\java" ...
reverse 123 321
reverse 456 654
reverse 789 987


Process finished with exit code 0
```

So, we have a good concept of lambda and functions as properties in Kotlin. Now, let us move ahead with high order functions.

High order functions

A high order function is a function which accepts another function as a parameter or returns another function. We just saw how we can use a function as a property, so it's quite easy to see that we can accept another function as a parameter or that we can return another function from a function. As stated previously, technically the function that receives or returns another function (it may be more than one) or does both is called a **high-order function**.

In our first lambda example in Kotlin, the `invokeSomeStuff` function was a high-order function.

The following is another example of high-order function:

```kotlin
fun performOperationOnEven(number:Int,operation:(Int)->Int):Int {
    if(number%2==0) {
        return operation(number)
    } else {
        return number
    }
}
fun main(args: Array<String>) {
    println("Called with 4,(it*2): ${performOperationOnEven(4,
            {it*2})}")
    println("Called with 5,(it*2): ${performOperationOnEven(5,
            {it*2})}")
}
```

In the preceding program, we created a high order function—performOperationOnEven which would take an `Int` and a lambda operation to execute on that `Int`. The only catch is that the function would only perform that operation on the provided `Int`, if that `Int` is an even number.

Isn't that easy enough? Let's have a look at the following output:

```
"C:\Program Files\Java\jdk1.8.0_131\bin\java" ...
Called with 4,(it*2): 8
Called with 5,(it*2): 5


Process finished with exit code 0
```

In all our previous examples, we saw how to pass a function (lambda) to another function. However, that's not the only feature of high order functions. A high order function also allows you to return a function from it.

So, let us explore it. Have a look at the following example:

```
fun getAnotherFunction(n:Int):(String)->Unit {
    return {
        println("n:$n it:$it")
    }
}
fun main(args: Array<String>) {
    getAnotherFunction(0)("abc")
    getAnotherFunction(2)("def")
    getAnotherFunction(3)("ghi")
}
```

In the preceding program, we created a function, getAnotherFunction, that would take an `Int` parameter and would return a function that takes a `String` value and returns `Unit`. That `return` function prints both its parameter (a `String`) and its parents parameter (an `Int`).

See the following output:

```
"C:\Program Files\Java\jdk1.8.0_131\bin\java" ...
n:0 it:abc
n:2 it:def
n:3 it:ghi


Process finished with exit code 0
```

 In Kotlin, technically you can have nested high order functions to any depth. However, that would do more harm than help, and would even destroy the readability. So, you should avoid them.

Pure functions and side effects

So, we have learned about lambda and high order functions. They are two of the most interesting and important topics of functional programming. In this section, we will be discussing side effects and pure functions.

So, let's start by defining side effects. We will then gradually move towards pure functions.

Side effects

In a computer program, when a function modifies any object/data outside its own scope, that is called a **side effect**. For instance, we often write functions that modify a global or static property, modify one of its arguments, raise an exception, write data to display or file, or even call another function which has a side effect.

For example, have a look at the following program:

```
class Calc {
    var a:Int=0
    var b:Int=0
    fun addNumbers(a:Int = this.a,b:Int = this.b):Int {
        this.a = a
        this.b = b
        return a+b
    }
}
```

```
    }
fun main(args: Array<String>) {
    val calc = Calc()
    println("Result is ${calc.addNumbers(10,15)}")
}
```

The preceding program is a simple object-oriented program. However, it contains side effects. The addNumbers() function modifies the state of the Calc class, which is bad practice in functional programming.

While we cannot avoid side effects in a few functions, especially where we are accessing IO and/or a database and so on, side effects should be avoided wherever possible.

Pure functions

The definition of a pure function says that, if the return value of a function is completely dependent on its arguments/parameters, then this function may be referred to as a **pure function**. So, if we declare a function as fun func1(x:Int):Int, then its return value will be strictly dependent on its argument, x; say, if you call func1 with a value of 3 N times, then, for every call, its return value will be the same.

The definition also says that a pure function should not actively or passively cause side effects, that is, it should not directly cause side effects, nor should it call any other function that causes side effects.

A pure function can be either a lambda or a named function.

So, why are they called pure functions? The reason is quite simple. Programming functions originated from mathematical functions. Programming functions, over time, evolved to contain multiple tasks and perform anonymous actions that are not directly related to the processing of passed arguments. So, those functions that still resemble mathematical functions are called pure functions.

So, let's modify our previous program to make it into a pure function:

```
fun addNumbers(a:Int = 0,b:Int = 0):Int {
    return a+b
}

fun main(args: Array<String>) {
    println()
}
```

Quite easy, isn't it? We are skipping the output, as the program is really easy.

Summary

In this chapter, we have learned about functions, how to use them, and their classifications. We also got introduced to lambda and high order functions. We learned about pure functions and side effects.

The next chapter will take you deeper into functions. As I already stated, you need to master functions in order to learn functional programming properly. So, what are you waiting for? Turn the page right now.

5
More on Functions

In the previous chapters, we covered many features of Kotlin's functions. But now we'll expand on these many features, most of them borrowed from other languages, but with a new twist to fully accommodate them into Kotlin's overall goals and flavour—type-safety and pragmatical conciseness.

Some features, such as **Domain Specific Languages (DSLs)**, let developers extend the language to domains that were not considered when Kotlin was first designed.

At the end of this chapter, you'll have a big picture of all function features, including:

- Extension functions
- Operator overloading
- Type-safe builders
- Inline functions
- Recursion and corecursion

Single-expression functions

Until now, all our examples were declared in a normal way.

The function sum takes two `Int` values and adds them. Declared in a normal way, we must provide a body with curly braces and an explicit `return`:

```
fun sum(a:Int, b:Int): Int {
    return a + b
}
```

Our `sum` function has its body declared inside curly braces with a `return` clause. But if our function is just one expression, it could have been written in a single line:

```
fun sum(a:Int, b:Int): Int = a + b
```

So, no curly braces, no `return` clause, and an equals (=) symbol. If you pay attention, it just looks similar to a lambda.

If you want to cut even more characters, you can use type inference too:

```
fun sum(a:Int, b:Int) = a + b
```

 Use type inference for a function's return when it is very evident which type you are trying to return. A good rule of thumb is to use it for simple types such as numeric values, Boolean, string, and simple `data class` constructors. Anything more complicated, especially if the function does any transformation, should have explicit types. Your future self will be glad!

Parameters

A function can have zero or more parameters. Our function, `basicFunction`, takes two parameters, as shown in the following code:

```
fun basicFunction(name: String, size: Int) {

}
```

Each parameter is defined as `parameterName: ParameterType`, in our example, `name: String` and `size: Int`. Nothing new here.

vararg

It gets interesting when parameters have two types that we have already covered—`vararg` and lambdas:

```
fun aVarargFun(vararg names: String) {
    names.forEach(::println)
}

fun main(args: Array<String>) {
    aVarargFun()
```

```
    aVarargFun("Angela", "Brenda", "Caroline")
}
```

A function with a parameter marked with the modifier, `vararg` can be called with zero or more values:

```
fun multipleVarargs(vararg names: String, vararg sizes: Int) {
// Compilation error, "Multiple vararg-parameters are prohibited"
}
```

A function can't have multiple `vararg` parameters, not even with different types.

Lambda

We already discussed how, if a function's last parameter is a lambda, it can't be passed outside the parenthesis and inside curly braces, as if the lambda itself is the body of a control structure.

We covered this `unless` function in Chapter 2, *Getting Started with Functional Programming*, in the section, *First-class and high-order functions*. Let's have a look at the following code:

```
fun unless(condition: Boolean, block: () -> Unit) {
    if (!condition) block()
}

unless(someBoolean) {
    println("You can't access this website")
}
```

Now, what happens if we combine `vararg` and lambda? Let's check it in the following code snippet:

```
fun <T, R> transform(vararg ts: T, f: (T) -> R): List<R> = ts.map(f)
```

Lambdas can be at the end of a function with a `vararg` parameter:

```
transform(1, 2, 3, 4) { i -> i.toString() }
```

Let's get a little adventurous, a `vararg` parameter of lambdas:

```
fun <T> emit(t: T, vararg listeners: (T) -> Unit) = listeners.forEach {
listener ->
    listener(t)
}

emit(1){i -> println(i)} //Compilation error. Passing value as a vararg is
only allowed inside a parenthesized argument list
```

We can't pass a lambda outside of the parenthesis, but we can pass many lambdas inside:

```
emit(1, ::println, {i -> println(i * 2)})
```

Named parameters

Ideally, our functions should not have too many parameters, but this isn't always the case. Some functions tend to be big, for example, the `data class` constructors (constructors are technically a function that returns a new instance).

What is the problem with functions with many parameters?

- They are hard to use. This can be alleviated or fixed with default parameters that we will cover in the next section, *Default parameters*.
- They are hard to read—named parameters to the rescue.
- They are probably doing too much. Are you sure that your function isn't too big? Try to refactor it and clean up. Look for possible side effects and other harmful practices. A special case is `data class` constructors, as they are just autogenerated assignments.

With named parameters, you can add readability to any function invocation.

Let's use a `data class` constructor as an example:

```
typealias Kg = Double
typealias cm = Int

data class Customer(val firstName: String,
                val middleName: String,
                val lastName: String,
                val passportNumber: String,
                val weight: Kg,
                val height: cm)
```

A normal invocation will look like this:

```
val customer1 = Customer("John", "Carl", "Doe", "XX234", 82.3, 180)
```

But including named parameters will increase the information available for the reader/maintainer and reduce mental work. We can also pass the parameters in any order that is more convenient or meaningful for the actual context:

```
val customer2 = Customer(
        lastName = "Doe",
        firstName = "John",
        middleName = "Carl",
        height = 180,
        weight = 82.3,
        passportNumber = "XX234")
```

Named parameters are very useful when they are combined with a `vararg` parameter:

```
fun paramAfterVararg(courseId: Int, vararg students: String,
roomTemperature: Double) {
    //Do something here
}

paramAfterVararg(68, "Abel", "Barbara", "Carl", "Diane", roomTemperature =
18.0)
```

Named parameters on high-order functions

Usually when we define a high-order function, we never name the parameters for the lambda(s):

```
fun high(f: (Int, String) -> Unit) {
    f(1, "Romeo")
}

high { q, w ->
    //Do something
}
```

But it is possible to add them. So, the `f` lambda now has its parameters named—`age` and `name`:

```
fun high(f: (age:Int, name:String) -> Unit) {
    f(1, "Romeo")
}
```

This doesn't change any behavior, it is just to give more clarity on the intended use of this lambda:

```
fun high(f: (age:Int, name:String) -> Unit) {
    f(age = 3, name = "Luciana") //compilation error
}
```

But it isn't possible to call a lambda with named parameters. In our example, invoking `f` with names produces a compilation error.

Default parameters

In Kotlin, function parameters can have default values. For the `Programmer,` the `favouriteLanguage` and `yearsOfExperience` data classes have default values (remember that a constructor is a function too):

```
data class Programmer(val firstName: String,
                      val lastName: String,
                      val favouriteLanguage: String = "Kotlin",
                      val yearsOfExperience: Int = 0)
```

So, `Programmer` can be created with just two parameters:

```
val programmer1 = Programmer("John", "Doe")
```

But if you want to pass `yearsOfExperience`, it must be as a named parameter:

```
val programmer2 = Programmer("John", "Doe", 12) //Error

val programmer2 = Programmer("John", "Doe", yearsOfExperience = 12) //OK
```

You can still pass all parameters if you want to, but they must be provided in the right order if you aren't using named arguments:

```
val programmer3 = Programmer("John", "Doe", "TypeScript", 1)
```

Extension functions

Definitively, one of the best features of Kotlin is extension functions. Extension functions let you modify existing types with new functions:

```
fun String.sendToConsole() = println(this)

fun main(args: Array<String>) {
    "Hello world! (from an extension function)".sendToConsole()
}
```

To add an extension function to an existing type, you must write the function's name next to the type's name, joined by a dot (.).

In our example, we add an extension function (sendToConsole()) to the String type. Inside the function's body, this refers the instance of String type (in this extension function, string is the receiver type).

Apart from the dot (.) and this, extension functions have the same syntax rules and features as a normal function. Indeed, behind the scenes, an extension function is a normal function whose first parameter is a value of the receiver type. So, our sendToConsole() extension function is equivalent to the next code:

```
fun sendToConsole(string: String) = println(string)

sendToConsole("Hello world! (from a normal function)")
```

So, in reality, we aren't modifying a type with new functions. Extension functions are a very elegant way to write utility functions, easy to write, very fun to use, and nice to read—a win-win. This also means that extension functions have one restriction—they can't access private members of this, in contrast with a proper member function that can access everything inside the instance:

```
class Human(private val name: String)

fun Human.speak(): String = "${this.name} makes a noise" //Cannot access
'name': it is private in 'Human'
```

Invoking an extension function is the same as a normal function—with an instance of the receiver type (that will be referenced as this inside the extension), invoke the function by name.

Extension functions and inheritance

There is a big difference between member functions and extension functions when we talk about inheritance.

The open class `Canine` has a subclass, `Dog`. A standalone function, `printSpeak`, receives a parameter of type `Canine` and prints the content of the result of the function `speak():` `String`:

```
open class Canine {
    open fun speak() = "<generic canine noise>"
}

class Dog : Canine() {
    override fun speak() = "woof!!"
}

fun printSpeak(canine: Canine) {
    println(canine.speak())
}
```

We already covered this in Chapter 1, *Kotlin – Data Types, Objects and Classes*, in the *Inheritance* section. Open classes with `open` methods (member functions) can be extended and alter their behavior. Invoking the `speak` function will act differently depending on which type is your instance.

The `printSpeak` function can be invoked with any instance of a class that *is-a* `Canine`, either `Canine` itself or any subclass:

```
printSpeak(Canine())
printSpeak(Dog())
```

If we execute this code, we can see this on the console:

```
<generic canine noise>
woof!!
```

Although both are `Canine`, the behavior of `speak` is different in both cases, as the subclass overrides the parent implementation.

But with extension functions, many things are different.

As with the previous example, `Feline` is an open class extended by the `Cat` class. But `speak` is now an extension function:

```
open class Feline

fun Feline.speak() = "<generic feline noise>"

class Cat : Feline()

fun Cat.speak() = "meow!!"

fun printSpeak(feline: Feline) {
   println(feline.speak())
}
```

Extension functions don't need to be marked as override, because we aren't overriding anything:

```
printSpeak(Feline())
printSpeak(Cat()
```

If we execute this code, we can see this on the console:

```
<generic feline noise>
<generic feline noise>
```

In this case, both invocations produce the same result. Although in the beginning it seems confusing, once you analyse what is happening, it becomes clear. We're invoking the `Feline.speak()` function twice; this is because each parameter that we pass is a `Feline` to the `printSpeak(Feline)` function:

```
open class Primate(val name: String)

fun Primate.speak() = "$name: <generic primate noise>"

open class GiantApe(name: String) : Primate(name)

fun GiantApe.speak() = "${this.name} :<scary 100db roar>"

fun printSpeak(primate: Primate) {
 println(primate.speak())
}

printSpeak(Primate("Koko"))
printSpeak(GiantApe("Kong"))
```

If we execute this code, we can see this on the console:

```
Koko: <generic primate noise>
Kong: <generic primate noise>
```

In this case, it is still the same behavior as with the previous examples, but using the right value for `name`. Speaking of which, we can reference `name` with `name` and `this.name`; both are valid.

Extension functions as members

Extension functions can be declared as members of a class. An instance of a class with extension functions declared is called the **dispatch receiver.**

The `Caregiver` open class internally defines, extension functions for two different classes, `Feline` and `Primate`:

```
open class Caregiver(val name: String) {
    open fun Feline.react() = "PURRR!!!"
    fun Primate.react() = "*$name plays with ${this@Caregiver.name}*"

    fun takeCare(feline: Feline) {
        println("Feline reacts: ${feline.react()}")
    }
    fun takeCare(primate: Primate){
        println("Primate reacts: ${primate.react()}")
    }
}
```

Both extension functions are meant to be used inside an instance of `Caregiver`. Indeed, it is a good practice to mark member extension functions as private, if they aren't open.

In the case of `Primate.react()`, we are using the `name` value from `Primate` and the `name` value from `Caregiver`. To access members with a name conflict, the extension receiver (`this`) takes precedence and to access members of the dispatcher receiver, the qualified `this` syntax must be used. Other members of the dispatcher receiver that don't have a name conflict can be used without qualified `this`.

Don't get confused by the various means of `this` that we have already covered:

- Inside a class, `this` means the instance of that class
- Inside an extension function, `this` means the instance of the receiver type like the first parameter in our utility function with nice syntax:

```
class Dispatcher {
    val dispatcher: Dispatcher = this

    fun Int.extension(){
        val receiver: Int = this
        val dispatcher: Dispatcher = this@Dispatcher
    }
}
```

Going back to our *Zoo* example, we instantiate a `Caregiver`, a `Cat`, and a `Primate`, and we invoke the function `Caregiver.takeCare` with both animal instances:

```
val adam = Caregiver("Adam")

val fulgencio = Cat()

val koko = Primate("Koko")

adam.takeCare(fulgencio)
adam.takeCare(koko)
```

If we execute this code, we can see this on the console:

```
Feline reacts: PURRR!!!
Primate reacts: *Koko plays with Adam*
```

Any zoo needs a veterinary surgeon. The class `Vet` extends `Caregiver`:

```
open class Vet(name: String): Caregiver(name) {
    override fun Feline.react() = "*runs away from $name*"
}
```

We override the `Feline.react()` function with a different implementation. We are also using the `Vet` class's name directly, as the `Feline` class doesn't have a property name:

```
val brenda = Vet("Brenda")

listOf(adam, brenda).forEach { caregiver ->
    println("${caregiver.javaClass.simpleName} ${caregiver.name}")
    caregiver.takeCare(fulgencio)
    caregiver.takeCare(koko)
}
```

After which, we get the following output:

```
Caregiver Adam
Feline reacts: PURRR!!!
Primate reacts: *Koko plays with Adam*
Vet Brenda
Feline reacts: *runs away from Brenda*
Primate reacts: *Koko plays with Brenda*
```

Extension functions with conflicting names

What happens when an extension function has the same name as a member function?

The `Worker` class has a function `work(): String` and a private function `rest(): String`. We also have two extension functions with the same signature, `work` and `rest`:

```
class Worker {
    fun work() = "*working hard*"

    private fun rest() = "*resting*"
}

fun Worker.work() = "*not working so hard*"

fun <T> Worker.work(t:T) = "*working on $t*"

fun Worker.rest() = "*playing video games*"
```

Having extension functions with the same signature isn't a compilation error, but a warning: `Extension is shadowed by a member: public final fun work(): String`

It is legal to declare a function with the same signature as a member function, but the member function always takes precedence, therefore, the extension function is never invoked. This behavior changes when the member function is private, in this case, the extension function takes precedence.

It is also possible to overload an existing member function with an extension function:

```
val worker = Worker()

println(worker.work())

println(worker.work("refactoring"))

println(worker.rest())
```

On execution, `work()` invokes the member function and `work(String)` and `rest()` are extension functions:

```
*working hard*
*working on refactoring*
*playing video games*
```

Extension functions for objects

In Kotlin, objects are a type, therefore they can have functions, including extension functions (among other things, such as extending interfaces and others).

We can add a `buildBridge` extension function to the object, `Builder`:

```
object Builder {

}

fun Builder.buildBridge() = "A shinny new bridge"
```

We can include companion objects. The class `Designer` has two inner objects, the `companion` object and `Desk` object:

```
class Designer {
    companion object {

    }
```

```
    object Desk {

    }
}


fun Designer.Companion.fastPrototype() = "Prototype"

fun Designer.Desk.portofolio() = listOf("Project1", "Project2")
```

Calling this functions works like any normal object member function:

```
Designer.fastPrototype()
Designer.Desk.portofolio().forEach(::println)
```

Infix functions

Functions (normal or extension) with just one parameter can be marked as `infix` and used with the `infix` notation. The `infix` notation is useful to express the code naturally for some domains, for example, math and algebra operations.

Let's add an `infix` extension function to the `Int` type, `superOperation` (which is just a regular sum with a fancy name):

```
infix fun Int.superOperation(i: Int) = this + i

fun main(args: Array<String>) {
    1 superOperation 2
    1.superOperation(2)
}
```

We can use the `superOperation` function with the `infix` notation or normal notation.

Another area where the `infix` notation is commonly used, is on assertion libraries, such as **HamKrest** (`https://github.com/npryce/hamkrest`) or **Kluent** (`https://github.com/MarkusAmshove/Kluent`). Writing specification code in a natural, easy to understand language is a huge advantage.

Kluent assertions look like natural English expressions:

```
"Kotlin" shouldStartWith "Ko"
```

Kluent also comes with a backtick version for even greater readability:

```
"Kotlin" `should start with` "Ko"
```

Backticks (`) let you write arbitrary identifiers, including words that are reserved in Kotlin. Now, you can write your own kaomoji functions:

```
infix fun String.`(ﾉ°□°)ﾉ︵┻━┻`(s: String) = "*$this flips table at $s*"

fun main(args: Array<String>) {
    "Adam" `(ﾉ°□°)ﾉ︵┻━┻` "Ben"
```

You can chain many `infix` functions to produce internal DSLs, or recreate classic memes:

```
object All {
    infix fun your(base: Pair<Base, Us>) {}
}

object Base {
    infix fun are(belong: Belong) = this
}

object Belong

object Us

fun main(args: Array<String>) {
    All your (Base are Belong to Us)
}
```

The `your` function, receives `Pair<Base, Us>` as a parameter (a kind of tuple that comes with and is widely used on the Kotlin standard library) and the `infix` extension function `<K, V> K.to(v: V)` returns a `Pair<K, V>` using the receiver as the first member and the parameter as the second parameter (`to` can be invoked with any combination of types).

Operator overloading

Operator overloading is a form of polymorphism. Some operators change behaviors on different types. The classic example is the operator plus (+). On numeric values, plus is a sum operation and on `String` is a concatenation. Operator overloading is a useful tool to provide your API with a natural surface. Let's say that we're writing a `Time` and `Date` library; it'll be natural to have the plus and minus operators defined on time units.

Kotlin lets you define the behavior of operators on your own or existing types with functions, normal or extension, marked with the `operator` modifier:

```
class Wolf(val name:String) {
    operator fun plus(wolf: Wolf) = Pack(mapOf(name to this, wolf.name to
wolf))
}

class Pack(val members:Map<String, Wolf>)

fun main(args: Array<String>) {
    val talbot = Wolf("Talbot")
    val northPack: Pack = talbot + Wolf("Big Bertha") //
talbot.plus(Wolf("..."))
}
```

The operator function plus returns a `Pack` value. To invoke it, you can use the `infix` operator way (`Wolf + Wolf`) or the normal way (`Wolf.plus(Wolf)`).

Something to be aware of about operator overloading in Kotlin—the operators that you can override in Kotlin are limited; you can't create arbitrary operators.

Binary operators

Binary operators receive a parameter (there are exceptions to this rule—`invoke` and indexed access).

The `Pack.plus` extension function receives a `Wolf` parameter and returns a new `Pack`. Note that `MutableMap` also has a plus (+) operator:

```
operator fun Pack.plus(wolf: Wolf) = Pack(this.members.toMutableMap() +
(wolf.name to wolf))

val biggerPack = northPack + Wolf("Bad Wolf")
```

The following table will show you all the possible binary operators that can be overloaded:

Operator	Equivalent	Notes
x + y	x.plus(y)	
x - y	x.minus(y)	
x * y	x.times(y)	

x / y	x.div(y)	
x % y	x.rem(y)	From Kotlin 1.1, previously mod.
x..y	x.rangeTo(y)	
x in y	y.contains(x)	
x !in y	!y.contains(x)	
x += y	x.plussAssign(y)	Must return Unit.
x -= y	x.minusAssign(y)	Must return Unit.
x *= y	x.timesAssign(y)	Must return Unit.
x /= y	x.divAssign(y)	Must return Unit.
x %= y	x.remAssign(y)	From Kotlin 1.1, previously modAssign. Must return Unit.
x == y	x?.equals(y) ?: (y === null)	Checks for null.
x != y	!(x?.equals(y) ?: (y === null))	Checks for null.
x < y	x.compareTo(y) < 0	Must return Int.
x > y	x.compareTo(y) > 0	Must return Int.
x <= y	x.compareTo(y) <= 0	Must return Int.
x >= y	x.compareTo(y) >= 0	Must return Int.

Invoke

Back in Chapter 2, *Getting Started with Functional Programming*, in the section *First-class and high-order functions*, when we introduced lambda functions, we show the definition of Function1:

```
/** A function that takes 1 argument. */
public interface Function1<in P1, out R> : Function<R> {
    /** Invokes the function with the specified argument. */
    public operator fun invoke(p1: P1): R
}
```

The invoke function is an operator, a curious one. The invoke operator can be called without name.

The class `Wolf` has an `invoke` operator:

```
enum class WolfActions {
    SLEEP, WALK, BITE
}

class Wolf(val name:String) {
    operator fun invoke(action: WolfActions) = when (action) {
        WolfActions.SLEEP -> "$name is sleeping"
        WolfActions.WALK -> "$name is walking"
        WolfActions.BITE -> "$name is biting"
    }
}

fun main(args: Array<String>) {
    val talbot = Wolf("Talbot")

    talbot(WolfActions.SLEEP) // talbot.invoke(WolfActions.SLEEP)
}
```

That's why we can call a lambda function directly with parenthesis; we are, indeed, calling the `invoke` operator.

The following table will show you different declarations of `invoke` with a number of different arguments:

Operator	Equivalent	Notes
x()	x.invoke()	
x(y)	x.invoke(y)	
x(y1, y2)	x.invoke(y1, y2)	
x(y1, y2..., yN)	x.invoke(y1, y2..., yN)	

Indexed access

The indexed access operator is the array read and write operations with square brackets (`[]`), that is used on languages with C-like syntax. In Kotlin, we use the `get` operators for reading and `set` for writing.

With the `Pack.get` operator, we can use `Pack` as an array:

```
operator fun Pack.get(name: String) = members[name]!!

val badWolf = biggerPack["Bad Wolf"]
```

Most of Kotlin data structures have a definition of the `get` operator, in this case, the `Map<K, V>` returns a `V?`.

The following table will show you different declarations of `get` with a different number of arguments:

Operator	Equivalent	Notes
x[y]	x.get(y)	
x[y1, y2]	x.get(y1, y2)	
x[y1, y2..., yN]	x.get(y1, y2..., yN)	

The `set` operator has similar syntax:

```
enum class WolfRelationships {
    FRIEND, SIBLING, ENEMY, PARTNER
}

operator fun Wolf.set(relationship: WolfRelationships, wolf: Wolf) {
    println("${wolf.name} is my new $relationship")
}

talbot[WolfRelationships.ENEMY] = badWolf
```

The operators `get` and `set` can have any arbitrary code, but it is a very well-known and old convention that indexed access is used for reading and writing. When you write these operators (and by the way, all the other operators too), use the principle of *least surprise*. Limiting the operators to their natural meaning on a specific domain, makes them easier to use and read in the long run.

The following table will show you different declarations of `set` with a different number of arguments:

Operator	Equivalent	Notes
`x[y] = z`	`x.set(y, z)`	Return value is ignored
`x[y1, y2] = z`	`x.set(y1, y2, z)`	Return value is ignored
`x[y1, y2..., yN] = z`	`x.set(y1, y2..., yN, z)`	Return value is ignored

Unary operators

Unary operators don't have parameters and act directly in the dispatcher.

We can add a `not` operator to the `Wolf` class:

```
operator fun Wolf.not() = "$name is angry!!!"

!talbot // talbot.not()
```

The following table will show you all the possible unary operators that can be overloaded:

Operator	Equivalent	Notes
`+x`	`x.unaryPlus()`	
`-x`	`x.unaryMinus()`	
`!x`	`x.not()`	
`x++`	`x.inc()`	Postfix, it must be a call on a `var`, should return a compatible type with the dispatcher type, shouldn't mutate the dispatcher.
`x--`	`x.dec()`	Postfix, it must be a call on a `var`, should return a compatible type with the dispatcher type, shouldn't mutate the dispatcher.
`++x`	`x.inc()`	Prefix, it must be a call on a `var`, should return a compatible type with the dispatcher type, shouldn't mutate the dispatcher.
`--x`	`x.dec()`	Prefix, it must be a call on a `var`, should return a compatible type with the dispatcher type, shouldn't mutate the dispatcher.

Postfix (increment and decrement) returns the original value and then changes the variable with the operator returned value. Prefix returns the operator's returned value and then changes the variable with that value.

Type-safe builders

With the two previous sections (`infix` functions and operator overloading), we have a good foundation for building fantastic DSLs. A **DSL** is a language that is specialized to a particular domain, in contrast to **general-purpose language** (**GPL**). Classic examples of DSLs (even when people don't realize it) are HTML (markup) and SQL (relational database queries).

Kotlin provides many features to create internal DSLs (a DSL that runs internally inside a host GPL), but there is one feature that we still need to cover, type-safe builders. Type-safe builders let us define data in a (semi) declarative way and are very useful to define GUIs, HTML markup, XML, and others.

An example of a beautiful Kotlin DSL is TornadoFX. **TornadoFX** (`https://tornadofx.io/`) is DSL for creating JavaFX applications.

We write an `FxApp` class that extends `tornadofx.App` and receives a `tornadofx.View` class (a class reference, not an instance):

```
import javafx.application.Application
import tornadofx.*

fun main(args: Array<String>) {
    Application.launch(FxApp::class.java, *args)
}

class FxApp: App(FxView::class)

class FxView: View() {
    override val root = vbox {
        label("Functional Kotlin")
        button("Press me")
    }
}
```

In less than 20 lines of code, including imports and main function, we can create a GUI application:

Of course, right now, it doesn't do anything, but it is simple to create a JavaFX Application with TornadoFX, if you compare it with Java. People with JavaFX experience could say that you can achieve something similar with FXML (a declarative XML language designed to build JavaFX layouts), but as with any other XML file, writing and maintaining is hard, and TornadoFX's DSL is simpler, flexible, and is compiled with Kotlin's type-safety.

But how do type-safe builders work?

Let's start with an example from the Kotlin Standard Library:

```
val joinWithPipe = with(listOf("One", "Two", "Three")){
    joinToString(separator = "|")
}
```

We can find `with` blocks in other languages, such as JavaScript and Visual Basic (including .Net). A `with` block is a language construct that lets us use any property or method on the value that we pass as a parameter. But in Kotlin, `with` is not a reserved keyword but rather a normal function with a special type of parameter.

Let's have a look at the `with` declaration:

```
public inline fun <T, R> with(receiver: T, block: T.() -> R): R {
    return receiver.block()
}
```

The first parameter is any value of type `T`, a receiver (as in extension function?) and the second one, `block`, is a function of type `T.() -> R`. In Kotlin's documentation, this kind of function is named **function type** with receiver and with any instance of `T`, we can call the `block` function. No worries about the `inline` modifier, we'll cover it in the next section.

 A trick to understanding the function type with receiver is to think of it as an extension function. Have a look at the declaration with that familiar dot (`.`), and inside the function, we can use any member of the receiver type using `this`, as in extension functions.

What about another example? Let's have a look at it:

```
val html = buildString {
    append("<html>\n")
    append("\t<body>\n")
    append("\t\t<ul>\n")
    listOf(1, 2, 3).forEach { i ->
        append("\t\t\t<li>$i</li>\n")
    }
    append("\t\t<ul>\n")
```

```
        append("\t</body>\n")
        append("</htm
```

```
l>")
        }
```

The `buildString` function receives a `StringBuilder.() -> Unit` parameter and returns a `String`; the declaration is astonishingly simple:

```
public inline fun buildString(builderAction: StringBuilder.() -> Unit):
String =
        StringBuilder().apply(builderAction).toString()
```

The `apply` function is an extension function similar to `with` but instead of returning R, returns the receiver instance. Usually, `apply` is used for *initializing* and *instance*:

```
public inline fun <T> T.apply(block: T.() -> Unit): T {
    block()
    return this
}
```

As you can see, all these functions are very simple to understand, but they increase Kotlin's usefulness and readability a great deal.

Creating a DSL

One of my big passions is cycling. The emotion of movement, the effort, the health benefits, and enjoying the landscape are some of the benefits (and I can keep going on and on).

I want to create a way to have a registry of my bikes and their components. For the prototype phase, I'll use XML, but later on we can change to a different implementation:

```xml
<bicycle description="Fast carbon commuter">
    <bar material="ALUMINIUM" type="FLAT">
    </bar>
    <frame material="CARBON">
        <wheel brake="DISK" material="ALUMINIUM">
        </wheel>
    </frame>
    <fork material="CARBON">
        <wheel brake="DISK" material="ALUMINIUM">
        </wheel>
    </fork>
</bicycle>
```

This is the perfect scenario to create a type-safe builder in Kotlin.

In the end, my `bicycle` DSL should look like this:

```kotlin
fun main(args: Array<String>) {
    val commuter = bicycle {
        description("Fast carbon commuter")
        bar {
            barType = FLAT
            material = ALUMINIUM
        }
        frame {
            material = CARBON
            backWheel {
                material = ALUMINIUM
                brake = DISK
            }
        }
        fork {
            material = CARBON
            frontWheel {
                material = ALUMINIUM
                brake = DISK
            }
        }
    }

    println(commuter)
}
```

My DSL is regular Kotlin code, is compiled fast, and my IDE will help me to autocomplete, and will complain when I make a mistake—a win-win situation.

Let's start with the program:

```kotlin
interface Element {
    fun render(builder: StringBuilder, indent: String)
}
```

All parts of my `bicycle` in my DSL will extend/implement the `Element` interface:

```
@DslMarker
annotation class ElementMarker

@ElementMarker
abstract class Part(private val name: String) : Element {
    private val children = arrayListOf<Element>()
    protected val attributes = hashMapOf<String, String>()

    protected fun <T : Element> initElement(element: T, init: T.() -> Unit):
T {
        element.init()
        children.add(element)
        return element
    }

    override fun render(builder: StringBuilder, indent: String) {
        builder.append("$indent<$name${renderAttributes()}>\n")
        children.forEach { c -> c.render(builder, indent + "\t") }
        builder.append("$indent</$name>\n")
    }

    private fun renderAttributes(): String = buildString {
        attributes.forEach { attr, value -> append(" $attr=\"$value\"") }
    }

    override fun toString(): String = buildString {
        render(this, "")
    }
}
```

`Part` is the base class for all my parts; it has `children` and `attributes` properties; it also inherits the `Element` interface with an XML implementation. Changing to a different format (JSON, YAML, and others) should not be too difficult.

The `initElement` function receives two parameters, an element `T` and an `init` function with receiver `T.() -> Unit`. Internally, the `init` function is executed and the element is added as children.

`Part` is annotated with an `@ElementMarker` annotation, that is itself annotated with `@DslMarker`. It prevents inner elements from reaching outer elements.

In this example, we can use `frame`:

```
val commuter = bicycle {
    description("Fast carbon commuter")
    bar {
        barType = FLAT
        material = ALUMINIUM
        frame {   } //compilation error
    }
```

It is still possible to do it explicitly with `this` qualified:

```
val commuter = bicycle {
    description("Fast carbon commuter")
    bar {
        barType = FLAT
        material = ALUMINIUM
        this@bicycle.frame{ }
    }
```

Now, several enumerations to describe materials, bar types, and brakes:

```
enum class Material {
    CARBON, STEEL, TITANIUM, ALUMINIUM
}

enum class BarType {
    DROP, FLAT, TT, BULLHORN
}

enum class Brake {
    RIM, DISK
}
```

Some of these parts have a `material` attribute:

```
abstract class PartWithMaterial(name: String) : Part(name) {
    var material: Material
        get() = Material.valueOf(attributes["material"]!!)
        set(value) {
            attributes["material"] = value.name
        }
}
```

We use a `material` property of type `Material` enumeration, and we store it inside the `attributes` map, transforming the value back and forth:

```
class Bicycle : Part("bicycle") {

    fun description(description: String) {
        attributes["description"] = description
    }

    fun frame(init: Frame.() -> Unit) = initElement(Frame(), init)

    fun fork(init: Fork.() -> Unit) = initElement(Fork(), init)

    fun bar(init: Bar.() -> Unit) = initElement(Bar(), init)
}
```

`Bicycle` defines a `description` function and functions for `frame`, `fork`, and `bar`. Each function receives an `init` function that we pass directly to `initElement`.

`Frame` has a function for the back wheel:

```
class Frame : PartWithMaterial("frame") {
    fun backWheel(init: Wheel.() -> Unit) = initElement(Wheel(), init)
}
```

`Wheel` has a property `brake` using the `Brake` enumeration:

```
class Wheel : PartWithMaterial("wheel") {
    var brake: Brake
        get() = Brake.valueOf(attributes["brake"]!!)
        set(value) {
            attributes["brake"] = value.name
        }
}
```

`Bar` has a property for its type, using the `BarType` enumeration:

```
class Bar : PartWithMaterial("bar") {

    var barType: BarType
        get() = BarType.valueOf(attributes["type"]!!)
        set(value) {
            attributes["type"] = value.name
        }
}
```

Fork defines a function for the front wheel:

```
class Fork : PartWithMaterial("fork") {
    fun frontWheel(init: Wheel.() -> Unit) = initElement(Wheel(), init)
}
```

We are close to the finish, the only thing that we need now is an entry function for our DSL:

```
fun bicycle(init: Bicycle.() -> Unit): Bicycle {
    val cycle = Bicycle()
    cycle.init()
    return cycle
}
```

And that's all. DSLs in Kotlin with the `infix` functions, operator overloading, and type-safe builders are extremely powerful, and the Kotlin community is creating new and exciting libraries every day.

Inline functions

High-order functions are very useful and fancy, but they come with a caveat—performance penalties. Remember, from Chapter 2, *Getting Started with Functional Programming*, in the section, *First-class and high-order functions*, that on compilation time, a lambda gets translated into an object that is allocated, and we are calling its `invoke` operator; those operations consume CPU power and memory, regardless of how small they are.

A function like this:

```
fun <T> time(body: () -> T): Pair<T, Long> {
    val startTime = System.nanoTime()
    val v = body()
    val endTime = System.nanoTime()
    return v to endTime - startTime
}

fun main(args: Array<String>) {
    val (_,time) = time { Thread.sleep(1000) }
    println("time = $time")
}
```

Once compiled, it will look like this:

```
val (_, time) = time(object : Function0<Unit> {
    override fun invoke() {
        Thread.sleep(1000)
    }
})
```

If performance is a priority for you (mission critical application, games, video streaming), you can mark a high-order function as `inline`:

```
inline fun <T> inTime(body: () -> T): Pair<T, Long> {
    val startTime = System.nanoTime()
    val v = body()
    val endTime = System.nanoTime()
    return v to endTime - startTime
}

fun main(args: Array<String>) {
    val (_, inTime) = inTime { Thread.sleep(1000) }
    println("inTime = $inTime")
}
```

Once compiled, it will look like this:

```
val startTime = System.nanoTime()
val v = Thread.sleep(1000)
val endTime = System.nanoTime()
val (_, inTime) = (v to endTime - startTime)
```

The whole function execution is replaced by the high-order function's body and the lambda's body. The `inline` functions are faster, albeit generating more bytecode:

```
time = 1005449985
inTime = 1003105225
```

2.3 milliseconds per execution doesn't look like a lot, but in the long run and with more optimizations, can create a noticeable compound effect.

Inline restrictions

Inline lambda functions have an important restriction—they can't be manipulated in any way (stored, copied, and others).

The `UserService` stores a list of listeners `(User) -> Unit`:

```
data class User(val name: String)

class UserService {
    val listeners = mutableListOf<(User) -> Unit>()
    val users = mutableListOf<User>()

    fun addListener(listener: (User) -> Unit) {
        listeners += listener
    }
}
```

Changing `addListener` into an `inline` function will produce a compilation error:

```
inline fun addListener(listener: (User) -> Unit) {
    listeners += listener //compilation error: Illegal use of inline-
parameter listener
}
```

If you think about it, it makes sense. When we inline a lambda, we're replacing it for its body, and that isn't something that we can store on a `Map`.

We can fix this problem with the `noinline` modifier:

```
//Warning: Expected performance impact of inlining addListener can be
insignificant
inline fun addListener(noinline listener: (User) -> Unit) {
    listeners += listener
}
```

Using `noinline` on an `inline` function will inline just the high-order function body but not the `noinline` lambda parameters (an `inline` high-order function can have both: `inline` and `noinline` lambdas). The resulting bytecode isn't as fast as a fully inline function, and the compiler will show a warning.

Inline lambda functions can't be used inside another execution context (local object, nested lambda).

In this example, we can't use `transform` inside the `buildUser` lambda:

```
inline fun transformName(transform: (name: String) -> String): List<User> {

    val buildUser = { name: String ->
        User(transform(name)) //compilation error: Can't inline transform
here
    }

    return users.map { user -> buildUser(user.name) }
}
```

To fix this problem, we need a `crossinline` modifier (alternatively, we can use `noinline` but with the associated performance lost):

```
inline fun transformName(crossinline transform: (name: String) -> String):
List<User> {

    val buildUser = { name: String ->
        User(transform(name))
    }

    return users.map { user -> buildUser(user.name) }
}

fun main(args: Array<String>) {
    val service = UserService()
    service.transformName(String::toLowerCase)
}
```

The generated code is quite complex. Many pieces are generated:

- A class that extends `(String) -> User` to represent `buildUser` and internally creates `User` using `String::toLowerCase` to transform the name
- A normal inline code to execute `List<User>.map()` using an instance of the class that represents `buildUser`
- `List<T>.map()` is `inline`, so that code gets generated too

Once you're aware of its restrictions, inline high-order functions are a great way to increase the execution speed of your code. Indeed, a lot of the high-order functions inside the Kotlin Standard Library are `inline`.

Recursion and corecursion

In Chapter 2, *Getting Started with Functional Programming,* in the section, *Recursion,* we cover recursion extensively (albeit there are recursion topics that are outside the scope of this book).

We used recursion to write classic algorithms such as Fibonacci (we're reusing `tailrecFib` from Chapter 2, *Getting Started with Functional Programming*):

```
fun tailrecFib(n: Long): Long {
    tailrec fun go(n: Long, prev: Long, cur: Long): Long {
        return if (n == 0L) {
            prev
        } else {
            go(n - 1, cur, prev + cur)
        }
    }

    return go(n, 0, 1)
}
```

And Factorial (same here, reusing `tailrecFactorial` from Chapter 2, *Getting Started with Functional Programming*):

```
fun tailrecFactorial(n: Long): Long {
    tailrec fun go(n: Long, acc: Long): Long {
        return if (n <= 0) {
            acc
        } else {
            go(n - 1, n * acc)
        }
    }

    return go(n, 1)
}
```

In both cases, we started with a number, and we reduced it to reach a base condition.

Another example that we looked at was `FunList`:

```
sealed class FunList<out T> {
    object Nil : FunList<Nothing>()

    data class Cons<out T>(val head: T, val tail: FunList<T>) : FunList<T>()

    fun forEach(f: (T) -> Unit) {
```

```
        tailrec fun go(list: FunList<T>, f: (T) -> Unit) {
            when (list) {
                is Cons -> {
                    f(list.head)
                    go(list.tail, f)
                }
                is Nil -> Unit//Do nothing
            }
        }

        go(this, f)
    }

    fun <R> fold(init: R, f: (R, T) -> R): R {
        tailrec fun go(list: FunList<T>, init: R, f: (R, T) -> R): R = when
(list) {
            is Cons -> go(list.tail, f(init, list.head), f)
            is Nil -> init
        }

        return go(this, init, f)
    }

    fun reverse(): FunList<T> = fold(Nil as FunList<T>) { acc, i -> Cons(i,
acc) }

    fun <R> foldRight(init: R, f: (R, T) -> R): R =
this.reverse().fold(init, f)

    fun <R> map(f:(T) -> R): FunList<R> = foldRight(Nil as FunList<R>){
tail, head -> Cons(f(head), tail) }

}
```

The functions, `forEach` and `fold`, are recursive. Starting with the complete list, we reduce it until we reach the end (represented with a `Nil`), the base case. The other functions—`reverse`, `foldRight`, and `map` are just using `fold` with different variations.

So, on one hand, recursion takes a complex value and reduces it to the desired answer and on the other hand, corecursion takes a value and builds on top of it to produce a compound value (including potentially infinite data structures such as `Sequence<T>`).

As we use a `fold` function for recursive operations, we can use an `unfold` function:

```
fun <T, S> unfold(s: S, f: (S) -> Pair<T, S>?): Sequence<T> {
    val result = f(s)
    return if (result != null) {
        sequenceOf(result.first) + unfold(result.second, f)
    } else {
        sequenceOf()
    }
}
```

The `unfold` function takes two parameters, an initial `s` value that represents the starting or base step, and an `f` lambda that takes that `s` step and produces a `Pair<T, S>?` (a nullable `Pair`) of the `T` value to add to the sequence and the next `S` step.

If the result of `f(s)` is null, we return an empty sequence, else we create a single value sequence and add the result of `unfold` with the new step.

Using `unfold`, we can create a function that repeats a single element many times:

```
fun <T> elements(element: T, numOfValues: Int): Sequence<T> {
    return unfold(1) { i ->
        if (numOfValues > i)
            element to i + 1
        else
            null
    }
}

fun main(args: Array<String>) {
    val strings = elements("Kotlin", 5)
    strings.forEach(::println)
}
```

The `elements` function takes the element to repeat any number of values. Internally, it uses `unfold`, passing 1 as the initial step and a lambda that takes the current step and compares it with `numOfValues`, returning `Pair<T, Int>` with the same element and the current step + 1 or null.

It is okay, but not very interesting. What about returning a Factorial sequence? We have you covered:

```
fun factorial(size: Int): Sequence<Long> {
    return sequenceOf(1L) + unfold(1L to 1) { (acc, n) ->
        if (size > n) {
            val x = n * acc
            (x) to (x to n + 1)
        } else
            null
    }
}
```

Same principle, the only difference is that our initial step is `Pair<Long, Int>` (the first element to carry the calculation and the second to evaluate against size) and therefore, our lambda should return `Pair<Long, Pair<Long, Int>>`.

Fibonacci will look similar:

```
fun fib(size: Int): Sequence<Long> {
    return sequenceOf(1L) + unfold(Triple(0L, 1L, 1)) { (cur, next</span>, n) ->
        if (size > n) {
            val x = cur + next
            (x) to Triple(next, x, n + 1)
        }
        else
            null
    }
}
```

Except that in this case, we use `Triple<Long, Long, Int>`.

The corecursive implementations to generate Factorial and Fibonacci sequences are a mirror of the recursive implementations to calculate a Factorial or a Fibonacci number, respectively—and some people can argue that is easier to understand.

Summary

With this chapter, we have already covered most of the Kotlin features for functional programming. We reviewed how to write shorter functions with single-expression functions, the different kind of parameters, how to extend our types with extension functions, and how to write natural and readable code with `infix` functions and operators. We also covered the basics of DSL authoring with type-safe builders and how to write efficient high-order functions. Last, but not least, we learned about recursion and corecursion.

In the next chapter, we will learn about Kotlin delegates.

6

Delegates in Kotlin

In the last two chapters, we learned about functions and function types in functional programming. We also learned about the various types of function Kotlin has to offer.

This chapter is based on delegates in Kotlin. Delegates are awesome features of Kotlin in favour of functional programming. If you are coming from a non-FP background such as Java, you are probably hearing about delegates for the first time. So in this chapter, we will try to untangle things for you.

We will start by learning the basics of delegation and then gradually move into implementations of delegates in Kotlin.

The following list contains the topics that will be covered in this chapter:

- Introduction to delegation
- Delegates in Kotlin
- Delegated properties
- Standard delegates
- Custom delegates
- Delegated map
- Local delegation
- Class delegation

So, let's get started with delegates.

Introduction to delegation

The origin of delegation in programming is from object composition. Object composition is a way to combine simple objects to derive a complex one. Object compositions are a critical building block of many basic data structures, including the tagged union, the linked list, and the binary tree.

To make object composition more reusable (as reusable as inheritance), a new pattern is incorporated—the **delegation pattern**.

This pattern allows an object to have a helper object, and that helper object is called a **delegate**. This pattern allows the original object to handle requests by delegating to the delegate helper object.

Though delegation is an object-oriented design pattern, not all languages have implicit support for delegation (such as Java, which doesn't support delegation implicitly). In those cases, you can still use *delegation* by explicitly passing the original object to the delegate to a method, as an argument/parameter.

But with the language support (such as in Kotlin), delegation becomes easier and often seems like using the original variable itself.

Understanding delegation

Over time, the delegation pattern has proven to be a better alternative of inheritance. Inheritance is a powerful tool for code reuse, especially in the context of the *Liskov Substitution* model. Moreover, the direct support of OOP languages makes it even stronger.

However, inheritance still has some limitations, such as a class can't change its superclass dynamically during program execution; also, if you perform a small modification to the super class, it'll be directly propagated to the child class, and that is not what we want every time.

Delegation, on the other hand, is flexible. You can think of delegation as a composition of multiple objects, where one object passes its method calls to another one and calls it a delegate. As I mentioned earlier, delegation is flexible; you can change the delegate at runtime.

For an example, think of the `Electronics` class and `Refrigerator` class. With inheritance, `Refrigerator` should implement/override the `Electronics` method calls and properties. With delegation however, the `Refrigerator` object would keep a reference of the `Electronics` object and would pass the method calls with it.

Now, since we know that Kotlin provides support for delegation, let's get started with delegation in Kotlin.

Delegates in Kotlin

Kotlin has out-of-the-box support for delegation. Kotlin provides you with some standard delegates for properties for most common programming needs. Most of the time, you'll find yourself using those standard delegates, instead of creating your own one; however, Kotlin also allows you to create your own delegate, as per your requirements.

Not only delegation for properties, Kotlin also allows you to have delegated classes.

So basically, there are two types of delegation in Kotlin, which are as follows:

- Property delegation
- Class delegation

So, let's have a look at the property delegation first, and then we will move ahead with class delegation.

Property delegation (standard delegates)

In the previous section, where we discussed delegation, we learned that delegation is a technique of method passing/forwarding.

For property delegates, it almost does the same. A property can pass its getter and setter calls to the delegate and the delegate can handle those calls on behalf of the property itself.

You're probably thinking, what is the benefit of passing getter and setter calls to the delegate? Only the delegate you're using can answer this question. Kotlin has multiple predefined standard delegations for most common use cases. Let's have a look at the following list, containing available standard delegates:

- The `Delegates.notNull` function and `lateinit`
- The `lazy` function
- The `Delegates.Observable` function
- The `Delegates.vetoble` function

The Delegates.notNull function and lateinit

Think of a situation where you need to declare a property at the class level, but you don't have the initial value for the variable there. You'll get the value at some later point, but before the property is actually used, and you're confident that the property will get initialised before using and it'll not be null. But, as per Kotlin syntax, you must initialize a property at the time of initializing. The quick fix is to declare it as a `nullable var` property, and assign a default null value. But as we mentioned earlier, since you are confident that the variable will not be null while using it, you are not willing to declare it as nullable.

`Delegates.notNull` is here to save you in this scenario. Have a look at the following program:

```
var notNullStr:String by Delegates.notNull<String>()

fun main(args: Array<String>) {
    notNullStr = "Initial value"
    println(notNullStr)
}
```

Focus on the first line—`var notNullStr:String by Delegates.notNull<String>()`, we declared a non-null `String var` property, but we didn't initialize it. Instead, we wrote `by Delegates.notNull<String>()`, but what does it mean? Let us inspect. The `by` operator is a reserved keyword in Kotlin, to be used with delegates. The `by` operator works with two operands, on the left-hand side of `by` will be the property/class that needs to be delegated, and on the right-hand side will be the delegate.

The delegate—`Delegates.notNull` allows you to temporarily go without initializing the property. It must be initialized before it is used (as we did on the very first line of the `main` method), otherwise it'll throw an exception.

So, let's modify the program by adding another property, which we will not initialize before using it, and see what happens:

```
var notNullStr:String by Delegates.notNull<String>()
var notInit:String by Delegates.notNull<String>()

fun main(args: Array<String>) {
    notNullStr = "Initial value"
    println(notNullStr)
    println(notInit)
}
```

The output looks like the following:

```
"C:\Program Files\Java\jdk1.8.0_131\bin\java" ...
Exception in thread "main" java.lang.IllegalStateException: Property
 notInit should be initialized before get.
    at kotlin.properties.NotNullVar.getValue(Delegates.kt:48)
    at com.rivuchk.packtpub.functionalkotlin.chapter06
.Chapter6_1_notnullKt.getNotInit(chapter6_1_notnull.kt)
    at com.rivuchk.packtpub.functionalkotlin.chapter06
.Chapter6_1_notnullKt.main(chapter6_1_notnull.kt:11)
Initial value

Process finished with exit code 1
```

So, the `notInit` property caused the exception—`Property notInit should be initialized before get`.

But doesn't the variable declaration—by `Delegates.notNull()` sound awkward? The Kotlin team also thought the same way. That's why from Kotlin 1.1 they added a simple keyword—`lateinit`, to achieve the same objective. As it simply states about late initialization, it should be simply `lateinit`.

So, let's modify the last program by replacing `by Delegates.notNull()` with `lateinit`. The following is the modified program:

```
lateinit var notNullStr1:String
lateinit var notInit1:String

fun main(args: Array<String>) {
    notNullStr1 = "Initial value"
    println(notNullStr1)
    println(notInit1)
}
```

In this program, we had to rename the variables, as you can't have two top-level (package-level variable, without any class/function) variables of the same name. Except variable names, the only thing that changed is we added `lateinit`, instead of `by Delegates.notNull()`.

So, now let's have a look at the following output to identify if there's any change:

```
"C:\Program Files\Java\jdk1.8.0_131\bin\java" ...
Initial value
Exception in thread "main" kotlin.UninitializedPropertyAccessException:
  lateinit property notInit1 has not been initialized
    at com.rivuchk.packtpub.functionalkotlin.chapter06
.Chapter6_2_lateinitKt.main(chapter6_2_lateinit.kt:11)

Process finished with exit code 1
```

The output is also identical, except it slightly changes the error message. It now says, `lateinit property notInit1 has not been initialized`.

The lazy function

The `lateinit` keyword works only on the `var` properties. The `Delegates.notNull()` function works properly only with `var` properties, too.

So, what should we do when using `val` properties? Kotlin provides you with another delegation—`lazy`, that's meant for `val` properties only. But it works in a slightly different way.

Unlike `lateinit` and `Delegates.notNull()`, you must specify how you want to initialize the variable at the time of declaration. So, what's the benefit? The initialization will not be called until the variable is actually used. That's why this delegate is called `lazy`; it enables lazy initialization of properties.

The following is a code example:

```
val myLazyVal:String by lazy {
    println("Just Initialised")
    "My Lazy Val"
}

fun main(args: Array<String>) {
    println("Not yet initialised")
    println(myLazyVal)
}
```

So in this program, we declared a `String val` property—myLazyVal with a `lazy` delegate. We used (printed) that property in the second line of the `main` function.

Now, let's focus on the variable declaration. The `lazy` delegate accepts a lambda that's expected to return the value of the property.

So, let's have a look at the output:

```
"C:\Program Files\Java\jdk1.8.0_131\bin\java" ...
Not yet initialised
Just Initialised
My Lazy Val

Process finished with exit code 0
```

Notice that the output clearly shows that the property got initialized after the first line of the `main` method executed, that is, when the property was actually used. This `lazy` initialization of properties can save your memory by a significant measure. It also comes as a handy tool in some situations, for example, think of a situation where you want to initialize the property with some other property/context, which would be available only after a certain point (but you have the property name); in that situation, you can simply keep the property as `lazy`, and then you can use it when it's confirmed that the initialization will be successful.

Observing property value change with Delegates.Observable

Delegates are not only for initializing properties lately/lazily. As we learned, delegation enables the forwarding of getter and setter calls of a property to the delegate. This enables delegates to offer more cool features than just lately/lazily initialization.

One such cool feature comes with `Delegates.observable`. Think of a situation where you need to look out for the value change of a property, and perform some action as soon as this occurs. The immediate solution that comes to our mind is to override the setter, but this would look nasty and make codes complex, whereas delegates are there to save our life.

Have a look at the following example:

```
var myStr:String by Delegates.observable("<Initial Value>") {
    property, oldValue, newValue ->
    println("Property `${property.name}` changed value from "$oldValue" to
"$newValue"")
}

fun main(args: Array<String>) {
    myStr = "Change Value"
    myStr = "Change Value again"
}
```

It's a simple example, we declared a `String` property—`myStr`, with the help of `Delegates.observable` (we will describe that initialization soon after having a look at the output), then, inside the `main` function, we changed the value of `myStr` twice.

Have a look at the following output:

```
"C:\Program Files\Java\jdk1.8.0_131\bin\java" ...
Property `myStr` changed value from "<Initial Value>" to "Change Value"
Property `myStr` changed value from "Change Value" to "Change Value again"

Process finished with exit code 0
```

In the output, we can see, that for both times we changed the value, a log got printed with the old and new value of the property. The `Delegates.observable` block in this program is responsible for that log in the output. So now, let's have a close look at the `Delegates.observable` block and understand how it works:

```
var myStr:String by Delegates.observable("<Initial Value>") {
    property, oldValue, newValue ->
    println("Property `${property.name}` changed value from "$oldValue" to
"$newValue"")
}
```

The `Delegates.observable` function takes two parameters to create the delegate. The first argument is the initial value of the property, and the second argument is the lambda that should be executed whenever the value change is noticed.

The lambda for `Delegates.observable` expects three parameters:

- The first one is an instance of `KProperty<out R>`

    `KProperty` is an interface in the Kotlin `stdlib`, `kotlin.reflect` package, it is a property; such as a named `val` or `var` declaration. Instances of this class are obtainable by the `::` operator. For more information,
    visit: `https://kotlinlang.org/api/latest/jvm/stdlib/kotlin.reflect /-k-property/`.

- The second parameter contains the old value of the property (the last value just before the assignment)
- The third parameter is the newest value assigned to the property (the new value used in the assignment)

So, as we've got the concept of `Delegates.observable`, let's move ahead with a new delegate, `Delegates.vetoable`.

The power of veto – Delegates.vetoable

`Delegates.vetoable` is another standard delegate that allows us to veto a value change.

    A **veto**, Latin for *I forbid,* is the power (for example, used by an officer of the state) to unilaterally stop an official action. There is more information here: `https://en.wikipedia.org/wiki/Veto`.

This right to veto allows us to have a logic check on each assignment of the property, where we can decide to continue with the assignment or not.

The following is an example:

```
var myIntEven:Int by Delegates.vetoable(0) {
    property, oldValue, newValue ->
    println("${property.name} $oldValue -> $newValue")
    newValue%2==0
}

fun main(args: Array<String>) {
    myIntEven = 6
    myIntEven = 3
    println("myIntEven:$myIntEven")
}
```

In this program, we created an `Int` property—`myIntEven`; this property should only accept even numbers as an assignment. The `Delegates.vetoable` delegate works almost the same as the `Delegates.observable` function, just there's a small change in the lambda. Here, the lambda is expected to return a Boolean; the assignment would be passed if that returned Boolean is `true`, else the assignment would be dismissed.

Have a look back at the program. While declaring the variable with the delegate `Delegates.vetoable`, we passed `0` as the initial value, then, in the lambda, we logged an assignment call, then we will return `true` if the new value is even and `false` if odd.

Here is the output:

```
"C:\Program Files\Java\jdk1.8.0_131\bin\java" ...
myIntEven 0 -> 6
myIntEven 6 -> 3
myIntEven:6

Process finished with exit code 0
```

So, in the output, we can see two logs of assignment, but when we printed the `myIntEven` property after the last assignment, we can see the last assignment wasn't successful.

Interesting, isn't it? Let us see another example of `Delegates.vetoable`. Have a look at the following code:

```
var myCounter:Int by Delegates.vetoable(0) {
    property, oldValue, newValue ->
    println("${property.name} $oldValue -> $newValue")
    newValue>oldValue
}

fun main(args: Array<String>) {
    myCounter = 2
    println("myCounter:$myCounter")
    myCounter = 5
    myCounter = 4
    println("myCounter:$myCounter")
    myCounter++
    myCounter--
    println("myCounter:$myCounter")
}
```

This program has a property—`myCounter`, which is expected to increase with each assignment.

In the lambda, we checked if the `newValue` value is greater than the `oldValue` value. Here is the output:

```
"C:\Program Files\Java\jdk1.8.0_131\bin\java" ...
myCounter 0 -> 2
myCounter:2
myCounter 2 -> 5
myCounter 5 -> 4
myCounter:5
myCounter 5 -> 6
myCounter 6 -> 5
myCounter:6


Process finished with exit code 0
```

The output which shows those assignments where the value was increased was successful, but those where the value decreased got dismissed.

Even when we used the increment and decrement operators, the increment operator was successful, but the decrement operator wasn't. This feature wouldn't be that easy to implement without delegates.

Delegated map

So, we learned how to use standard delegates, but Kotlin has to offer more with delegation. The map delegation is among those awesome features that comes with delegation. So, what is it? It is the freedom of passing a map as a single parameter instead of numbers of parameters in a function/class constructor. Let's have a look. The following is a program applying *map delegation*:

```
data class Book (val delegate:Map<String,Any?>) {
    val name:String by delegate
    val authors:String by delegate
    val pageCount:Int by delegate
    val publicationDate:Date by delegate
    val publisher:String by delegate
}

fun main(args: Array<String>) {
    val map1 = mapOf(
            Pair("name","Reactive Programming in Kotlin"),
            Pair("authors","Rivu Chakraborty"),
            Pair("pageCount",400),
Pair("publicationDate",SimpleDateFormat("yyyy/mm/dd").parse("2017/12/05")),
            Pair("publisher","Packt")
    )
    val map2 = mapOf(
            "name" to "Kotlin Blueprints",
            "authors" to "Ashish Belagali, Hardik Trivedi, Akshay
Chordiya",
            "pageCount" to 250,
            "publicationDate" to
SimpleDateFormat("yyyy/mm/dd").parse("2017/12/05"),
            "publisher" to "Packt"
    )

    val book1 = Book(map1)
    val book2 = Book(map2)

    println("Book1 $book1 nBook2 $book2")
}
```

The program is simple enough; we defined a `Book` data class, and in the constructor, instead of taking all member values one by one, we took a map and then delegated all to the map delegate.

One thing to be cautious here is to mention all member variables in the map, and the key name should exactly match the property name.

Here is the output:

```
"C:\Program Files\Java\jdk1.8.0_131\bin\java" ...
Book1 Book(delegate={name=Reactive Programming in Kotlin, authors=Rivu
 Chakraborty, pageCount=400, publicationDate=Tue Dec 05 00:00:00 IST
 2017, publisher=Packt})
Book2 Book(delegate={name=Kotlin Blueprints, authors=Ashish Belagali,
 Hardik Trivedi, Akshay Chordiya, pageCount=230, publicationDate=Sun Dec
 10 00:00:00 IST 2017, publisher=Packt})

Process finished with exit code 0
```

Simple enough, isn't it? Yes, delegations are that much powerful. But are you curious about what will happen if we skip mentioning any of the properties in the map? It will simply avoid the properties you skipped, and if you explicitly try to access them, then it'll throw an exception—`java.util.NoSuchElementException`.

Custom delegation

So far in this chapter, we have seen the standard delegations available with Kotlin. However, Kotlin does allow us to write our own custom delegates, to suit our custom needs.

For example, in the program, where we checked for the `Even` with `Delegates.vetoable`, we could only discard the value assignment, but there's no way to automatically assign the next even number to the variable.

In the following program, we used `makeEven`, a custom delegate which would automatically assign the next even number if an odd number is passed to the assignment, otherwise if an even number is passed to the assignment, it would pass that.

Have a look at the following program:

```
var myEven:Int by makeEven(0) {
    property, oldValue, newValue, wasEven ->
    println("${property.name} $oldValue -> $newValue, Even:$wasEven")
}

fun main(args: Array<String>) {
    myEven = 6
    println("myEven:$myEven")
    myEven = 3
    println("myEven:$myEven")
    myEven = 5
    println("myEven:$myEven")
    myEven = 8
    println("myEven:$myEven")
}
```

Here is the output:

```
"C:\Program Files\Java\jdk1.8.0_131\bin\java" ...
myEven 6 -> 6, Even:true
myEven:6
myEven 3 -> 3, Even:false
myEven:4
myEven 5 -> 5, Even:false
myEven:6
myEven 8 -> 8, Even:true
myEven:8


Process finished with exit code 0
```

The output clearly shows that whenever we assigned an even number to myEven, it got assigned, but when we assigned an odd number, the next even number (+1) got assigned.

For this delegate, we used almost the same lambda as the Delegates.observable we just added one more parameter—wasEven:Boolean, which will contain true if the assigned number was even, or false otherwise.

Eager to know how we created the delegate? Here is the code:

```
abstract class MakeEven(initialValue: Int):ReadWriteProperty<Any?,Int> {
    private var value:Int = initialValue

    override fun getValue(thisRef: Any?, property: KProperty<*>) = value

    override fun setValue(thisRef: Any?, property: KProperty<*>, newValue:
Int) {
        val oldValue = newValue
        val wasEven = newValue %2==0
        if(wasEven) {
            this.value = newValue
        } else {
            this.value = newValue +1
        }
        afterAssignmentCall(property,oldValue, newValue,wasEven)
    }

    abstract fun afterAssignmentCall (property: KProperty<*>, oldValue:
Int, newValue: Int, wasEven:Boolean):Unit
}
```

For creating a delegate on `var` properties, you need to implement the `ReadWriteProperty` interface.

That interface has two functions to be overridden—`getValue` and `setValue`. These functions are actually delegated functions of the getters and setters of the property. You can return your desired value from the `getValue` function, which will then be forwarded as the return value of the property. Every time the property is accessed, the `getValue` function will be called. Similarly, every time the property is assigned a value, the `setValue` function will get called, and whatever we return from the `setValue` function will actually be the value the property is finally assigned. For example, assume a property `a` is assigned `X`, but from the `setValue` function, we returned `Y`, so after the assignment statement, the property `a` will actually hold `Y` instead of `X`.

So, if you want to return the property's value from your delegate's `getValue` function, you must keep the value of the property stored somewhere (yes, you would not be able to pull the value from the original property, maybe because the original property will not even store the value, as the property knows that it would be delegated). In this program, we used a mutable `var` property—`value`, to store the value of the property. We are returning `value` from the `getValue` function.

Inside the `setValue` function, we checked whether the assigned `newValue` is even or not. If even, we assigned that `newValue` to the value property (which will be returned from the `getValue` function), and if the `newValue` is odd, we assigned `newValue+1` to the `value` property.

In the `MakeEven` class, we have an abstract function—`afterAssignmentCall`. We called this function during the end of the `setValue` function. This function is meant for logging purposes.

So, the delegate is almost ready, but what about the abstract function? We need to extend this class to apply the delegate, right? But remember the code where we used it like `by makeEven(0) {...}`, so there must be a function there, mustn't there? Yes, there's a function, the following is the definition:

```
   inline fun makeEven(initialValue: Int, crossinline onAssignment:(property:
KProperty<*>, oldValue: Int, newValue: Int,
wasEven:Boolean)->Unit):ReadWriteProperty<Any?, Int>
         =object : MakeEven(initialValue){
      override fun afterAssignmentCall(property: KProperty<*>, oldValue: Int,
newValue: Int, wasEven: Boolean)
             = onAssignment(property,oldValue,newValue,wasEven)
   }
```

We created an anonymous object of `MakeEven` and passed it as a delegate, and we passed the argument lambda—`onAssignment`, as the abstract function—`afterAssignmentCall`.

So, we've got to grip with delegates, let's move ahead and try our hands on some more interesting aspects of delegates.

Local delegates

Delegation is powerful, we've already seen that, but think of a common situation where inside a method we declare and initialize a property, then we apply a logic which will either use the property or will continue without it. For example, the following is such a program:

```
fun useDelegate(shouldPrint:Boolean) {
    val localDelegate = "Delegate Used"
    if(shouldPrint) {
        println(localDelegate)
    }
    println("bye bye")
}
```

In this program, we will use the `localDelegate` property, only if the `shouldPrint` value is `true`, else we won't use it. But it would always take space in memory since it is declared and initialized. An option to avoid this memory blockage is to have the property inside the `if` block, but it's a simple dummy program, and here we can easily afford to move the variable declaration inside the `if` block, whereas in many real-life scenarios, moving the variable declaration inside the `if` block is not possible.

So, what's the solution? Yes, using `lazy` delegation can save our life here. But it wasn't possible in Kotlin before the arrival of Kotlin 1.1.

So, the following is the updated program:

```
fun useDelegate(shouldPrint:Boolean) {
    val localDelegate by lazy {
        "Delegate Used"
    }
    if(shouldPrint) {
        println(localDelegate)
    }
    println("bye bye")
}
```

Though we only used `lazy` for this example, from Kotlin 1.1, we can have any delegation applied in local properties.

Class delegation

Class delegation is another interesting feature of Kotlin. How? Just think of the following situation.

You have an interface, *I*, and two classes, *A* and *B*. Both *A* and *B* implement *I*. In your code, you've an instance of *A* and you want to create an instance of *B* from that *A*.

In traditional inheritance, it is not directly possible; you have to write a bunch of nasty codes to achieve that, but class delegation is there to save you.

Go through the following code:

```
interface Person {
    fun printName()
}

class PersonImpl(val name:String):Person {
```

```
        override fun printName() {
            println(name)
        }
    }

    class User(val person:Person):Person by person {
        override fun printName() {
            println("Printing Name:")
            person.printName()
        }
    }

    fun main(args: Array<String>) {
        val person = PersonImpl("Mario Arias")
        person.printName()
        println()
        val user = User(person)
        user.printName()
    }
```

In this program, we created the instance of `User`, with its member property—`person`, which is an instance of the `Person` interface. In the main function, we passed an instance of `PersonImpl` to the user to create the instance of `User`.

Now, have a look at the declaration of `User`. After color (`:`), the phrase `Person by person` indicates that the class `User` extends `Person` and is expected to copy `Person` behaviors from the provided `person` instance.

Here is the output:

```
"C:\Program Files\Java\jdk1.8.0_131\bin\java" ...
Mario Arias


Printing Name:
Mario Arias


Process finished with exit code 0
```

The output shows the overriding works as expected, and we can also access properties and functions of the `person`, just like a normal property.

A really awesome feature, isn't it?

Summary

In this chapter, we learned about delegates and we saw how to use delegates in various ways to make our code efficient and clean. We learned about different features and parts of delegates, and how to use them.

The next chapter is about coroutines, a path-breaking feature of Kotlin, to enable seamless asynchronous processing while keeping the developer's life easy and straightforward.

So, don't wait long, start with the next chapter now.

7
Asynchronous Programming with Coroutines

Today's software development landscape makes asynchronous processing one of the most important topics. The ever-increasing number of processors and cores and the massive consumption of external services (which has grown in recent years with the adoption of microservices architectures) are some of the factors that we should keep an eye on and strive to use a good asynchronous approach.

Kotlin's implementation of coroutines is an excellent tool to build asynchronous applications.

In this chapter, we'll cover the following topics:

- Coroutines
- Alternative approaches
- Asynchronous processing
- Channels and actors

Introduction to coroutines

Let's start with a simple example without coroutines:

```
import kotlin.concurrent.thread

fun main(args: Array<String>) {
    thread {
        Thread.sleep(1000)
        println("World!")
    }
    print("Hello ")
    Thread.sleep(2000)
}
```

The `thread` function executes a block of code in a different thread. Inside the block, we are simulating an expensive I/O computation (such as accessing data from a microservice over HTTP) with `Thread.sleep`. `Thread.sleep` will block the current thread for the number of milliseconds passed as a parameter. In this example, we don't wait until the computation finishes to keep working on other things; we print another message, `"Hello"`, while the other computation is being executed. At the end, we wait for two seconds until the computation is finished.

That's not a pretty code, and we can do better:

```
fun main(args: Array<String>) {
    val computation = thread {
        Thread.sleep(1000)
        println("World!")
    }
    print("Hello ")
    computation.join()
}
```

In this version, we have a reference to our thread called, `computation`; at the end, we wait for the `join()` method to finish. This is smarter than just waiting for a fixed amount of time, as real-life computations could have different execution times.

Understanding JVM threads

Threads are the building blocks of asynchronous concurrent applications on JVM (and other platforms, too). A JVM thread is, most of the time, backed by a hardware thread (such as a core inside a processor). A hardware thread can support several software threads (a JVM thread is a kind of software thread), but only one software thread is executed at any given time.

The OS (or the JVM) decides which software thread is executed on each hardware thread and switches quickly among the live threads, thereby, giving the appearance that there are several software threads executing at the same time, when in reality there are as many active software threads being executed as there are hardware threads. But, in most circumstances, it is useful to think that all software threads are being performed at the same time.

Threads in JVM are very fast and responsive, but they come at a cost. Each Thread has a cost in CPU time and memory on creation, disposal (when garbage is collected), and context switch (the process to store and recover a thread's state when it becomes the executing thread or stops being it). Because this cost is relatively high, a JVM application can't have a significant number of threads.

A JVM application on a typical development machine can easily handle 100 threads:

```
fun main(args: Array<String>) {
    val threads = List(100){
        thread {
            Thread.sleep(1000)
            print('.')
        }
    }
    threads.forEach(Thread::join)
}
```

If you use any external application to monitor the JVM application, such as VisualVM or JConsole (among others), you'll see a graphic like this:

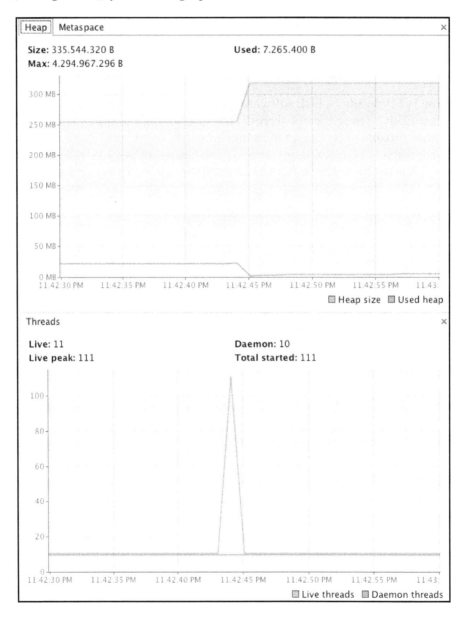

We can increase our threads to 1,000 as shown in the following screenshot:

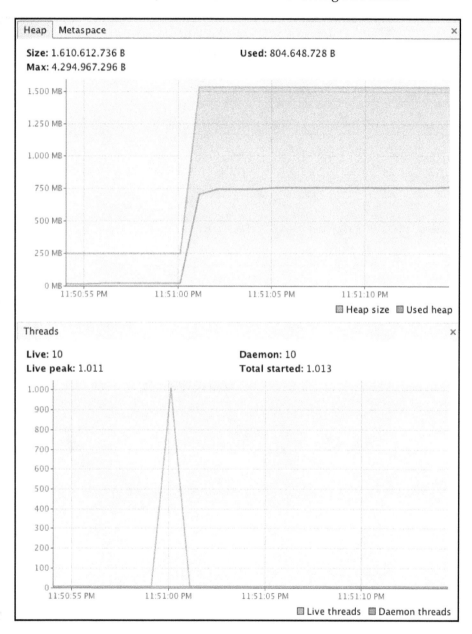

The amount of memory is growing at a fast rate, reaching more than 1.5 GB.

Can we increase our threads to 10,000? Take a look at the following screenshot:

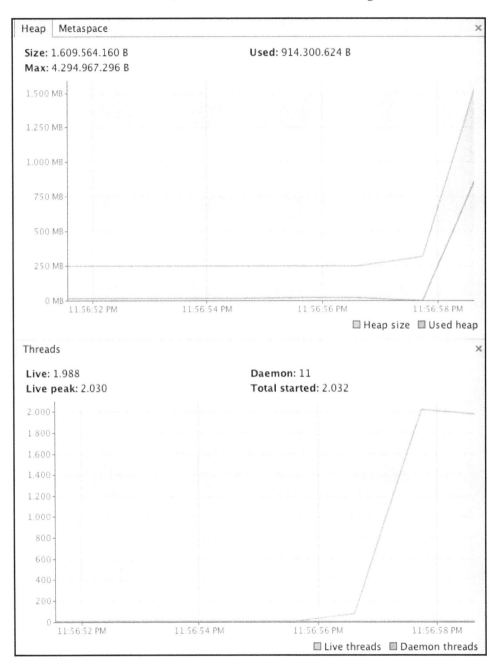

The answer is a blunt no; around 2,020 threads were created when the application died with OutOfMemoryError (this application was running with default settings; those settings can be changed at startup time).

Let's try with 1,900, a fair estimate of what we can execute safely:

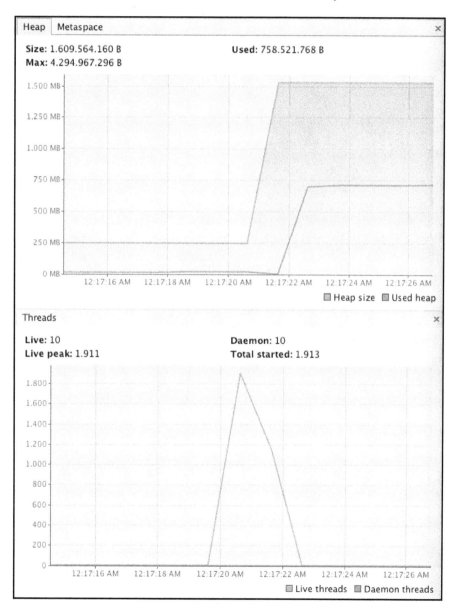

Yes, we can run 1,900 concurrent threads.

In modern JVM applications, creating and destroying threads is considered a bad practice; instead, we use `Executor`, an abstraction that lets us manage and reuse threads, reducing the cost of creation and disposal:

```
import java.util.concurrent.Executors
import java.util.concurrent.TimeUnit

fun main(args: Array<String>){
    val executor = Executors.newFixedThreadPool(1024)
    repeat(10000){
        executor.submit {
            Thread.sleep(1000)
            print('.')
        }
    }
    executor.shutdown()
}
```

We created an `executor` value that, internally, has a thread pool of up to 1,024 threads. Then, we submit 10,000 tasks; at the end, we shut down `Executor`. When we shut down `Executor`, it can't accept new tasks and executes all pending ones as follows:

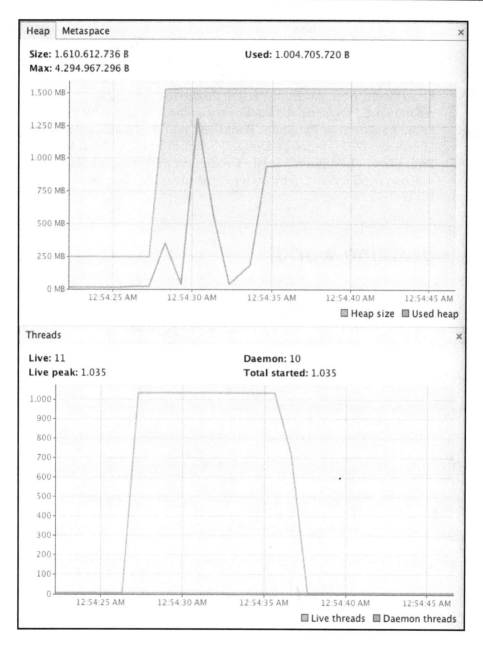

There are many options to fine-tune and play with, `Executor`, such as the number of threads and the type of pool or its actual implementation.

There is a lot more theory on JVM threads than is possible to cover in this book. If you want to read and learn more about threads and concurrency, we recommend the classic book, *Java Concurrency in Practice (2006)* by Dough Lea, David Holmes, Joseph Bower, Joshua Block, Tim Peierls, and Brian Goetz, from Addison-Wesley Professional. We also recommend *Programming Concurrency on the JVM (2011)* by Venkat Subramanian from Pragmatic Bookshelf, and the *Java Concurrency LiveLessons (2015)* video by Douglas Schmidt from Addison-Wesley Professional. Last but not least, we suggest the series of books and videos, *Java Concurrency* by Javier Fernández Gonzáles, published by Packt.

Hello, coroutine world!

Now, let's rewrite our `Hello World` application with coroutines.

But, hey! What is a coroutine? Basically, a coroutine is a very light thread that runs a block of code and has a similar life cycle, but can complete with a return value or an exception. Technically, a coroutine is an instance of a suspendable computation, a computation that may suspend. Coroutines aren't bound to a particular thread and can suspend in one `Thread` and resume execution in a different one:

```
import kotlinx.coroutines.experimental.delay
import kotlinx.coroutines.experimental.launch
import kotlinx.coroutines.experimental.runBlocking

fun main(args: Array<String>) = runBlocking {
    launch {
        delay(1000)
        println("World")
    }
    print("Hello ")
    delay(2000)
}
```

There are a few things to cover here:

- `runBlocking`: This function creates a coroutine and blocks the current `Thread` until the coroutine finishes, returning its result value (`Unit` in this case).
- `launch`: This function creates a new coroutine without blocking the current `Thread` and returns `Job` (ignored here).
- `delay`: This function is a suspending (more on this later) function that delays the current coroutine without blocking the current thread.
- `suspend`: A suspending function is a function that may suspend the execution of a coroutine, without blocking the current `Thread`; therefore a suspending function must be called inside a coroutine—it can't be invoked from normal code. The function must be marked with the `suspend` modifier. So, `delay` can be invoked inside `runBlocking` and `launch`, both functions (among others) take a suspending lambda as the last parameter—a suspending lambda is a lambda marked with the `suspend` modifier.

Let's summarize what we know now, and a few other concepts before going further:

Concept	Description
Coroutine	A very light thread that can return a value and can suspend and resume.
Suspending function	A function marked with a `suspend` modifier. It can suspend a coroutine without blocking the thread. Suspending functions must be invoked inside a coroutine, for example `delay`.
Suspending lambda	A lambda function marked with a `suspend` modifier. It can suspend a coroutine without blocking the thread.
Coroutine builder	A function that takes a suspending lambda, creates a coroutine and may return a result, for example `runBlocking`.
Suspension point	A point where a suspending function is invoked.
Continuation	The state of a suspended coroutine at a suspension point, it represents the rest of its execution after suspension point.

Let's get back to business.

As we discussed previously, computations can have different execution times. So, `delay` isn't ideal in our `Hello World` example:

```
fun main(args: Array<String>) = runBlocking {
    val job = launch {
        delay(1000)
        println("World")
    }
    print("Hello ")
    job.join()
}
```

As with our example with threads, we take the reference to the job created by `launch`, and we suspend it at the end with the suspending function `join`.

So far, so good. But are coroutines so very light? Can we have 10,000 coroutines?

Let's try it by executing the following code snippet:

```
fun main(args: Array<String>) = runBlocking {
    val jobs = List(10000) {
        launch {
            delay(1000)
            print('.')
        }
    }
    jobs.forEach { job -> job.join() }
}
```

Oh, indeed! It works:

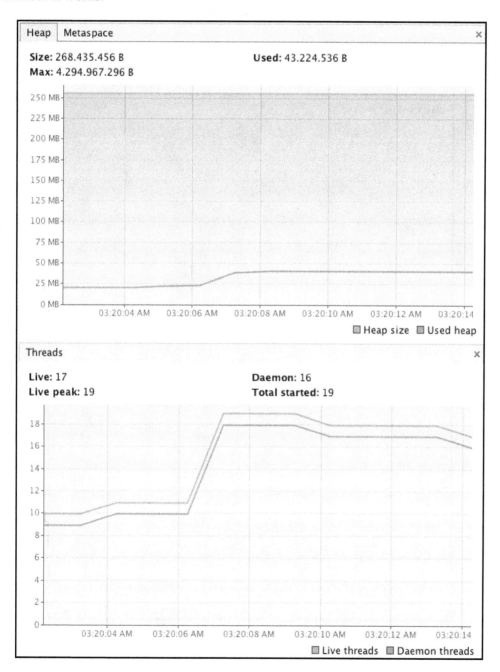

They are orders of magnitude faster than the `Executor` solution, a lot less memory, fewer threads (barely seven threads) and, on top of that, are very easy to read.

Let's go with 1 million coroutines:

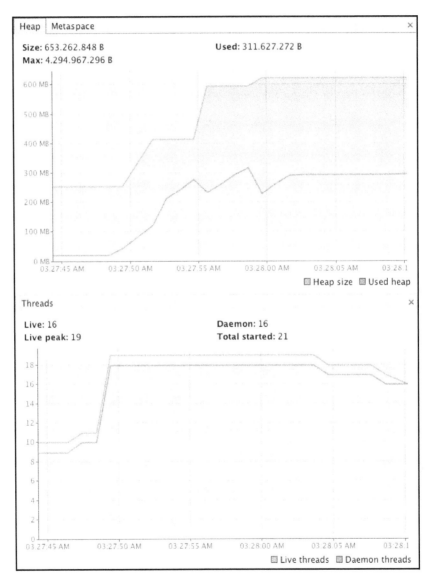

Less than 2,000 threads need more than 1.5 GB of memory. 1 million coroutines need less than 700 MB of memory—I rest my case. The verdict is that the coroutines are very, very light.

Using coroutines in real life

Microbenchmarks are very funny and they give us an idea of the power of Kotlin coroutines, but they don't represent a real-case scenario.

Let's introduce our real-case scenario:

```
enum class Gender {
    MALE, FEMALE;

    companion object {
        fun valueOfIgnoreCase(name: String): Gender =
valueOf(name.toUpperCase())
    }
}

typealias UserId = Int

data class User(val id: UserId, val firstName: String, val lastName:
String, val gender: Gender)

data class Fact(val id: Int, val value: String, val user: User? = null)

interface UserService {
    fun getFact(id: UserId): Fact
}
```

Our `UserService` interface has just one method—`getFact` will return a Chuck Norris-style fact about our user, identified by the user ID.

The implementation should check first on a local database for a user; if the user doesn't exist in the database, it should get it from the **RandomUser API** service, (`https://randomuser.me/documentation`), and then store for future use. Once the service has a user, it should check again in the database for a fact related to that user; if the fact doesn't exist in the database, it should get it from The **Internet Chuck Norris Database API** service, (`http://www.icndb.com/api/`), and store it in the database. Once the service has a fact, it could be returned. The service must try to reduce the number of external calls (database, API services) without using a cache.

Now, let's introduce other interfaces, HTTP clients—`UserClient` and `FactClient`:

```
interface UserClient {
    fun getUser(id: UserId): User
}

interface FactClient {
    fun getFact(user: User): Fact
}
```

Our clients will be implemented using `http4k` (`https://www.http4k.org/`) for HTTP communication, and Kotson (`https://github.com/SalomonBrys/Kotson`) for JSON processing. Both libraries are being designed for Kotlin, but any other library should work fine:

```
import com.github.salomonbrys.kotson.*
import com.google.gson.GsonBuilder
import org.http4k.client.ApacheClient

abstract class WebClient {
    protected val apacheClient = ApacheClient()

    protected val gson = GsonBuilder()
        .registerTypeAdapter<User> {
            deserialize { des ->
                val json = des.json
                User(json["info"]["seed"].int,
json["results"][0]["name"]["first"].string.capitalize(),
json["results"][0]["name"]["last"].string.capitalize(),
Gender.valueOfIgnoreCase(json["results"][0]["gender"].string))

            }
        }
        .registerTypeAdapter<Fact> {
            deserialize { des ->
                val json = des.json
                Fact(json["value"]["id"].int,
                    json["value"]["joke"].string)
            }
        }.create()!!
}
```

Both clients will extend a common parent class that contains `http4k ApacheClient` and a `Gson` value configured with Kotson DSL:

```
import org.http4k.core.Method
import org.http4k.core.Request

class Http4KUserClient : WebClient(), UserClient {
    override fun getUser(id: UserId): User {
        return gson.fromJson(apacheClient(Request(Method.GET,
"https://randomuser.me/api")
                .query("seed", id.toString()))
                .bodyString())
    }
}
```

`Http4KUserClient` is very simple, both libraries are easy to use, and we move a lot of code to the parent class:

```
class Http4KFactClient : WebClient(), FactClient {
    override fun getFact(user: User): Fact {
        return gson.fromJson<Fact>(apacheClient(Request(Method.GET,
"http://api.icndb.com/jokes/random")
                .query("firstName", user.firstName)
                .query("lastName", user.lastName))
                .bodyString())
                .copy(user = user)
    }
}
```

`Http4KFactClient` sets the user value inside the `Fact` instance, using the `copy` method.

These classes are very nicely implemented, but to test the actual performance of our algorithm, we will mock these interfaces:

```
class MockUserClient : UserClient {
    override fun getUser(id: UserId): User {
        println("MockUserClient.getUser")
        Thread.sleep(500)
        return User(id, "Foo", "Bar", Gender.FEMALE)
    }
}

class MockFactClient : FactClient {
    override fun getFact(user: User): Fact {
        println("MockFactClient.getFact")
        Thread.sleep(500)
        return Fact(Random().nextInt(), "FACT ${user.firstName},
```

```
${user.lastName}", user)
    }
}
```

Take a look at the following database repositories, `UserRepository` and `FactRepository`:

```
interface UserRepository {
    fun getUserById(id: UserId): User?
    fun insertUser(user: User)
}

interface FactRepository {
    fun getFactByUserId(id: UserId): Fact?
    fun insertFact(fact: Fact)
}
```

For our repositories, we'll use `JdbcTemplate` of Spring 5. Spring 5 comes with support for Kotlin, including extension functions for easy and idiomatic Kotlin use (you can use `JdbcTemplate` in any application, it doesn't need to be a Spring one):

```
import org.springframework.dao.EmptyResultDataAccessException
import org.springframework.jdbc.core.JdbcTemplate

abstract class JdbcRepository(protected val template: JdbcTemplate) {
    protected fun <T> toNullable(block: () -> T): T? {
        return try {
            block()
        } catch (_: EmptyResultDataAccessException) {
            null
        }
    }
}
```

As with the clients, both repositories will have a parent class—in this case, with a function to transform, `EmptyResultDataAccessException`; (spring's way to indicate a non-existing record) into a nullable—idiomatic Kotlin.

Both implementations are straightforward, as follows:

```
import org.springframework.jdbc.core.queryForObject

class JdbcUserRepository(template: JdbcTemplate) :
JdbcRepository(template), UserRepository {
    override fun getUserById(id: UserId): User? {
        return toNullable {
            template.queryForObject("select * from USERS where id = ?", id) {
```

```
resultSet, _ ->
            with(resultSet) {
               User(getInt("ID"),
                      getString("FIRST_NAME"),
                      getString("LAST_NAME"),
                      Gender.valueOfIgnoreCase(getString("GENDER")))
            }
        }
      }
   }

   override fun insertUser(user: User) {
      template.update("INSERT INTO USERS VALUES (?,?,?,?)",
            user.id,
            user.firstName,
            user.lastName,
            user.gender.name)
   }
}

class JdbcFactRepository(template: JdbcTemplate) :
JdbcRepository(template), FactRepository {
   override fun getFactByUserId(id: Int): Fact? {
      return toNullable {
         template.queryForObject("select * from USERS as U inner join FACTS
as F on U.ID = F.USER where U.ID = ?", id) { resultSet, _ ->
            with(resultSet) {
               Fact(getInt(5),
                      getString(6),
                      User(getInt(1),
                            getString(2),
                            getString(3),
                            Gender.valueOfIgnoreCase(getString(4))))
            }
         }
      }
   }

   override fun insertFact(fact: Fact) {
      template.update("INSERT INTO FACTS VALUES (?,?,?)", fact.id,
fact.value, fact.user?.id)
   }
}
```

For our database, we are using the H2 in-memory database, but any database will work (you can make this application work with some different persistence mechanisms, such as NoSQL database or any cache):

```
fun initJdbcTemplate(): JdbcTemplate {
    return JdbcTemplate(JdbcDataSource()
        .apply {
setUrl("jdbc:h2:mem:facts_app;DB_CLOSE_DELAY=-1;DB_CLOSE_ON_EXIT=false")
        })
        .apply {
            execute("CREATE TABLE USERS (ID INT AUTO_INCREMENT PRIMARY KEY,
FIRST_NAME VARCHAR(64) NOT NULL, LAST_NAME VARCHAR(64) NOT NULL, GENDER
VARCHAR(8) NOT NULL);")
            execute("CREATE TABLE FACTS (ID INT AUTO_INCREMENT PRIMARY KEY,
VALUE_ TEXT NOT NULL, USER INT NOT NULL,  FOREIGN KEY (USER) REFERENCES
USERS(ID) ON DELETE RESTRICT)")
        }
}
```

The function `initJdbcTemplate` creates `JdbcTemplate` with an H2 `DataSource`, and, once it is ready, it creates the tables inside the `apply` extension function. The `apply` extension function is useful to configure properties and call initialization code, returning the same value:

```
public inline fun <T> T.apply(block: T.() -> Unit): T {
    block()
    return this
}
```

As with the clients, for testing, we will use mocks:

```
class MockUserRepository : UserRepository {
    private val users = hashMapOf<UserId, User>()

    override fun getUserById(id: UserId): User? {
        println("MockUserRepository.getUserById")
        Thread.sleep(200)
        return users[id]
    }

    override fun insertUser(user: User) {
        println("MockUserRepository.insertUser")
        Thread.sleep(200)
        users[user.id] = user
    }
}
```

```
class MockFactRepository : FactRepository {

    private val facts = hashMapOf<UserId, Fact>()

    override fun getFactByUserId(id: UserId): Fact? {
        println("MockFactRepository.getFactByUserId")
        Thread.sleep(200)
        return facts[id]
    }

    override fun insertFact(fact: Fact) {
        println("MockFactRepository.insertFact")
        Thread.sleep(200)
        facts[fact.user?.id ?: 0] = fact
    }

}
```

With these mocks, our worst case scenario is around 1,600 milliseconds:

- `UserRepository.getUserById = 200ms ~`
- `UserClient.getUser = 500ms ~`
- `UserRepository = 200ms ~`
- `FactClient.getFact = 500ms ~`
- `FactRepository.insertRepository = 200ms ~`

Now, we'll implement `UserService` with different styles of asynchronicity, including a synchronous implementation, our baseline.

Synchronous implementation

Synchronous code is easy to write, predictable, and easy to test, but in some cases, it doesn't use system resources in an optimal manner:

```
class SynchronousUserService(private val userClient: UserClient,
                    private val factClient: FactClient,
                    private val userRepository: UserRepository,
                    private val factRepository: FactRepository) :
UserService {

    override fun getFact(id: UserId): Fact {
        val user = userRepository.getUserById(id)
        return if (user == null) {
            val userFromService = userClient.getUser(id)
```

```
                userRepository.insertUser(userFromService)
                getFact(userFromService)
            } else {
                factRepository.getFactByUserId(id) ?: getFact(user)
            }
        }
    }

    private fun getFact(user: User): Fact {
        val fact = factClient.getFact(user)
        factRepository.insertFact(fact)
        return fact
    }
}
```

There's nothing fancy here, just your normal, old boring code:

```
fun main(args: Array<String>) {
    fun execute(userService: UserService, id: Int) {
        val (fact, time) = inTime {
            userService.getFact(id)
        }
        println("fact = $fact")
        println("time = $time ms.")
    }
    val userClient = MockUserClient()
    val factClient = MockFactClient()
    val userRepository = MockUserRepository()
    val factRepository = MockFactRepository()

    val userService = SynchronousUserService(userClient,
        factClient,
        userRepository,
        factRepository)

    execute(userService, 1)
    execute(userService, 2)
    execute(userService, 1)
    execute(userService, 2)
    execute(userService, 3)
    execute(userService, 4)
    execute(userService, 5)
    execute(userService, 10)
    execute(userService, 100)
}
```

We execute the `UserService.getFact` method 10 times to warm up the JVM (JVM optimizations make the application run faster after a while). Needless to say, execution time is 1,600 milliseconds, no surprises here.

Callbacks

A popular style of asynchronous code is to execute the code in a separate thread and invoke a `callback` function when the aforementioned thread finishes its execution. One downside of the callback style is that our asynchronous functions now need an extra parameter. Callback style is easy to write in Kotlin with its support for lambdas.

For our callback implementation, we'll need adapters for our clients and repositories:

```kotlin
import kotlin.concurrent.thread

class CallbackUserClient(private val client: UserClient) {
    fun getUser(id: Int, callback: (User) -> Unit) {
        thread {
            callback(client.getUser(id))
        }
    }
}

class CallbackFactClient(private val client: FactClient) {
    fun get(user: User, callback: (Fact) -> Unit) {
        thread {
            callback(client.getFact(user))
        }
    }
}

class CallbackUserRepository(private val userRepository: UserRepository) {
    fun getUserById(id: UserId, callback: (User?) -> Unit) {
        thread {
            callback(userRepository.getUserById(id))
        }
    }

    fun insertUser(user: User, callback: () -> Unit) {
        thread {
            userRepository.insertUser(user)
            callback()
        }
    }
}
```

```
    }

    class CallbackFactRepository(private val factRepository: FactRepository) {
        fun getFactByUserId(id: Int, callback: (Fact?) -> Unit) {
            thread {
                callback(factRepository.getFactByUserId(id))
            }
        }

        fun insertFact(fact: Fact, callback: () -> Unit) {
            thread {
                factRepository.insertFact(fact)
                callback()
            }
        }
    }
}
```

These adapters execute our code in a separate thread and invoke the callback, lambda, once it is completed:

```
class CallbackUserService(private val userClient: CallbackUserClient,
                          private val factClient: CallbackFactClient,
                          private val userRepository: CallbackUserRepository,
                          private val factRepository: CallbackFactRepository) :
UserService {

    override fun getFact(id: UserId): Fact {
        var aux: Fact? = null
        userRepository.getUserById(id) { user ->
            if (user == null) {
                userClient.getUser(id) { userFromClient ->
                    userRepository.insertUser(userFromClient) {}
                    factClient.get(userFromClient) { fact ->
                        factRepository.insertFact(fact) {}
                        aux = fact
                    }

                }
            } else {
                factRepository.getFactByUserId(id) { fact ->
                    if (fact == null) {
                        factClient.get(user) { factFromClient ->
                            factRepository.insertFact(factFromClient) {}
                            aux = factFromClient
                        }
                    } else {
                        aux = fact
                    }
```

```
                    }
                }
            }
        }
        while (aux == null) {
            Thread.sleep(2)
        }
        return aux!!
    }
}
```

Callback style tends to be very obscure and hard to read; when several callbacks are nested, it is even worse (affectionately known in the community as callback hell). The `while` block at the end with `Thread.sleep` looks very hacky. It is also very fast with an execution time of 1,200 milliseconds but with many threads created and memory consumption to match it.

A callback implementation that creates a thread per function call will quickly consume all the application's resources in a production scenario; therefore, it should be based on some `Executor` implementation or similar.

Java Futures

As callback style tends to be hard to maintain, other styles have emerged in recent years. One of these styles is futures. A **future** is a computation that may complete in the future. When we invoke the `Future.get` method, it will obtain its result, but we also block the thread:

```
import java.util.concurrent.ExecutorService
import java.util.concurrent.Executors

class FutureUserService(private val userClient: UserClient,
                private val factClient: FactClient,
                private val userRepository: UserRepository,
                private val factRepository: FactRepository) : UserService
{
    override fun getFact(id: UserId): Fact {

        val executor = Executors.newFixedThreadPool(2)

        val user = executor.submit<User?> { userRepository.getUserById(id)
}.get()
        return if (user == null) {
            val userFromService = executor.submit<User> {
userClient.getUser(id) }.get()
            executor.submit { userRepository.insertUser(userFromService) }
```

```
        getFact(userFromService, executor)
    } else {
      executor.submit<Fact> {
        factRepository.getFactByUserId(id) ?: getFact(user, executor)
      }.get()
    }.also {
      executor.shutdown()
    }
  }

  private fun getFact(user: User, executor: ExecutorService): Fact {
    val fact = executor.submit<Fact> { factClient.getFact(user) }.get()
    executor.submit { factRepository.insertFact(fact) }
    return fact
  }
}
```

The implementation with futures is very similar to our synchronous implementation, but with those weird `submit` and `get` functions all over the place. We also have `Executor` that we need to take care of. Total time is around 1,200 milliseconds, with many threads created, more than in the callback example. One possible option is to have `Executor` per instance or globally, but in that case, we also need to have some way to manage its life cycle.

Promises with Kovenant

Another option to write asynchronous code is to use promises. A **promise** is similar to a future (in many frameworks, futures and promises are synonymous), as it represents a computation that may complete in the future. We have a blocking method to obtain its result, but we can also react to its result, callback style.

Kovenant (http://kovenant.komponents.nl/) is an implementation of promises for Kotlin:

```
import nl.komponents.kovenant.Promise
import nl.komponents.kovenant.task
import nl.komponents.kovenant.then

class PromiseUserService(private val userClient: UserClient,
                private val factClient: FactClient,
                private val userRepository: UserRepository,
                private val factRepository: FactRepository) :
UserService {

  override fun getFact(id: UserId): Fact {

    return (task {
```

```
                userRepository.getUserById(id)
        } then { user ->
            if (user == null) {
                task {
                    userClient.getUser(id)
                } success  { userFromService ->
                    userRepository.insertUser(userFromService)
                } then { userFromService ->
                    getFact(userFromService).get()
                }
            } else {
                task { factRepository.getFactByUserId(id) ?:
    getFact(user).get() }
            }
        }).get().get()
    }

    private fun getFact(user: User): Promise<Fact, Exception> = task {
        factClient.getFact(user)
    } success  { fact ->
        factRepository.insertFact(fact)
    }
}
```

The function `task` creates `Promise<T, Exception>` (something that we didn't cover previously in our other implementations). We can interact with `Promise<T, Exception>` in several ways:

- `get(): T`: This blocks the current thread and returns the promise's result.
- `then(bind: (T) -> R): Promise<R, Exception>`: This is similar to `map` on functional collections; it returns a new `Promise` value with a new type.
- `success(callback: (T) -> Unit): Promise<T, Exception>`: This is callback on successful `Promise` execution. It's useful for side effects
- `fail(callback: (Exception) -> Unit): Promise<T, Exception>`: This is callback on fail, like a `catch` block.
- `always(callback: () -> Unit): Promise<T, Exception>`: This always executes, like a `finally` block.

The codes feel difficult to grasp at first sight, but, once you get used to the promise idioms, it is easy to read. Also, notice that a promise is a future, so you can write something similar to our future's example but without messing around with `Executors`. Java 8 includes a new type of future named `CompletableFuture<T>` which can be considered a promise.

Execution time is around 1,350 milliseconds for the first execution (Kovenant initialization phase), and then it stabilizes around 1,200 milliseconds. On its default configuration, Kovenant uses as many threads as possible, resulting in a high use of memory, but Kovenant can be fine-tuned to use fewer threads.

Coroutines

Now, let's rework our example with coroutines:

```
import kotlinx.coroutines.experimental.Deferred
import kotlinx.coroutines.experimental.async
import kotlinx.coroutines.experimental.launch
import kotlinx.coroutines.experimental.runBlocking

class CoroutineUserService(private val userClient: UserClient,
                   private val factClient: FactClient,
                   private val userRepository: UserRepository,
                   private val factRepository: FactRepository) :
UserService {
   override fun getFact(id: UserId): Fact = runBlocking {
      val user = async { userRepository.getUserById(id) }.await()
      if (user == null) {
         val userFromService = async { userClient.getUser(id) }.await()
         launch { userRepository.insertUser(userFromService) }
         getFact(userFromService)
      } else {
         async { factRepository.getFactByUserId(id) ?: getFact(user)
}.await()
      }
   }

   private suspend fun getFact(user: User):Fact {
      val fact: Deferred<Fact> = async { factClient.getFact(user) }
      launch { factRepository.insertFact(fact.await()) }
      return fact.await()
   }
}
```

Our code is more straightforward than our `Future` example, getting very close to our synchronous code. We covered `runBlocking` and `launch` in the previous section, but a new coroutine builder is introduced here, `async`.

The `async` coroutine builder takes a block of code and executes it asynchronously, returning `Deferred<T>`. A `Deferred` is a `Future` with an `await` method that blocks the coroutine until completion but not the thread; `Deferred` also extends from `Job` so inherits all its methods, such as `join`.

Coroutine code feels natural yet it is explicit when we are using asynchronous code, but due to the low cost on resources, we can use as many coroutines as we want in our code; for example, `CoroutineUserService` uses less than half of threads and memory than any other implementation.

Now that we have all implementations, we can compare code complexity and resource consumption:

	Code complexity	Resource consumption
Synchronous	There is very low code complexity.	The resource consumption is very low with slow performance.
Callbacks	Very high adapters are needed; duplication is expected; nested callbacks are hard to read; and there are various hacks.	The resource consumption is high. It could improve using a shared `Executor`, but it will add more code complexity.
Futures	Code complexity is medium. `Executors` and `get()` are noisy but it is still readable.	Resource consumption is high, but it can be fine-tuned using different `Executor` implementations and sharing executors but this adds code complexity.
Promises	Code complexity is medium using promise style (`then`, `success`). Using a futures style (`get`), it can be as slick as coroutines without affecting performance.	Resource consumption is very high, with top performance, but it can be fine-tuned without altering the code.
Coroutines	Code complexity is low; it's the same size as synchronous style with explicit blocks for asynchronous operations.	Resource consumption is low, with top performance out of the box.

Overall, coroutines are a clear winner, with Kovenant promises coming in a close second.

Coroutine context

Coroutines always run in a context. All coroutine builders have context specified by default, and that context is available through the value `coroutineContext`, inside the coroutine body:

```kotlin
import kotlinx.coroutines.experimental.*

fun main(args: Array<String>) = runBlocking {
    println("run blocking coroutineContext = $coroutineContext")
    println("coroutineContext[Job] = ${coroutineContext[Job]}")
    println(Thread.currentThread().name)
    println("-----")

    val jobs = listOf(
        launch {
            println("launch coroutineContext = $coroutineContext")
            println("coroutineContext[Job] = ${coroutineContext[Job]}")
            println(Thread.currentThread().name)
            println("-----")
        },
        async {
            println("async coroutineContext = $coroutineContext")
            println("coroutineContext[Job] = ${coroutineContext[Job]}")
            println(Thread.currentThread().name)
            println("-----")
        },
        launch(CommonPool) {
            println("common launch coroutineContext = $coroutineContext")
            println("coroutineContext[Job] = ${coroutineContext[Job]}")
            println(Thread.currentThread().name)
            println("-----")
        },
        launch(coroutineContext) {
            println("inherit launch coroutineContext = $coroutineContext")
            println("coroutineContext[Job] = ${coroutineContext[Job]}")
            println(Thread.currentThread().name)
            println("-----")
        }
    )

    jobs.forEach { job ->
        println("job = $job")
        job.join()
    }
}
```

Each coroutine context also includes `CoroutineDispatcher` that decides which thread the coroutine runs. Coroutines builders, such as `async` and `launch`, use the `DefaultDispatcher` dispatcher as default (in the current coroutines version, 0.2.1, `DefaultDispatcher` is equal to `CommonPool`; however, this behavior can change in the future).

The coroutine context can also hold values; for example, you can recover the coroutine's job by using `coroutineContext[Job]`.

Coroutine contexts can be used to control its children. Our 1 million coroutines example can be reworked to join all its children:

```
fun main(args: Array<String>) = runBlocking {

    val job = launch {
        repeat(1_000_000) {
            launch(coroutineContext) {
                delay(1000)
                print('.')
            }
        }
    }

    job.join()
}
```

Instead of each one of the million coroutines having its own context, we can set a shared coroutine context that actually comes from the external `launch` coroutine context. When we join the outer `launch` job, it joins all its coroutine children, too.

Channels

One way for two coroutines to communicate (or for a coroutine to the external world as with `async`) is through `Deferred<T>`:

```
import kotlinx.coroutines.experimental.delay
import kotlinx.coroutines.experimental.launch
import kotlinx.coroutines.experimental.runBlocking

fun main(args: Array<String>) = runBlocking {
    val result = CompletableDeferred<String>()

    val world = launch {
        delay(500)
```

```
        result.complete("World (from another coroutine)")
    }

    val hello =launch {
        println("Hello ${result.await()}")
    }

    hello.join()
    world.join()
}
```

Deferreds are fine for single values, but sometimes we want to send a sequence or a stream. In that case, we can use `Channel`. `Channel` which is similar to `BlockingQueue`, but with suspending operations instead of blocking ones, also `Channel` can be `close`:

```
import kotlinx.coroutines.experimental.channels.*

fun main(args: Array<String>) = runBlocking<Unit> {
    val channel = Channel<String>()

    val world = launch {
        delay(500)
        channel.send("World (from another coroutine using a channel)")
    }

    val hello = launch {
        println("Hello ${channel.receive()}")
    }

    hello.join()
    world.join()
}
```

Let's write our 1 million coroutines example with channels as follows:

```
fun main(args: Array<String>) = runBlocking<Unit> {

    val channel = Channel<Char>()

    val jobs = List(1_000_000) {
        launch {
            delay(1000)
            channel.send('.')
        }
    }

    repeat(1_000_000) {
```

Chapter 7

```
        print(channel.receive())
    }

    jobs.forEach { job -> job.join() }
}
```

Of course, this isn't the intended use case for channels. Usually, a single coroutine (or many) sends messages to the channel:

```
fun main(args: Array<String>) = runBlocking<Unit> {

    val channel = Channel<Char>()

    val sender = launch {
        repeat(1000) {
            delay(10)
            channel.send('.')
            delay(10)
            channel.send(',')
        }
        channel.close()
    }

    for (msg in channel) {
        print(msg)
    }

    sender.join()

}
```

A channel is itself an Iterator, so it can be used on the `for` blocks.

A simpler way to write this code is by using the `produce` builder as follows:

```
fun dotsAndCommas(size: Int) = produce {
    repeat(size) {
        delay(10)
        send('.')
        delay(10)
        send(',')
    }
}

fun main(args: Array<String>) = runBlocking<Unit> {
    val channel = dotsAndCommas(1000)

    for (msg in channel) {
```

[181]

```
        print(msg)
    }
  }
```

The `produce` builder returns `ReceiveChannel<T>`, a channel type just for receiving. A `Channel<T>` extends both types, `SendChannel<T>` and `ReceiveChannel<T>`.

Channel pipelines

When we have channels, we can have related patterns, such as pipelines. A **pipeline** is a series of channels connecting consumers and producers, similar to Unix pipes or **Enterprise Integration Patterns** (EIP).

Let's write our own sales system using EIPs. Let's first take a look at the models:

```
data class Quote(val value: Double, val client: String, val item: String,
val quantity: Int)

data class Bill(val value: Double, val client: String)

data class PickingOrder(val item: String, val quantity: Int)
```

Now, let's take a look at the patterns:

```
import kotlinx.coroutines.experimental.CoroutineContext

fun calculatePriceTransformer(coroutineContext: CoroutineContext,
quoteChannel: ReceiveChannel<Quote>) = produce(coroutineContext) {
    for (quote in quoteChannel) {
        send(Bill(quote.value * quote.quantity, quote.client) to
PickingOrder(quote.item, quote.quantity))
    }
}
```

The `calculatePriceTransformer` function receives quotes from a channel and transforms it into `Pair<Bill, PickingOrder>`:

```
fun cheapBillFilter(coroutineContext: CoroutineContext, billChannel:
ReceiveChannel<Pair<Bill, PickingOrder>>) = produce(coroutineContext) {
    billChannel.consumeEach { (bill, order) ->
        if (bill.value >= 100) {
            send(bill to order)
        } else {
            println("Discarded bill $bill")
        }
```

```
        }
    }
```

The `cheapBillFilter` function well filters the `bill` value below `100`:

```
suspend fun splitter(filteredChannel: ReceiveChannel<Pair<Bill,
PickingOrder>>,
                accountingChannel: SendChannel<Bill>,
                warehouseChannel: SendChannel<PickingOrder>) = launch {
    filteredChannel.consumeEach { (bill, order) ->
        accountingChannel.send(bill)
        warehouseChannel.send(order)
    }
}
```

`splitter` splits `Pair<Bill, PickingOrder>` into their own channels:

```
suspend fun accountingEndpoint(accountingChannel: ReceiveChannel<Bill>) =
launch {
    accountingChannel.consumeEach { bill ->
        println("Processing bill = $bill")
    }
}

suspend fun warehouseEndpoint(warehouseChannel:
ReceiveChannel<PickingOrder>) = launch {
    warehouseChannel.consumeEach { order ->
        println("Processing order = $order")
    }
}
```

Both `accountingEndpoint` and `warehouseEndpoint` process their respective messages by printing, but, in a real-life scenario, we could be storing these messages into our database, sending emails or sending messages to other systems using **JMS**, **AMQP**, or **Kafka**:

```
fun main(args: Array<String>) = runBlocking {

    val quoteChannel = Channel<Quote>()
    val accountingChannel = Channel<Bill>()
    val warehouseChannel = Channel<PickingOrder>()
    val transformerChannel = calculatePriceTransformer(coroutineContext,
quoteChannel)

    val filteredChannel = cheapBillFilter(coroutineContext,
transformerChannel)
```

```
        splitter(filteredChannel, accountingChannel, warehouseChannel)

        warehouseEndpoint(warehouseChannel)

        accountingEndpoint(accountingChannel)

        launch(coroutineContext) {
            quoteChannel.send(Quote(20.0, "Foo", "Shoes", 1))
            quoteChannel.send(Quote(20.0, "Bar", "Shoes", 200))
            quoteChannel.send(Quote(2000.0, "Foo", "Motorbike", 1))
        }
        delay(1000)
        coroutineContext.cancelChildren()
    }
```

The `main` method assembles our sales system and tests it.

Many other channel messages patterns can be implemented with coroutine channels, such as fan-in, fan-out, and `actors`. We'll cover `actors` in our next section.

Managing mutable state

The main concern (and nightmare fuel) when we deal with asynchronous code is how to handle mutable state. We covered how to reduce mutable state with a functional style in Chapter 3, *Immutability - It's Important*. But sometimes it is impossible to use a functional immutable style. Coroutines offer some alternatives to this problem.

In the following example, we'll use several coroutines to update a counter:

```
import kotlin.system.measureTimeMillis

suspend fun repeatInParallel(times: Int, block: suspend () -> Unit) {
    val job = launch {
        repeat(times) {
            launch(coroutineContext) {
                block()
            }
        }
    }
    job.join()
}

fun main(args: Array<String>) = runBlocking {
    var counter = 0
```

```
    val time = measureTimeMillis {
        repeatInParallel(1_000_000) {
            counter++
        }
    }
    println("counter = $counter")
    println("time = $time")
}
```

On smaller numbers, `counter` is right, but once we start increasing the size, we'll see wacky numbers.

Now we can have a look at the alternatives that coroutines provide us.

Switching contexts

Our first option is to use a different context for our update operation:

```
import kotlinx.coroutines.experimental.*

fun main(args: Array<String>) = runBlocking {
    var counter = 0

    val counterContext = newSingleThreadContext("CounterContext")

    val time = measureTimeMillis {
        repeatInParallel(1_000_000) {
            withContext(counterContext) {
                counter++
            }
        }
    }
    println("counter = $counter")
    println("time = $time")
}
```

The `withContext` function executes a block in a specific coroutine context—in this case, a single-threaded one. Switching context is a powerful technique that lets us manipulate, in a fine-grained way, how our code runs.

Thread safe structures

From Java 5 and onwards, we have access to some atomic thread safe structures, that are still useful with coroutines:

```
import java.util.concurrent.atomic.AtomicInteger

fun main(args: Array<String>) = runBlocking {
    val counter = AtomicInteger(0)

    val time = measureTimeMillis {
        repeatInParallel(1_000_000) {
            counter.incrementAndGet()
        }
    }
    println("counter = ${counter.get()}")
    println("time = $time")
}
```

`AtomicInteger` gives us many atomic operations that are thread safe. There are more thread safe structures such as other atomic primitives and concurrent collections.

Mutexes

A `Mutex` (mutual exclusion) object allows access to multiple coroutines to share the same resource but not simultaneously:

```
import kotilnx.coroutines.experimental.sync.Mutex
import kotlinx.coroutines.experimental.sync.withLock

fun main(args: Array<String>) = runBlocking {
    val mutex = Mutex()
    var counter = 0

    val time = measureTimeMillis {
        repeatInParallel(1_000_000) {
            mutex.withLock {
                counter++
            }
        }
    }
    println("counter = $counter")
    println("time = $time")
}
```

A `Mutex` object works similarly to a synchronized control structure, but, instead of blocking the thread, it just blocks the coroutine.

Actors

An `actor` is kind of object that interacts with other actors and with the external world through messages. An `actor` object can have a private internal mutable state that can be modified and accessed externally through messages, but not directly. Actors are growing in popularity in recent years due to their consistent programming model, and have been tested successfully in multi-million user applications, such as **WhatsApp** that is built with **Erlang**, the language that brings actors into the limelight:

```
import kotlinx.coroutines.experimental.channels.actor

sealed class CounterMsg
object IncCounter : CounterMsg()
class GetCounter(val response: CompletableDeferred<Int>) : CounterMsg()

fun counterActor(start:Int) = actor<CounterMsg> {
    var counter = start
    for (msg in channel) {
        when (msg) {
            is IncCounter -> counter++
            is GetCounter -> msg.response.complete(counter)
        }
    }
}
```

To write an `actor`, first, we need to define which messages we want to send. Here, we are creating two messages, `IncCounter` and `GetCounter`. `GetCounter` has a `CompletableDeferred<Int>` value that will let us know the counter value outside the `actor`.

We can use the `actor<CounterMsg>` builder to create `actor`. Inside our `actor` coroutine, we have access to the `channel` property, `ReceiveChannel<CounterMsg>`, to receive the messages and react to them. The `counterActor(Int)` function will return `SendChannel<CounterMsg>`; therefore, the only functions that we can call are `send(CounterMsg)` and `close()`:

```
fun main(args: Array<String>) = runBlocking {
    val counterActor = counterActor(0)

    val time = measureTimeMillis {
```

```
        repeatInParallel(1_000_000) {
            counterActor.send(IncCounter)
        }
    }
    val counter = CompletableDeferred<Int>()
    counterActor.send(GetCounter(counter))
    println("counter = ${counter.await()}")
    println("time = $time")
}
```

Actors can be hard to grasp at the beginning but once, you understand, the `actor` model is straightforward for creating complex and powerful systems.

 In the example code for this book, you can find an implementation of our `UserService` example using `actors`. You can watch it online at `https://github.com/MarioAriasC/FunctionalKotlin/blob/master/Chapter07/src/main/kotlin/com/packtpub/functionalkotlin/chapter07/facts.kt#L377`.

Summary

Coroutines show a high potential to transform the way we think about asynchronous code and execution. In this chapter, we covered how to write coroutines and how to use coroutine contexts and channels. We also took a comprehensive look at how to deal with asynchronous shared mutable state.

In our next chapter, we'll learn about functional collections and their operations.

8

Collections and Data Operations in Kotlin

In the previous chapters, we have covered a wide range of topics, starting from data types, classes, and objects in Kotlin and moving on to immutability, functions, delegates, and coroutines in the last chapter. In this chapter, we are going to discuss the collections framework and data operations in Kotlin. Kotlin inherits collections framework from Java, but has significant changes from it in favor of functional programming.

The collections framework that Kotlin provides is more functional than Java and, as the signature of Kotlin, it is easier to use and understand.

We will start this chapter with the fundamentals of collections and gradually move on to data operations that collections support in Kotlin. The following is the list of topics that we are going to cover in this chapter:

- An introduction to collections
- The `Iterator` and `Iterable` interfaces
- Collection types in Kotlin—`Array`, `List`, `Map`, and `Set`
- Mutability and immutability
- Working with lists
- Various data operations—`map`, `sort`, `filter`, `flatMap`, `partition`, `fold`, and `group by`

So, what are we waiting for? Let's get started with collections.

An introduction to collections

The **collections framework** is a set of classes and interfaces that provides a unified architecture for performing common groups of data related operations, such as the following:

- Searching
- Sorting
- Insertion
- Deletion
- Manipulation

All the lists, maps, and sets we use in our programs everyday are part of this collections framework.

All collections frameworks contain the following things:

- **Interfaces**: These are abstract data types are used to represent collections. Interfaces allow collections to be manipulated independent of the details of their representation. In object-oriented languages, these are generally interfaces form a hierarchy.
- **Implementations**: These are concrete implementations of the collection of interfaces. In essence, these are reusable data structures.
- **Algorithms**: Methods that perform useful computations, such as searching and sorting (as listed earlier), on objects that implement collection interfaces. These algorithms are said to be **polymorphic**. The same method can be used on many different implementations of the appropriate collection interface. In short, algorithms are a reusable functionality.

Apart from the Java and Kotlin collections framework, the best-known examples of collections framework are the **C++ Standard Template Library** (**STL**) and Smalltalk's collection hierarchy.

The advantages of a collections framework

So, what is the benefit of having a collections framework? There are several benefits, but, most importantly, it reduces the programming time and effort. The collections framework provides a developer with high-quality (in terms of performance and code optimization) implementations of useful data structures and algorithms, while providing you with interoperability between unrelated APIs. You can use these implementations in your program, thus reducing your programming effort and time.

So, as we have got to know what the collections framework is, let us now have a look at the hierarchy of classes and interfaces in the collections framework.

So, let's go through the following figure:

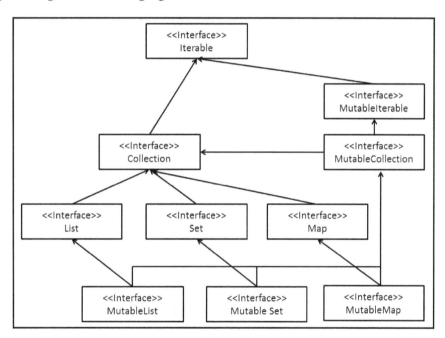

As we mentioned earlier, the collections framework is a set of data types and classes that lets us work with a group (or groups) of data. That group may be in the form of a simple list/map/set or any other data structure.

The preceding figure represents the collections framework of Kotlin. Just like Java, all collection interfaces in Kotlin are originated from the `Iterable` interface. However, the Kotlin collections framework is a bit different than that of Java; Kotlin distinguishes between mutable and immutable collections.

Kotlin has two base collection interfaces, namely `Iterable` and `MutableIterable`. The `Iterable` interface is extended by the `Collection` interface, which defines basic read-only collection operations (like `size`, `isEmpty()`, `contains()`, and so on).

The `MutableCollection` interface extends the `Collection` interface and the `MutableIterable` interface, adding the read-write feature.

Before the collections framework was introduced in Java, developers used to use arrays, vectors, and HashTables to work with a group of data. The problem with this approach was that none of them have some common methods. The collections framework was thus created to make a developer's life easier by providing common methods and operations across various types of collections.

 The collection framework was introduced in Java before formation of the Kotlin language and it has been included in Kotlin from the very beginning.

Aren't you curious about why there are so many collection types? Let's find out the purpose of some of the most commonly used collection types as we cover them in the following sections.

List and MutableList

List is one of the most commonly used collection data types. It is an implementation of the `Collection` interface used to work with a group of ordered data.

 The data in a list may be ordered based on when it was added (like if we add 3 after 4 to an `Int List`, then 4 will appear in the list before 3, much like an array) or may even be ordered based on other ordering algorithms.

As we mentioned earlier, Kotlin distinguishes between mutable and read-only collection types; so, the `List` interface, which is immutable, contains only the read-only functions, as follows:

- `fun get(index: Int):E`: This method is used to get an element from the list at the given index.
- `fun indexOf(element: @UnsafeVariance E):Int`: This method is used to identify the index of an element in the list. This method will search for the specified element inside the whole list and return the position of the element if it's in the list. Otherwise, it will return −1.
- `fun listIterator(): ListIterator<E>`: In case you want to get an instance of `ListIterator` (this will be covered later in this chapter, while we discuss `Iterator` and `Iterable`).
- `fun subList(fromIndex: Int, toIndex: Int): List<E>`: Returns a portion of the list with the specified `fromIndex` and `toIndex` value.

So considering this, it contains only read-only functions, how can we have a list with data? While you cannot put data into an immutable list after it gets created, you can definitely create an immutable list with pre-populated data (obviously, otherwise there wouldn't be any purpose in having immutable lists). You can achieve that in many ways, but the most popular one is to use the `listOf` function.

The `listOf` function declaration looks like the following (which can be found inside `Collections.kt`, in the `kotlin.collections` package):

```
public fun <T> listOf(vararg elements: T): List<T>
```

As we can see in the function declaration, the function takes a `vararg` parameter of a generic type as an element; the function will return a `list` instance containing those elements. As you already know, the significance of a `vararg` argument is that it can contain 0 to almost 64K arguments (if each argument is of 1 byte, a function can have a maximum of 64K bytes allocation, so actually it would be less) within it; so, while creating `list` with the `listOf` function, you can call it even without parameters to create an empty list, or call the function with as many arguments as you need (assuming you don't need more than 64K bytes) to create the read-only `list` with them.

The following program is an example of the `listOf` function:

```
fun main(args: Array<String>) {
    val list = listOf<Int>(1,2,3,4,5,6,7,8,9,10)
    for (i in list) {
        println("Item $i")
    }
}
```

In the preceding program, we created a `list` value containing numbers 1 through 10. We then used a `for` loop to loop through each element in the `list` value and print it.

Let's have a look at the following output to validate that:

```
"C:\Program Files\Java\jdk1.8.0_131\bin\java" ...
Item 1
Item 2
Item 3
Item 4
Item 5
Item 6
Item 7
Item 8
Item 9
Item 10

Process finished with exit code 0
```

The `i in list` inside the braces of the `for` loop, tells the `for` loop to iterate through all the elements inside the `list` value and copy the element to a temporary variable `i` for each of the iterations.

We will look at more ways to work with collections later in this chapter, but first let us learn different types of collections.

So, continuing our discussions on lists, we've seen how to create an immutable list with pre-defined elements; now, we will look at how to create and work with mutable lists, but before that let's have a look at the ways to create an empty list.

Let's go through the following program:

```
fun main(args: Array<String>) {
    val emptyList1 = listOf<Any>()      val emptyList2 = emptyList<Any>()
    println("emptyList1.size = ${emptyList1.size}")
    println("emptyList2.size = ${emptyList2.size}")
}
```

So, in the preceding program, we created empty lists, one with a `listOf` function with no arguments, another one is with an `emptyList` function. Please note that the `listOf` function, if called without any arguments, calls an `emptyList` function internally.

The following is the screenshot of the output:

```
"C:\Program Files\Java\jdk1.8.0_131\bin\java" ...
emptyList1.size = 0
emptyList2.size = 0

Process finished with exit code 0
```

So, we've seen how to work with immutable lists with a pre-defined bunch of elements, but what if we need to add items to the `list` value dynamically? Kotlin provides you with mutable lists for this purpose.

The following example will help you understand immutable lists:

```
fun main(args: Array<String>) {
    val list = mutableListOf(1,2,4) //(1)

    for (i in list) {
        println("for1 item $i")
    }

    println("-----Adding Items-----")

    list.add(5) //(2)      list.add(2,3) //(3)      list.add(6) //(4)

    for (i in list) {
        println("for2 item $i")
    }
}
```

The following is the output of the program:

```
"C:\Program Files\Java\jdk1.8.0_131\bin\java" ...
for1 item 1
for1 item 2
for1 item 4
-----Adding Items-----
for2 item 1
for2 item 2
for2 item 3
for2 item 4
for2 item 5
for2 item 6


Process finished with exit code 0
```

Now, let us explain the program. So, at first, we created the `list` value with `mutableListOf` function on comment (1), with the items 1, 2, and 4. Note, we skipped the type parameter here, it's not important if you pass the elements to the function, as Kotlin has type interference. We printed the `list` values before moving ahead to add items.

For `listOf` or any other collections function, type interference is an issue. So, you'll not need to specify the generic type of the collection in use if you pass the elements or if you've provided the type of the collection itself.

On comment (2), we added item 5 to the `list`, with the `List$add()` function, which appends the provided item to the `list` array.

Then, on comment (3), we used the `add` function with an index parameter, to add item 4 to the second position (counting from 0, as usual).

Then, again we appended the `list` array with 5.

So, we added elements to a `list` array and accessed all the items through the `for` loop, but what about accessing a single element? Let's have an example to access and modify single elements in Kotlin. Go through the following example:

```
fun main(args: Array<String>) {
    val list = listOf(
            "1st Item",
            "2nd Item",
            "3rd Item",
            "4th Item",
            "5th Item"
    )

    println("3rd Item on the list - ${list.get(2)}")
    println("4rd Item on the list - ${list[3]}")
}
```

We accessed the third element with index 2 and the fourth element with index 3. The reason is simple and straightforward as, with arrays and in lists, counting begins at 0.

The thing to notice here is that Kotlin provides out-of-the-box support for lists and provides you with a square bracket operator (`[ ]`) to access elements of the `list` value just like an array. In the first `get` statement, we used the `get` function with an index to get the element of that index; in the second `get` statement, we used the square brackets, which, in turn, call that `get` function.

As lists store items as per their order/index, it's easy to get items from a list with an index; you can easily skip a loop if you want just a particular element from that list and if you know the index for the element you want. Just pass the element to the `get` function and you have the element. This `get` element by index is not supported by other collection interfaces like `set` (though `OrderedSet` supports them), which doesn't support the ordering of elements.

So, as we have got a little grip on lists, let us move ahead and have a look at the sets.

Set and MutableSet

Just like `List`, `Set` also has the following two variants in Kotlin:

- `Set`
- `MutableSet`

`Set` is read-only and `MutableSet` is the mutable version of `Set`, which contains the read-write functionalities.

> Just like with list, set values also have read-only functions and properties like `size`, `iterator()`, and so on. We are skipping mentioning them here to avoid redundant contents in this book. Also, please note that set doesn't do ordering like list (unless you use `OrderedSet`). So, it lacks the functions which involve orders like `indexOf(item)`, `add(index, item)`, and so on.

Sets in collections represent mathematical sets (as in set theory).

The following is an example with `MutableSet`:

```
fun main(args: Array<String>) {
    val set = mutableSetOf(1,2,3,3,2)

    println("set $set")

    set.add(4)
    set.add(5)
    set.add(5)
    set.add(6)

    println("set $set")
}
```

The following is the output:

```
"C:\Program Files\Java\jdk1.8.0_131\bin\java" ...
set [1, 2, 3]
set [1, 2, 3, 4, 5, 6]


Process finished with exit code 0
```

The output clearly shows that, even though we added multiple duplicate items to the `set`, both at the time of initialization and later, only unique items got inserted and all duplicate items got ignored.

Now, you may be curious as to whether the same will happen with custom classes and data classes; let us check with the following example:

```kotlin
data class MyDataClass (val someNumericValue:Int, val
someStringValue:String)
class MyCustomClass (val someNumericValue:Int, val someStringValue:String)
{
    override fun toString(): String {
        return "MyCustomClass(someNumericValue=$someNumericValue,
someStringValue=$someStringValue)"
    }
}
fun main(args: Array<String>) {
    val dataClassSet = setOf(
            MyDataClass(1,"1st obj"),
            MyDataClass(2,"2nd obj"),
            MyDataClass(3,"3rd obj"),
            MyDataClass(2,"2nd obj"),
            MyDataClass(4,"4th obj"),
            MyDataClass(5,"5th obj"),
            MyDataClass(2,"will be added"),
            MyDataClass(3,"3rd obj")
    )
    println("Printing items of dataClassSet one by one")
    for(item in dataClassSet) {
      println(item)
    }
    val customClassSet = setOf(
      MyCustomClass(1,"1st obj"),
      MyCustomClass(2,"2nd obj"),
      MyCustomClass(3,"3rd obj"),
      MyCustomClass(2,"2nd obj"),
      MyCustomClass(4,"4th obj"),
      MyCustomClass(5,"5th obj"),
      MyCustomClass(5,"5th Obj"),
      MyCustomClass(3,"3rd obj")
    )
    println("Printing items of customClassSet one by one")
    for(item in customClassSet) {
      println(item)
    }
}
```

In this program, we first created a data class and a custom class, then we created sets with them and inserted duplicate items.

Let us see the following output to check whether the sets are free of duplicate items:

```
"C:\Program Files\Java\jdk1.8.0_131\bin\java" ...
Printing items of dataClassSet one by one
MyDataClass(someNumericValue=1, someStringValue=1st obj)
MyDataClass(someNumericValue=2, someStringValue=2nd obj)
MyDataClass(someNumericValue=3, someStringValue=3rd obj)
MyDataClass(someNumericValue=4, someStringValue=4th obj)
MyDataClass(someNumericValue=5, someStringValue=5th obj)
MyDataClass(someNumericValue=2, someStringValue=will be
 added)
Printing items of customClassSet one by one true
MyCustomClass(someNumericValue=1, someStringValue=1st obj)
MyCustomClass(someNumericValue=2, someStringValue=2nd obj)
MyCustomClass(someNumericValue=3, someStringValue=3rd obj)
MyCustomClass(someNumericValue=4, someStringValue=4th obj)
MyCustomClass(someNumericValue=5, someStringValue=5th obj)

Process finished with exit code 0
```

Have a look at the preceding output carefully. While, as is the case with data classes, `set` ignored the duplicate items, when trying the same with a normal class, it was unable to detect the duplicate insertions and kept them.

 The last item that got added in `dataClassSet`—`MyDataClass(2, "will be added")` if you think it was a duplicate item then check again, while the value of `someNumericValue` for this object is identical to a previous one, the `someStringValue` value differs from that previous object's `someStringValue`.

Why is this an anomaly? The answer is short and simple—the collections framework internally uses `hashCode()` and `equals()` functions to perform equality checks while adding items to the `set` values and they are missing from the custom class.

In Kotlin, the compiler automatically extracts the `hashCode()` and `equals()` functions. Thus, the `set` values were able to distinguish between duplicate items without custom implementations of those functions. For more information on data classes visit the following link: `https://kotlinlang.org/docs/reference/data-classes.html`

So, if we implement those functions, then `set` will be able to distinguish between the duplicate items in the `customClassSet` values as well. Obviously, that's how it works for data classes as well. Just add the following code to the `MyCustomClass` definition and run the program to see the difference yourself:

```
override fun hashCode() =
someStringValue.hashCode()+someNumericValue.hashCode()

    override fun equals(other: Any?): Boolean {
        return other is MyCustomClass && other.someNumericValue ==
someNumericValue && other.someStringValue==someStringValue
    }
```

Cool, isn't it? So, we are done with `List` and `Set`. Let us now have a look at the `Map` interface; then, we will discuss the data operation functions provided by the collections framework.

Map and MutableMap

The `Map` interface in the collections framework is a bit different than all others interfaces we have covered earlier; unlike others it works with key-value pairs. No, this is not similar to `Pair`; `Pair` is just a pair of two values combined together, while a map is a collection of key-value pairs.

In a map, keys are unique and cannot be duplicated. If you add two values with the same key, then the later one will replace the previous one. Values, on the other hand can be redundant/duplicate. The reason behind this behavior is that in a map, a value is stored and retrieved with respect to its key, so redundant keys will make it impossible to distinguish them from each-other and to fetch their values.

The declaration of `Map` in Kotlin reads like interface `Map<K, out V>`, the `K` value is the generic type of the key and `V` is the generic type of value.

To learn more about collections, let us have a look at a few of the functions and properties. Go through the following list:

- `val size: Int`: This function indicates the size of the `Map` interface, that is, the number of key-value pairs residing inside the map.
- `fun isEmpty(): Boolean`: This function helps in checking whether a `Map` interface is empty or not.
- `fun containsKey(key: K): Boolean`: This function checks for the provided `key` inside the collection of key-value pairs it has and returns `true` if it is found.
- `operator fun get(key: K): V?`: This function cum operator (if used by square brackets (`[]`) like an array) returns the value corresponding to a key or null if the key doesn't exist within it.
- `val keys: Set<K>`: This function indicates the collection of keys available in that map at that point of time. As keys cannot be duplicated and they are not ordered, a `Set` value is the best data-structure to hold them.
- `val values: Collection<V>`: Contains all the values of the `map` value as a collection.
- `interface Entry<out K, out V>`: This function is defined inside the `Map` interface. An `Entry` represents a single key-value pair in the `Map` interface. The key-value pairs are stored as an entry inside the `map` value.
- `val entries: Set<Map.Entry<K, V>>`: This function gets you all the entries in the map.

The previous were read-only interfaces of `Map` as it only supports read-only operations. For read-write access, you've to use the `mutableMap` function. So, let us now have a look at the read-write interfaces provided by `mutableMap` as seen in the following list:

- `fun put(key: K, value: V): V?` : This interface adds a key-value pair to the `Map` and returns the previous value associated with the key (if any or null if the key wasn't present in the `Map` earlier).
- `fun remove(key: K): V?` : This interface removes a key-value pair from the map with the key and returns the value and returns null if the key doesn't exist in the `Map` interface.
- `fun putAll(from: Map<out K, V>): Unit` : This interface adds the key-value pairs from the provided `map` value.
- `fun clear(): Unit`: As the name suggests, this instance clears the `map` value. It removes everything that the `map` value contains—every key and every value.

So, as we now know the interfaces and functions the `Map` interfaces has to offer, let's now have an example with `Map`.

Let's go through the following example:

```kotlin
fun main(args: Array<String>) {
    val map = mapOf(
            "One".to(1),
            "Two".to(2),
            "Three".to(3),
            "Four".to(4),
            "Five".to(0),//(1) We placed 0 instead of 5 here, will be
replaced later
            "Six".to(6),
            "Five".to(5)//(2) This will replace earlier map of "Five".to(0)
            )

    println("The value at Key `Four` is ${map["Four"]}")

    println("Contents in map")
    for(entry in map) {
        println("Key ${entry.key}, Value ${entry.value}")
    }

    val mutableMap = mutableMapOf<Int,String>()

    mutableMap.put(1,"Item 1")
    mutableMap.put(2,"Item 2")
    mutableMap.put(3,"Item 3")
    mutableMap.put(4,"Item 4")

    println("Replacing value at key 1 - ${mutableMap.put(1,"Item
5")}")//(3)

    println("Contents in mutableMap")
    for(entry in mutableMap) {
        println("Key ${entry.key}, Value ${entry.value}")
    }
}
```

So, we demonstrated the use of the following two types of maps:

- Read-only `Map`
- Read-write `MutableMap`

Kotlin provides you with a version of the `mapOf()` function that accepts `vararg` parameters of the `Pair` type. This makes it easy for you to create read-only maps—just pass the key-value pairs as the instances of `Pair` to the `mapOf()` function.

Let us see the output before further inspecting and discussing the program. See the following screenshot:

```
"C:\Program Files\Java\jdk1.8.0_131\bin\java" ...
The value at Key `Four` is 4
Contents in map
Key One, Value 1
Key Two, Value 2
Key Three, Value 3
Key Four, Value 4
Key Five, Value 5
Key Six, Value 6
Replacing value at key 1 - Item 1
Contents in mutableMap
Key 1, Value Item 5
Key 2, Value Item 2
Key 3, Value Item 3
Key 4, Value Item 4


Process finished with exit code 0
```

While creating the map, on comment `(1)`, we passed a `"Five".to(0)` pair and on comment `(2)`, we passed the `"Five".to(5)` pair to the same `mapOf` function, to check which value the `map` stores for the `"Five"` key; the output suggests that the `map` took the second value—5, as we described earlier that a `map` value always takes the last value for the same key.

Also note that Kotlin supports array-like square brackets in `Map` as well. Instead of an index, you can pass the key.

So, as we got our hands dirty with three most important interfaces in Kotlin's collection framework: `List`, `Set`, and `Map`. Let's now move forward and get ourselves introduced to data operations in a collection.

Data operations in a collection

Kotlin provides out-of-the-box support for its collection framework. As a result, the collections framework in Kotlin is full of interesting features that make it stand apart from the collections framework in other languages, such as Java. You already got introduced with some of those features, such as separate interfaces for read-only and mutable collections, square box operator-like arrays, and so on. What I'm going to introduce now is probably the most interesting feature of Kotlin's collections framework, but goes mostly unnoticed—data operation functions.

Kotlin supports data operation functions for all of its collections framework interfaces, objects, and classes. By data operation functions, I mean the operators and functions by which we can access, process or operate on data from a collection; if you are familiar with ReactiveX framework/RxJava/RxKotlin, you'll find it similar as Kotlin picked them mostly from there.

The following is a list of a few of the collection data operation functions that we are going to cover here:

- The `map` function
- The `filter` function
- The `flatMap` function
- The `drop` functions
- The `take` functions
- The `zip` functions

So, what are we waiting for? Let us get started.

Though, the data operation functions with collections make you feel like you're working with streams/Rx, they are in no way similar to streams/Rx. What they do is simply use high order functions and extension functions to provide you with stream-like interfaces and internally they operate on the same loops (yes, you read it right, they use loops to produce results and then return it from the function just like a simple imperial program). It is advisable to avoid bigger chains of these functions in your program, as you'll end up with multiple loops. Using `forEach` or your own loop in such scenarios is a better choice, as you will be able to perform multiple operations with a single loop with `forEach` or with your own loop. However, for a single operation or small chains, you can definitely use these functions to make your code well organized.

The map function

The map function allows you to apply an algorithm to a collection all-together and obtain the results as a resultant set. It's helpful in making your code well-organized and writing loops (though it'll use loop internally, you're freed from writing those boilerplate codes).

The map function receives all the elements of the collection as each iteration and should return the computed resultant item that should be placed in the resultant list in place of the passed item.

Go through the following example:

```
fun main(args: Array<String>) {
    val list = listOf<Int>(1,2,3,4,5,6,7,8,9,10)
    val modifiedList = list.map { it*2 }

    println("modifiedList -> $modifiedList")
}
```

So, we had a list of Int, we needed to multiply each item from the list value with 2, and we did it with ease with just a single line of code—list.map { it*2 }, which would normally take us two or three lines more of boilerplate. Insane, isn't it?

The following is the output of the program:

```
"C:\Program Files\Java\jdk1.8.0_131\bin\java" ...
modifiedList -> [2, 4, 6, 8, 10, 12, 14, 16, 18, 20]

Process finished with exit code 0
```

As expected, the map function applied the provided lambda to each of the elements of the list and returned the resultant list.

The filter function

Think of a situation where you need to filter the items in a collection. For example, when you want to obtain only even numbers from a list of integers. The filter function is there to help you in these scenarios.

The `filter` function receives all the elements of the collection as each iteration and should return `true` or `false`, based on its determination of whether the passed item should be on the resultant list or not.

Go through the following program:

```
fun main(args: Array<String>) {
    val list = 1.until(50).toList()//(1)
    val filteredListEven = list.filter { it%2==0 }//(2)

    println("filteredListEven -> $filteredListEven")

    val filteredListPSquare = list.filter {
        val sqroot = sqrt(it.toDouble()).roundToInt()
        sqroot*sqroot==it
    }//(3)

    println("filteredListPSquare -> $filteredListPSquare")
}
```

In this program, we first obtained a list of `Int` containing numbers from 1 to 50 with the help of `IntRange`. We then filtered the list to obtain even numbers on comment `(2)` and printed them. On comment `(3)`, we filtered the list (the original list containing `Int` values from 1 to 50) to obtain perfect squares and printed them.

The following is the output of the program:

```
"C:\Program Files\Java\jdk1.8.0_131\bin\java" ...
filteredListEven -> [2, 4, 6, 8, 10, 12, 14, 16,
 18, 20, 22, 24, 26, 28, 30, 32, 34, 36, 38, 40,
 42, 44, 46, 48]
filteredListPSquare -> [1, 4, 9, 16, 25, 36, 49]

Process finished with exit code 0
```

The previous code snippet and its output show just how much boilerplate code can be eliminated with the help of these data operation functions.

The flatMap function

Another awesome function available with collections framework is the `flatMap` function.

Like the `map` function, it receives each of the items in the collection as an iteration, but, unlike the `map` function, it should return another collection for each of the items passed. These returned collections are then combined to create the resultant collection.

Have a look at the following example:

```
fun main(args: Array<String>) {
    val list = listOf(10,20,30)

    val flatMappedList = list.flatMap {
        it.rangeTo(it+2).toList()
    }

    println("flatMappedList -> $flatMappedList")
}
```

The output looks like the following:

```
"C:\Program Files\Java\jdk1.8.0_131\bin\java" ...
flatMappedList -> [10, 11, 12, 20, 21, 22, 30, 31, 32]

Process finished with exit code 0
```

While the original list contained only three numbers—10, 20, and 30, the resultant list contains three more numbers for each of the numbers in the original list, all thanks to the `flatMap` function.

The drop functions

There may be some scenarios when you want to drop a portion (say, the first 5 or the last 10) of the collection and work on the remaining parts. Kotlin's collection framework provides you with a set of the `drop` functions that can help you in these scenarios. Have a look at the following program:

```
fun main(args: Array<String>) {
    val list = 1.until(50).toList()
```

```
        println("list.drop(25) -> ${list.drop(25)}")//(1)
        println("list.dropLast(25) -> ${list.dropLast(25)}")//(2)
    }
```

In the preceding program, we've dropped the first 25 items from the list on comment (1), and on comment (2), I've dropped the last 25 items.

The following screenshot shows the output of the program:

```
"C:\Program Files\Java\jdk1.8.0_131\bin\java" ...
list.drop(25) -> [26, 27, 28, 29, 30, 31, 32, 33, 34,
    35, 36, 37, 38, 39, 40, 41, 42, 43, 44, 45, 46, 47,
    48, 49]
list.dropLast(25) -> [1, 2, 3, 4, 5, 6, 7, 8, 9, 10,
    11, 12, 13, 14, 15, 16, 17, 18, 19, 20, 21, 22, 23, 24]

Process finished with exit code 0
```

Worked perfectly, didn't it?

The take functions

The take functions work in just the opposite way to the drop functions. You can take a selection from the collection and ignore the rest.

Have a look at the following program:

```
fun main(args: Array<String>) {
    val list = 1.until(50).toList()

    println("list.take(25) -> ${list.take(25)}")//(1)
    println("list.takeLast(25) -> ${list.takeLast(25)}")//(2)
    println("list.takeWhile { it<=10 } -> ${list.takeWhile { it<=10
}}")//(3)
    println("list.takeLastWhile { it>=40 } -> ${list.takeLastWhile { it>=40
}}")//(4)
}
```

While statements on comment (1) and comment (2) are opposite to the drop functions earlier, they just take and print the 25 items from the list.

The statement on comment (3) is a bit different, here we used the `takeWhile` function. The `takeWhile` function takes a predicate and keeps taking items on the resultant collection while the predicate returns `true`; once the predicate returns `false` the `takeWhile` value will stop checking for any more items and will return the resultant collection.

The `takeLastWhile` values work in a similar way but in reverse.

The following is a screenshot of the output:

```
"C:\Program Files\Java\jdk1.8.0_131\bin\java" ...
list.take(25) -> [1, 2, 3, 4, 5, 6, 7, 8, 9, 10, 11,
 12, 13, 14, 15, 16, 17, 18, 19, 20, 21, 22, 23, 24, 25]
list.takeLast(25) -> [25, 26, 27, 28, 29, 30, 31, 32,
 33, 34, 35, 36, 37, 38, 39, 40, 41, 42, 43, 44, 45,
 46, 47, 48, 49]
list.takeWhile { it<=10 } -> [1, 2, 3, 4, 5, 6, 7, 8,
 9, 10]
list.takeLastWhile { it>=40 } -> [40, 41, 42, 43, 44,
 45, 46, 47, 48, 49]


Process finished with exit code 0
```

Let's now move ahead with the `zip` functions.

The zip function

The `zip` function does exactly what it sounds like, it zips collections. Confusing? Let's have a look at the following example:

```
fun main(args: Array<String>) {
    val list1 = listOf(1,2,3,4,5)
    val list2 = listOf(
            "Item 1",
            "Item 2",
            "Item 3",
            "Item 4",
            "Item 5"
    )
```

```
    val resultantList = list1.zip(list2)

    println(resultantList)
}
```

We created two lists—one with `Int` and the other with `String`. We then created a resultant list by zipping the `Int` list with the `String` list and printed the resultant list.

So, what does the `resultantList` value contain? What operation did the `zip` function perform?

Let us decide it ourselves by having a look at the following output:

```
"C:\Program Files\Java\jdk1.8.0_131\bin\java
[(1, Item 1), (2, Item 2), (3, Item 3),
 (4, Item 4), (5, Item 5)]


Process finished with exit code 0
```

Amazing, isn't it? The `zip` function takes another collection, combines the source collection with the provided collection, and creates a `Pair` value for each of the items. But what if the collections differ in item counts? What if we want to combine each item in a list with the next item in the same list?

Let's take another example. Have a look at the following code:

```
fun main(args: Array<String>) {
    val list1 = listOf(1,2,3,4,5,6,7,8)
    val list2 = listOf(
            "Item 1",
            "Item 2",
            "Item 3",
            "Item 4",
            "Item 5"
    )

    println("list1.zip(list2)-> ${list1.zip(list2)}")

    println("list1.zipWithNext() -> ${list1.zipWithNext()}")
}
```

So, the first `println` statement here answers our first question—it tries to combine two lists with asymmetrical item counts.

On the second `println` statement, we used the `zipWithNext` function, which zips one item of a collection with the next item of the same collection. So, let's have a look at the output to find out what happens.

The following is the output:

```
"C:\Program Files\Java\jdk1.8.0_131\bin\java" ...
list1.zip(list2)-> [(1, Item 1), (2, Item 2),
 (3, Item 3), (4, Item 4), (5, Item 5)]
list1.zipWithNext() -> [(1, 2), (2, 3), (3, 4),
 (4, 5), (5, 6), (6, 7), (7, 8)]


Process finished with exit code 0
```

So, the `zip` operator only zipped those items of `list1`, for which it could find a pair in `list2` and skipped the remaining. The `zipWithNext` operator on the other hand, worked as expected.

So, we are done with data operation functions in Kotlin collection framework. However, Kotlin provides you with more capabilities for collections; so, let's move ahead and see what more it has to offer.

Grouping collections

Kotlin's collection framework allows you to group collections based on your requirements. For example, if you have a list of strings and want to group them with respect to their size, you can easily do that with the help of the `groupBy` function, which groups a collection based on the logic provided and returns `Map` with that group of collections.

So, the following is a short example:

```
fun main(args: Array<String>) {
    val list = 1.rangeTo(50).toList()

    println(list.groupBy { it%5 })
}
```

So, what we did here is as follows: we created a list of `Int` containing numbers from 1 to 50 (both inclusive) then, we tried to group them based on their remnants when divided by 5.

So, there should be five groups, from 0 to 5, and each of them should contain 10 numbers. Let's check the following output to see if that happened or not:

```
"C:\Program Files\Java\jdk1.8.0_131\bin\java" ...
{1=[1, 6, 11, 16, 21, 26, 31, 36, 41, 46],
 2=[2, 7, 12, 17, 22, 27, 32, 37, 42, 47],
 3=[3, 8, 13, 18, 23, 28, 33, 38, 43, 48],
 4=[4, 9, 14, 19, 24, 29, 34, 39, 44, 49],
 0=[5, 10, 15, 20, 25, 30, 35, 40, 45, 50]}

Process finished with exit code 0
```

So, the `groupBy` function just worked as expected and returned `Map<Int,List<Int>>` that contained the grouped list.

Summary

So, this chapter was on collections and data operations in Kotlin. We started the chapter by exploring the collection framework in Kotlin and data structure of collections, and we gradually moved towards learning the data operations and functions that Kotlin collection framework provides out of the box.

In the next chapter, we will learn how to work with functional programming, reactive programming, and OOP altogether. We believe Kotlin is the best language for this, as it lets you take the benefits of both worlds—functional programming and OOP. In the next chapter, we will see how to take advantage of this.

In the next chapter, we will also introduce ourselves to the ReactiveX framework, which is among the most popular frameworks for functional reactive programming.

So, lets move ahead; the next chapter is just a page turn away.

9

Functional Programming and Reactive Programming

So far, we've made good progress over the last eight chapters. You've already learned the concepts of **functional programming** (**FP**) and some awesome Kotlin features such as coroutines and delegates, which are not exactly from FP theories (in fact, delegates are from the OOP paradigm), but all of them enable us to get more benefits out of FP.

This short chapter is dedicated to combining other programming principles/paradigms with FP to get the best output from them. Here's a list of the topics that we will cover in this chapter:

- Combining FP with OOP
- Functional reactive programming
- Introduction to RxKotlin

So, let's get started.

Combining FP with OOP

FP and OOP are both old age programming paradigms, having their set of benefits and disadvantages. For instance, it is difficult to strictly follow FP without any side effects and all pure functions, especially for beginners in FP and with complex project requirements. However, with OOP systems, it is difficult to avoid side effects; also, OOP systems are often termed as a nightmare for concurrent programs.

FP doesn't acknowledge state, whereas in real life, states cannot be avoided.

All these hassles can be avoided by using/combining OOP with FP. The most general style of mixing OOP and FP that has been professed can be summarized as functional in the small, object-oriented in the large. This is a simple and the most efficient idea of combining OOP with FP. This concept talks about using OOP at a higher level in your code, that is, in the modular architecture, and you can use OOP for classes and interfaces, while using FP at the lower level, that is, while writing methods/functions.

To break this concept, consider a structure where you are writing classes and interfaces as you normally do with OOP, and then while writing functions/methods, you follow the FP style of working with pure functions, monads, and immutability.

As stated earlier in this book, we believe that Kotlin is the best language if you want a mixture of OOP and FP.

Functional reactive programming

The concept of functional reactive programming emerged by combining FP paradigms with reactive programming.

The definition of **functional reactive programming** says it is a programming paradigm for reactive programming (asynchronous dataflow programming) using the building blocks of FP (for example, `map`, `reduce`, and `filter`).

So, let's begin by defining reactive programming, and then we will discuss combining them with FP.

Reactive programming is a modern programming paradigm, which talks about propagation of change, that is, instead of representing the world as a series of states, reactive programming models behavior.

Reactive programming is an asynchronous programming paradigm that revolves around data streams and the propagation of change. In simpler words, those programs which propagate all the changes that affected its data/data streams to all the interested parties (such as end users, components and sub-parts, and other programs that are somehow related) are called **reactive programs**.

Reactive programming is best defined with Reactive Manifesto, as described in the following section.

The Reactive Manifesto

The **Reactive Manifesto** (`http://www.reactivemanifesto.org`) is a document, defining the four reactive principles, which are as follows:

- **Responsive**: The system responds in a timely manner. Responsive systems focus on providing rapid and consistent response times, so they deliver a consistent quality of service.
- **Resilient**: In case the system faces any failure, it stays responsive. Resilience is achieved by replication, containment, isolation, and delegation. Failures are contained within each component, isolating components from each other, so when failure occurs in a component, it will not affect the other components or the system as a whole.
- **Elastic**: Reactive systems can react to changes and stays responsive under varying workloads. Reactive systems achieve elasticity in a cost-effective way on commodity hardware and software platforms.
- **Message-driven**: In order to establish the resilient principle, reactive systems need to establish a boundary between components by relying on asynchronous message-passing.

By implementing all the preceding four principles, a system becomes reliable and responsive, thus reactive.

Functional reactive frameworks for Kotlin

For writing reactive programs, we need a library. There are several reactive programming libraries for Kotlin out there to help us on these. Here's a list of the available libraries:

- RxKotlin
- Reactor-Kotlin
- Redux-Kotlin
- RxKotlin/RxJava and other Reactive Java (ReactiveX) frameworks can also be used with Kotlin (as Kotlin is 100% interoperable with Java-bidirectional)

In this book, we will focus on RxKotlin.

Getting started with RxKotlin

RxKotlin is a specific implementation of reactive programming for Kotlin, which is influenced by FP. It favors function composition, the avoidance of global state, and side effects. It relies on the observer pattern of producer/consumer, with a lot of operators that allow composing, scheduling, throttling, transforming, error handling, and life cycle management. ReactiveX frameworks are backed by a large community and Netflix.

Reactor-Kotlin is also based on FP; it is widely accepted and is backed by Spring Framework. Both RxKotlin and Reactor-Kotlin share a lot of similarities (probably because of **Reactive Streams** specifications).

Downloading and setting up RxKotlin

You can download and build RxKotlin from GitHub (`https://github.com/ReactiveX/RxKotlin`). It does not require any other dependencies. The documentation on the GitHub Wikipedia page is well-structured. Here is how you can check out the project from GitHub and run the build as follows:

```
$ git clone https://github.com/ReactiveX/RxKotlin.git
$ cd RxKotlin/
$ ./gradlew build
```

You can also use Maven and Gradle, as instructed on the page.

 We are using RxKotlin version 2.2.0 for this book.

Now, let's take a look at what RxKotlin is all about. We will begin with something well-known, and gradually we will get into the secrets of the library.

Comparing the Pull mechanism with the RxJava Push mechanism

RxKotlin revolves around the `Observable` type that represents a system of real-life events and data, intended for push mechanisms, thus it is lazy and can be used in both ways—synchronously and asynchronously.

It'll be easier for us to understand if we start with a simple example that works with a list of data:

```
fun main(args: Array<String>) {
    var list:List<Any> = listOf(1, "Two", 3, "Four", "Five", 5.5f) // 1
    var iterator = list.iterator() // 2
    while (iterator.hasNext()) { // 3
        println(iterator.next()) // Prints each element 4
    }
}
```

The output is as follows:

```
"C:\Program Files\Java\jdk1.8.0_131\bin\java" ...
1
Two
3
Four
Five
5.5

Process finished with exit code 0
```

Let's go through the program line by line to understand how it works.

At comment 1, we created a list with seven items (the list contains data of mixed data types with the help of Any class). At comment 2, we created iterator from the list, so that we can iterate over the data. In comment 3, we created a while loop to pull data from the list with the help of an iterator, and then at comment 4, we printed it.

The thing to notice here is that we're pulling data from the list while the current thread is blocked till the data is received and ready. For instance, think of getting that data from a network call/database query instead of just a list, and in that case, how long the thread will be blocked. You can obviously create a separate thread for those operations, but that too will increase complexity.

Just give it a thought, which one is a better approach, making the program wait for data or pushing data to the program whenever it's available?

The building blocks of the ReactiveX framework (be it RxKotlin or RxJava) are the observables. The `Observable` class is opposite to Iterator. It has an underlying collection or computation that produces values that can be consumed by a consumer. But the difference is that the consumer doesn't pull these values from the producer like in the Iterator pattern; instead the producer pushes the values as notifications to the consumer.

So, let's take the same example again, this time with `observable`:

```
fun main(args: Array<String>) {
    var list = listOf(1, "Two", 3, "Four", "Five", 5.5f) // 1
    var observable = list.toObservable();

    observable.subscribeBy(  // named arguments for lambda Subscribers
            onNext = { println(it) },
            onError =  { it.printStackTrace() },
            onComplete = { println("Done!") }
    )
}
```

This program's output is the same as the previous one; it prints all the items in the list. The difference is in its approach. So, let's see how it actually works:

1. Created a list (the same as the previous one)
2. An `Observable` instance is created by the `list`
3. We subscribe to the observer (we're using named arguments for lambda; we will cover them in detail later)

As we subscribe to the `observable` variable, each data will be pushed to `onNext` as it gets ready; it'll call `onComplete` when all the data is pushed, and `onError` if any error occurs.

So, you learned how to use the `Observable` instances and that they are quite similar to the Iterator instances, something we're quite familiar with. We can use these `Observable` instances for building asynchronous streams and pushing data updates to their subscribers (even to multiple subscribers). This was a simple implementation of the reactive programming paradigm. The data is being propagated to all the interested parties—the subscribers.

Observables

As we discussed earlier, in reactive programming, Observable has an underlying computation that produces values that can be consumed by a consumer (Observer). The most important thing here is that the consumer (Observer) doesn't pull values here; rather, Observable pushes the values to the consumer. So, we can say that an Observable interface is a push-based, composable Iterator that emits its items through a series of operators to the final Observer, which finally consumes the items. Let's now break these things down sequentially to understand it better:

- Observer subscribes to Observable
- Observable starts emitting the items that it has in it
- Observer reacts to whatever item the Observable emits

So, let's delve into how Observable works through its events/methods, namely onNext, onComplete, and onError.

How Observable works

As we stated earlier, an Observable value has the following three most important events/methods:

- onNext: The Observable interface passes all the items one by one to this method
- onComplete: When all the items have gone through the onNext method, the Observable calls the onComplete method
- onError: When the Observable faces any error, it calls the onError method to deal with the error, if defined

One thing to note here is that the item in Observable that we are talking about can be anything; it is defined as Observable<T>, where T can be any class. Even an array/list can be assigned as Observable.

Let's look at the following diagram:

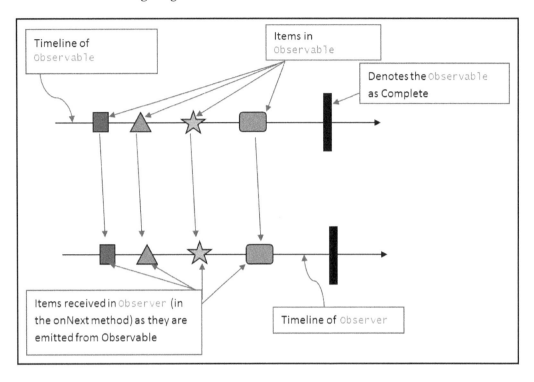

Here's a code example to understand it better:

```kotlin
fun main(args: Array<String>) {

    val observer = object :Observer<Any>{//1
    override fun onComplete() {//2
        println("All Completed")
    }

        override fun onNext(item: Any) {//3
            println("Next $item")
        }

        override fun onError(e: Throwable) {//4
            println("Error Occured $e")
        }

        override fun onSubscribe(d: Disposable) {//5
            println("Subscribed to $d")
        }
```

```
    }

    val observable = listOf(1, "Two", 3, "Four", "Five",
5.5f).toObservable() //6

    observable.subscribe(observer)//7

    val observableOnList = Observable.just(listOf("One", 2, "Three",
"Four", 4.5, "Five", 6.0f),
            listOf("List with 1 Item"),
            listOf(1,2,3))//8



    observableOnList.subscribe(observer)//9
}
```

In the preceding example, we declared the observer instance of the `Any` datatype at comment 1.

 Here, we take the benefit of the `Any` datatype. In Kotlin, every class is a child class of `Any`. Also, in Kotlin, everything is a class and object; there is no separate primitive datatype.

The `Observer` interface has four methods declared in it. The `onComplete()` method at comment 2 gets called when `Observable` is finished with all its items without any error. At comment 3, we defined the `onNext(item: Any)` function, which will be called by the `observable` value for each item it has to emit. In that method, we printed the data to the console. At comment 4, we defined the `onError(e: Throwable)` method, which will be called in case the `Observable` interface faces an error. At comment 5, the `onSubscribe(d: Disposable)` method will get called whenever the `Observer` subscribes to `Observable`. At comment 6, we created an `Observable` from a list (`val observable`) and subscribed to the `observable` value with the `observer` value at comment 7. At comment 8, we again created observable (`val observableOnList`), which holds lists as items.

The output of the program is as follows:

```
"C:\Program Files\Java\jdk1.8.0_131\bin\java" ...
Subscribed to io.reactivex.internal.operators.observable
 .ObservableFromIterable$FromIterableDisposable@759ebb3d
Next 1
Next Two
Next 3
Next Four
Next Five
Next 5.5
All Completed
Subscribed to io.reactivex.internal.operators.observable
 .ObservableFromArray$FromArrayDisposable@4cdf35a9
Next [One, 2, Three, Four, 4.5, Five, 6.0]
Next [List with 1 Item]
Next [1, 2, 3]
All Completed

Process finished with exit code 0
```

So, as you can see in the output, for the first subscription (comment 7), when we subscribe to the observable value, it calls the onSubscribe method, then the Observable property starts emitting items, as observer starts receiving them on the onNext method and prints them. When all the items are emitted from the Observable property, it calls the onComplete method to denote that all the items have been successfully emitted. It is the same with the second one, except that here, each item is a list.

As we gained some grip on Observables, you can now learn a few ways to create Observable factory methods for Observable.

The Observable.create method

At any time, you can create your own custom implementation of Observable with the Observable.create method. This method takes an instance of the ObservableEmitter<T> interface as a source to observe. Take a look at the following code example:

```
fun main(args: Array<String>) {

    val observer: Observer<String> = object : Observer<String> {
        override fun onComplete() {
            println("All Completed")
        }

        override fun onNext(item: String) {
            println("Next $item")
        }

        override fun onError(e: Throwable) {
            println("Error Occured => ${e.message}")
        }

        override fun onSubscribe(d: Disposable) {
            println("New Subscription ")
        }
    }//Create Observer

    val observable:Observable<String> = Observable.create<String> {//1
        it.onNext("Emitted 1")
        it.onNext("Emitted 2")
        it.onNext("Emitted 3")
        it.onNext("Emitted 4")
        it.onComplete()
    }

    observable.subscribe(observer)

    val observable2:Observable<String> = Observable.create<String> {//2
        it.onNext("Emitted 1")
        it.onNext("Emitted 2")
        it.onError(Exception("My Exception"))
    }

    observable2.subscribe(observer)
}
```

First, we created an instance of the Observer interface as the previous example. I will not elaborate the observer value, as we have already seen an overview in the previous example, and will see this in detail later in this chapter. At comment 1, we created an Observable value with the Observable.create method. We have emitted four strings from the Observable value with the help of onNext method, then notified it is complete with the onComplete method. At comment 2, we almost did the same except here, instead of calling onComplete, we called onError with a custom Exception function.

Here is the output of the program:

```
"C:\Program Files\Java\jdk1.8.0_131\bin\java" ...
New Subscription
Next Emitted 1
Next Emitted 2
Next Emitted 3
Next Emitted 4
All Completed
New Subscription
Next Emitted 1
Next Emitted 2
Error Occured => My Exception


Process finished with exit code 0
```

The Observable.create method is useful, especially when you are working with a custom data structure and want to have a control over which values are getting emitted. You can also emit values to the observer from a different thread.

The **Observable contract**
(http://reactivex.io/documentation/contract.html) states that Observables must issue notifications to observers serially (not in parallel). They may issue these notifications from different threads, but there must be a formal happens-before relationship between the notifications.

The Observable.from methods

The `Observable.from` methods are comparatively simpler than the `Observable.create` method. You can create the `Observable` instances from nearly every Kotlin structure with the help of from methods.

 In RxKotlin 1, you will have `Observale.from` as a method; however, from RxKotlin 2.0 (as with RxJava2.0), operator overloads have been renamed with a postfix, such as `fromArray`, `fromIterable`, and `fromFuture`.

Let's take a look at the following code:

```kotlin
fun main(args: Array<String>) {

    val observer: Observer<String> = object : Observer<String> {
        override fun onComplete() {
            println("Completed")
        }

        override fun onNext(item: String) {
            println("Received-> $item")
        }

        override fun onError(e: Throwable) {
            println("Error Occured => ${e.message}")
        }

        override fun onSubscribe(d: Disposable) {
            println("Subscription")
        }
    }//Create Observer

    val list = listOf("Str 1","Str 2","Str 3","Str 4")
    val observableFromIterable: Observable<String> =
Observable.fromIterable(list)//1
    observableFromIterable.subscribe(observer)


    val callable = object : Callable<String> {
        override fun call(): String {
            return "I'm From Callable"
        }

    }
    val observableFromCallable:Observable<String> =
```

```
Observable.fromCallable(callable)//2
    observableFromCallable.subscribe(observer)

    val future:Future<String> = object : Future<String> {
        val retStr = "I'm from Future"

        override fun get() = retStr

        override fun get(timeout: Long, unit: TimeUnit?)  = retStr

        override fun isDone(): Boolean = true

        override fun isCancelled(): Boolean = false

        override fun cancel(mayInterruptIfRunning: Boolean): Boolean =
false

    }
    val observableFromFuture:Observable<String> =
Observable.fromFuture(future)//3
    observableFromFuture.subscribe(observer)
}
```

At comment 1, we used the `Observable.fromIterable` method to create `Observable` from an `Iterable` instance (here, `list`). At comment 2. We called the `Observable.fromCallable` method to create `Observable` from a `Callable` instance, we did the same at comment 3, where we called the `Observable.fromFuture` method to derive `Observable` from a `Future` instance.

Here is the output:

```
Subscription
Received-> Str 1
Received-> Str 2
Received-> Str 3
Received-> Str 4
Completed
Subscription
Received-> I'm From Callable
Completed
Subscription
Received-> I'm from Future
Completed

Process finished with exit code 0
```

Iterator<T>.toObservable

Thanks to the extension functions of Kotlin, you can turn any Iterable instance, such as list, to Observable without much effort. We have already used this method in Chapter 1, *Kotlin – Data Types, Objects, and Classes*, but again take a look at this:

```kotlin
fun main(args: Array<String>) {
    val observer: Observer<String> = object : Observer<String> {
        override fun onComplete() {
            println("Completed")
        }

        override fun onNext(item: String) {
            println("Received-> $item")
        }

        override fun onError(e: Throwable) {
            println("Error Occured => ${e.message}")
        }

        override fun onSubscribe(d: Disposable) {
            println("Subscription")
        }
    }//Create Observer
    val list:List<String> = listOf("Str 1","Str 2","Str 3","Str 4")

    val observable: Observable<String> = list.toObservable()

    observable.subscribe(observer)

}
```

The output is as follows:

```
"C:\Program Files\Java\jdk1.8.0_131\bin\java" ...
Subscription
Received-> Str 1
Received-> Str 2
Received-> Str 3
Received-> Str 4
Completed


Process finished with exit code 0
```

So, aren't you curious to look into the `toObservable` method? Let's do it. You can find this method inside the `observable.kt` file provided with the `RxKotlin` package:

```
fun <T : Any> Iterator<T>.toObservable(): Observable<T> =
toIterable().toObservable()
fun <T : Any> Iterable<T>.toObservable(): Observable<T> =
Observable.fromIterable(this)
fun <T : Any> Sequence<T>.toObservable(): Observable<T> =
asIterable().toObservable()

fun <T : Any> Iterable<Observable<out T>>.merge(): Observable<T> =
Observable.merge(this.toObservable())
fun <T : Any> Iterable<Observable<out T>>.mergeDelayError(): Observable<T>
= Observable.mergeDelayError(this.toObservable())
```

So, it uses the `Observable.from` method internally, thanks again to the extension functions of Kotlin.

Subscriber – the Observer interface

In RxKotlin 1.x, the `Subscriber` operator essentially became an `Observer` type in RxKotlin 2.x. There is an `Observer` type in RxKotlin 1.x, but the `Subscriber` value is what you pass to the `subscribe()` method, and it implements `Observer`. In RxJava 2.x, a `Subscriber` operator only exists when talking about `Flowables`.

As you can see in the previous examples in this chapter, an `Observer` type is an interface with four methods in it, namely `onNext(item:T)`, `onError(error:Throwable)`, `onComplete()`, and `onSubscribe(d:Disposable)`. As stated earlier, when we connect `Observable` to `Observer`, it looks for these four methods in the `Observer` type and calls them. Here is a short description of the following four methods:

- `onNext`: The `Observable` calls this method of `Observer` to pass each of the items one by one
- `onComplete`: When the `Observable` wants to denote that it's done with passing items to the `onNext` method, it calls the `onComplete` method of `Observer`
- `onError`: When `Observable` faces any error, it calls the `onError` method to deal with the error if defined in the `Observer` type, otherwise it throws the exception
- `onSubscribe`: This method is called whenever a new `Observable` subscribes to `Observer`

Subscribing and disposing

So, we have `Observable` (the thing that should be observed upon) and we have the `Observer` type (that should be observed), now what? How do we connect them? `Observable` and `Observer` are like an input device (be it keyboard or mouse) and the computer; we need something to connect them (even wireless input devices have some connectivity channels, be it Bluetooth or Wi-Fi).

The `subscribe` operator serves the purpose of the media by connecting an `Observable` interface to `Observer`. We can pass one to three methods (`onNext`, `onComplete`, and `onError`) to the `subscribe` operator, or we can pass an instance of the `Observer` interface to the subscribe operator to get the `Observable` interface connected with `Observer`.

So, let's look at an example now:

```kotlin
fun main(args: Array<String>) {
    val observable = Observable.range(1,5)//1

    observable.subscribe({//2
        //onNext method
        println("Next-> $it")
    },{
        //onError Method
        println("Error=> ${it.message}")
    },{
        //onComplete Method
        println("Done")
    })

    val observer: Observer<Int> = object : Observer<Int> {//3
    override fun onComplete() {
        println("All Completed")
    }

        override fun onNext(item: Int) {
            println("Next-> $item")
        }

        override fun onError(e: Throwable) {
            println("Error Occurred=> ${e.message}")
        }

        override fun onSubscribe(d: Disposable) {
            println("New Subscription ")
```

```
        }
    }

    observable.subscribe(observer)
}
```

In this example, we have created an `Observable` instance (at comment 1) and used it twice with different overload `subscribe` operators. At comment 2, we passed three methods as arguments to the `subscribe` method. The first parameter is the `onNext` method, the second one is the `onError` method, and the last one is `onComplete`. At comment 2, we passed an instance of the `Observer` interface.

The output can be easily predicted, so we are skipping it.

So, we have got the concepts of subscribing, and can do it now. What about if you want to stop the emissions after some period of subscription? There must be a way, right? So, let's inspect this.

Remember the `onSubscribe` method of `Observer`? There was a parameter on that method which we haven't discussed yet. While you subscribe, if you pass the methods instead of the `Observer` instance, then the `subscribe` operator will return an instance of `Disposable`, or if you use an instance of `Observer`, then you will get the instance of `Disposable` in the parameter of the `onSubscribe` method.

You can use the instance of the `Disposable` interface to stop emissions at any given time. Let's look at an example:

```
fun main(args: Array<String>) {

    val observale = Observable.interval(100, TimeUnit.MILLISECONDS)//1
    val observer = object : Observer<Long> {

        lateinit var disposable: Disposable//2

        override fun onSubscribe(d: Disposable) {
            disposable = d//3
        }

        override fun onNext(item: Long) {
            println("Received $item")
            if (item >= 10 && !disposable.isDisposed) {//4
                disposable.dispose()//5
                println("Disposed")
            }
        }
```

```
        override fun onError(e: Throwable) {
            println("Error ${e.message}")
        }

        override fun onComplete() {
            println("Complete")
        }

    }
    runBlocking {
        observale.subscribe(observer)
        delay(1500)//6
    }

}
```

Here, we used the `Observable.interval` factory method. This method takes two parameters describing the interval period and time unit; it then emits integers sequentially starting from zero. `Observable` created with `interval` never completes and never stops until you dispose off them, or the program stops execution. I thought it would be the perfect fit in this scenario as we want to stop the `Observable` midway here.

So, in this example, at comment 1, we created `Observable` with the `Observable.interval` factory method that will emit an integer after each `100` milliseconds interval.

At comment 2, I have declared `lateinit var disposable` of the `Disposable` type (`lateinit` means the variable will get initialized at a later point in time). At comment 3, inside the `onSubscribe` method, we will assign the received parameter value to the `disposable` variable.

We intend to stop the execution after the sequence reached `10`, that is, after `10` is emitted, the emission should be stopped immediately. To achieve this, we placed a check inside the `onNext` method, where we are checking the value of the emitted item. We check whether it's equal to or greater than `10`, and if the emission is not already stopped (disposed), then we dispose the emission (comment 5).

Here is the output:

```
"C:\Program Files\Java\jdk1.8.0_131\bin\java" ...
Received 0
Received 1
Received 2
Received 3
Received 4
Received 5
Received 6
Received 7
Received 8
Received 9
Received 10
Disposed


Process finished with exit code 0
```

From the output, we can see that no integer got emitted after the `disposable.dispose()` method was called, though the execution waited for 500 milliseconds more (100*10 = 1000 milliseconds to print the sequence till `10`, and we called the delay method with `1500`, thus 500 milliseconds after emitting `10`).

If you are curious to know the `Disposable` interface, then the following is the definition:

```
interface Disposable {
  /**
  * Dispose the resource, the operation should be idempotent.
  */
  fun dispose()
  /**
  * Returns true if this resource has been disposed.
  * @return true if this resource has been disposed
  */
  val isDisposed:Boolean
}
```

It has one property that denotes that the emission is already notified to stop (disposed) and a method to notify the emission to stop (dispose).

Summary

In this chapter, you learned about combining FP concepts with OOP and reactive programming. We even discussed RxKotlin and covered the setup and basic usage of RxKotlin.

The next chapter is about more advanced FP concepts—monads, functors, and applicatives, and how to implement them with Kotlin. Monads, functors, and applicatives are some of the must-know concepts and are often referred to as the building blocks of FP. So, don't skip the next chapter if you are truly willing to learn about FP. Turn the page now.

10
Functors, Applicatives, and Monads

Functors, applicatives, and monads are among the most searched words related to functional programming, which makes sense if you consider that no-one knows what they mean (not really, there are bright people that know what they're talking about). The confusion about monads, in particular, has become a joke/meme in the programming community:

> *"A monad is a monoid in the category of endofunctors, what's the problem?"*

This quote is fictionally attributed to Philip Wadler by James Iry on his classic blog post, *A Brief, Incomplete and Mostly Wrong History of Programming Languages,* (`http://james-iry.blogspot.co.uk/2009/05/brief-incomplete-and-mostly-wrong.html`).

In this chapter, we will cover the following topics:

- Functors
- Options, lists, and functions as functors
- Monads
- Applicatives

Functors

What if I told you that you already use functors in Kotlin? Surprised? Let's have a look at the following code:

```
fun main(args: Array<String>) {
    listOf(1, 2, 3)
            .map { i -> i * 2 }
            .map(Int::toString)
            .forEach(::println)
}
```

The `List<T>` class has a function, `map(transform: (T) -> R): List<R>`. Where does the name `map` come from? It came from category theory. What we do when we transform from `Int` to `String`, is we map from the `Int` category to the `String` category. In the same sense, in our example, we transform from `List<Int>` to `List<Int>` (not that exciting), and then from `List<Int>` to `List<String>`. We didn't change the external type, just the internal value.

And that is a functor. A **functor** is a type that defines a way to transform or to map its content. You can find different definitions of a functor, more or less academic; but in principle, all point to the same direction.

Let's define a generic interface for a functor type:

```
interface Functor<C<_>> { //Invalid Kotlin code
    fun <A,B> map(ca: C<A>, transform: (A) -> B): C<B>
}
```

And, it doesn't compile because Kotlin doesn't support higher-kinded types.

 You'll find more information on higher-kinded types for Kotlin, including alternatives and the future of Kotlin, in `Chapter 13`, *Arrow Types*.

In languages that support higher-kinded types, such as **Scala** and **Haskell**, it is possible to define a `Functor` type, for example, the Scala cats functor:

```
trait Functor[F[_]] extends Invariant[F] { self =>
  def map[A, B](fa: F[A])(f: A => B): F[B]

  //More code here
```

In Kotlin, we don't have those features, but we can simulate them by convention. If a type has a function or an extension function, then `map` is a functor (this is called **structural typing**, defining a type by its structure rather than its hierarchy).

We can have a simple `Option` type:

```
sealed class Option<out T> {
    object None : Option<Nothing>() {
        override fun toString() = "None"
    }

    data class Some<out T>(val value: T) : Option<T>()

    companion object
}
```

Then, you can define a `map` function for it:

```
fun <T, R> Option<T>.map(transform: (T) -> R): Option<R> = when (this) {
    Option.None -> Option.None
    is Option.Some -> Option.Some(transform(value))
}
```

And use it in the following way:

```
fun main(args: Array<String>) {
    println(Option.Some("Kotlin")
            .map(String::toUpperCase)) //Some(value=KOTLIN)
}
```

Now, an `Option` value will behave differently for `Some` and `None`:

```
fun main(args: Array<String>) {
    println(Option.Some("Kotlin").map(String::toUpperCase))
//Some(value=KOTLIN)
    println(Option.None.map(String::toUpperCase)) //None
}
```

Extension functions are so flexible that we can write a `map` function for a function type, `(A) -> B`, therefore, transforming functions into functors:

```
fun <A, B, C> ((A) -> B).map(transform: (B) -> C): (A) -> C = { t ->
transform(this(t)) }
```

What we are changing here is the return type from B to C by applying the parameter function, transform: (B) -> C to the result of the function (A) -> B itself:

```
fun main(args: Array<String>) {
    val add3AndMultiplyBy2: (Int) -> Int = { i: Int -> i + 3 }.map { j -> j
* 2 }
    println(add3AndMultiplyBy2(0)) //6
    println(add3AndMultiplyBy2(1)) //8
    println(add3AndMultiplyBy2(2)) //10
}
```

If you have experience in other functional programming languages, recognize this behavior as forward function composition (more on function composition in Chapter 12, *Getting Started with Arrow).*

Monads

A **monad** is a functor type that defines a flatMap (or bind, in other languages) function, that receives a lambda that returns the same type. Let me explain it with an example. Luckily for us, List<T> defines a flatMap function:

```
fun main(args: Array<String>) {
    val result = listOf(1, 2, 3)
            .flatMap { i ->
                listOf(i * 2, i + 3)
            }
            .joinToString()
    println(result) //2, 4, 4, 5, 6, 6
}
```

In a map function, we just transform the List value's content, but in flatMap, we can return a new List type with less or more items, making it a lot more potent than map.

So, a generic monad will look like this (just remember that we don't have higher-kinded types):

```
interface Monad<C<_>>: Functor<C> { //Invalid Kotlin code
    fun <A, B> flatMap(ca:C<A>, fm:(A) -> C<B>): C<B>
}
```

Now, we can write a `flatMap` function for our `Option` type:

```
fun <T, R> Option<T>.flatMap(fm: (T) -> Option<R>): Option<R> = when (this)
{
    Option.None -> Option.None
    is Option.Some -> fm(value)
}
```

If you pay close attention, you can see that `flatMap` and map look very similar; so similar that we can rewrite map using `flatMap`:

```
fun <T, R> Option<T>.map(transform: (T) -> R): Option<R> = flatMap { t ->
Option.Some(transform(t)) }
```

And now we can use a `flatMap` function's power in cool ways that will be impossible with a plain map:

```
fun calculateDiscount(price: Option<Double>): Option<Double> {
    return price.flatMap { p ->
        if (p > 50.0) {
            Option.Some(5.0)
        } else {
            Option.None
        }
    }
}

fun main(args: Array<String>) {
    println(calculateDiscount(Option.Some(80.0))) //Some(value=5.0)
    println(calculateDiscount(Option.Some(30.0))) //None
    println(calculateDiscount(Option.None)) //None
}
```

Our function, `calculateDiscount`, receives and returns `Option<Double>`. If the price is higher than `50.0`, we return a discount of `5.0` wrapped on `Some`, and `None` if it doesn't.

One cool trick with `flatMap` is that it can be nested:

```
fun main(args: Array<String>) {
    val maybeFive = Option.Some(5)
    val maybeTwo = Option.Some(2)

    println(maybeFive.flatMap { f ->
        maybeTwo.flatMap { t ->
            Option.Some(f + t)
        }
    }) // Some(value=7)
}
```

In the inner `flatMap` function, we have access to both values and operate over them.

We can write this example in a slightly shorter way by combining `flatMap` and `map`:

```
fun main(args: Array<String>) {
    val maybeFive = Option.Some(5)
    val maybeTwo = Option.Some(2)

    println(maybeFive.flatMap { f ->
        maybeTwo.map { t ->
            f + t
        }
    }) // Some(value=7)
}
```

As such, we can rewrite our first `flatMap` example as a composition of two lists—one of numbers and another one of functions:

```
fun main(args: Array<String>) {
    val numbers = listOf(1, 2, 3)
    val functions = listOf<(Int) -> Int>({ i -> i * 2 }, { i -> i + 3 })
    val result = numbers.flatMap { number ->
        functions.map { f -> f(number) }
    }.joinToString()

    println(result) //2, 4, 4, 5, 6, 6
}
```

This technique of nesting several `flatMap` or combinations of `flatMap` with `map` is very powerful and is the primary idea behind another concept named monadic comprehensions, which allow us to combine monadic operations (more about comprehensions in `Chapter 13`, *Arrow Types*).

Applicatives

Our previous example, invoking a lambda inside a wrapper with a parameter inside the same kind of wrapper, is the perfect way to introduce applicatives.

An **applicative** is a type that defines two functions, a `pure(t: T)` function that returns the `T` value wrapped in the applicative type, and an `ap` function (`apply`, in other languages) that receives a lambda wrapped in the applicative type.

In the previous section, when we explained monads, we made them extend directly from a functor but in reality, a monad extends from an applicative and an applicative extends from a functor. Therefore, our pseudo code for a generic applicative, and the entire hierarchy, will look like this:

```
interface Functor<C<_>> { //Invalid Kotlin code
    fun <A,B> map(ca:C<A>, transform:(A) -> B): C<B>
}

interface Applicative<C<_>>: Functor<C> { //Invalid Kotlin code
    fun <A> pure(a:A): C<A>

    fun <A, B> ap(ca:C<A>, fab: C<(A) -> B>): C<B>
}

interface Monad<C<_>>: Applicative<C> { //Invalid Kotlin code
    fun <A, B> flatMap(ca:C<A>, fm:(A) -> C<B>): C<B>
}
```

In short, an applicative is a more powerful functor, and a monad is a more powerful applicative.

Now, let's write an `ap` extension function for `List<T>`:

```
fun <T, R> List<T>.ap(fab: List<(T) -> R>): List<R> = fab.flatMap { f ->
this.map(f) }
```

And we can revisit our last example from the *Monads* section:

```
fun main(args: Array<String>) {
    val numbers = listOf(1, 2, 3)
    val functions = listOf<(Int) -> Int>({ i -> i * 2 }, { i -> i + 3 })
    val result = numbers.flatMap { number ->
        functions.map { f -> f(number) }
    }.joinToString()

    println(result) //2, 4, 4, 5, 6, 6
}
```

Let's rewrite it with the `ap` function:

```
fun main(args: Array<String>) {
    val numbers = listOf(1, 2, 3)
    val functions = listOf<(Int) -> Int>({ i -> i * 2 }, { i -> i + 3 })
    val result = numbers
            .ap(functions)
            .joinToString()
    println(result) //2, 4, 6, 4, 5, 6
}
```

Easier to read, but with a caveat—the result is in a different order. We need to be aware and choose which option is appropriate for our particular case.

We can add `pure` and `ap` to our `Option` class:

```
fun <T> Option.Companion.pure(t: T): Option<T> = Option.Some(t)
```

`Option.pure` is just a simple alias for the `Option.Some` constructor.

Our `Option.ap` function is fascinating:

```
//Option
fun <T, R> Option<T>.ap(fab: Option<(T) -> R>): Option<R> = fab.flatMap { f
-> map(f) }

//List
fun <T, R> List<T>.ap(fab: List<(T) -> R>): List<R> = fab.flatMap { f ->
this.map(f) }
```

Both `Option.ap` and `List.ap` have the same body, using a combination of `flatMap` and `map`, which is precisely how we combine monadic operations.

With monads, we summed two Option<Int> using flatMap and map:

```
fun main(args: Array<String>) {
    val maybeFive = Option.Some(5)
    val maybeTwo = Option.Some(2)

    println(maybeFive.flatMap { f ->
        maybeTwo.map { t ->
            f + t
        }
    }) // Some(value=7)
}
```

Now, using applicatives:

```
fun main(args: Array<String>) {
    val maybeFive = Option.pure(5)
    val maybeTwo = Option.pure(2)

    println(maybeTwo.ap(maybeFive.map { f -> { t: Int -> f + t } })) //
Some(value=7)
}
```

That is not very easy to read. First, we map maybeFive with a lambda (Int) -> (Int)
-> Int (technically, a curried function, and there is more information about curried
functions in Chapter 12, *Getting Started with Arrow*), that returns an Option<(Int) ->
Int> that can be passed as a parameter for maybeTwo.ap.

We can make things easier to read with a little trick (that I'm borrowing from Haskell):

```
infix fun <T, R> Option<(T) -> R>.`(*)`(o: Option<T>): Option<R> = flatMap
{ f: (T) -> R -> o.map(f) }
```

The infix extension function Option<(T) -> R>.`(*)` will let us read the sum
operation from left to right; how cool is that? Now, let's look at the following code,
summing two Option<Int> using applicatives

```
fun main(args: Array<String>) {
    val maybeFive = Option.pure(5)
    val maybeTwo = Option.pure(2)

    println(Option.pure { f: Int -> { t: Int -> f + t } } `(*)` maybeFive
`(*)` maybeTwo) // Some(value=7)
}
```

We wrap the `(Int) -> (Int) -> Int` lambda with the `pure` function and then we apply `Option<Int>`, one by one. We use the name `` `(*)` `` as a homage to Haskell's `<*>`.

So far, you can see that applicatives let you do some cool tricks, but monads are more powerful and flexible. When do use one or the other? It obviously depends on your particular problem, but our general advice is to use the abstraction with the least amount of power possible. You can start with a functor's `map`, then an applicative's `ap`, and lastly a monad's `flatMap`. Everything can be done with `flatMap` (as you can see `Option`, `map`, and `ap` were implemented using `flatMap`), but most of the time `map` and `ap` can be more accessible to reason about it.

Coming back to functions, we can make a function behave as an applicative. First, we should add a pure function:

```
object Function1 {
    fun <A, B> pure(b: B) = { _: A -> b }
}
```

First, we create an object `Function1`, as the function type `(A) -> B` doesn't have a companion object to add new extension functions as we did with `Option`:

```
fun main(args: Array<String>) {
    val f: (String) -> Int = Function1.pure(0)
    println(f("Hello,"))    //0
    println(f("World"))     //0
    println(f("!"))         //0
}
```

`Function1.pure(t: T)` will wrap a `T` value in a function and will return it, regardless of the parameter that we use. If you have experience with other functional languages, you'll recognize function's `pure` as an `identity` function (more about `identity` functions in `Chapter 12`, *Getting Started with Arrow*).

Let's add `flatMap`, an `ap`, to a function `(A) -> B`:

```
fun <A, B, C> ((A) -> B).map(transform: (B) -> C): (A) -> C = { t ->
transform(this(t)) }

fun <A, B, C> ((A) -> B).flatMap(fm: (B) -> (A) -> C): (A) -> C = { t ->
fm(this(t))(t) }

fun <A, B, C> ((A) -> B).ap(fab: (A) -> (B) -> C): (A) -> C = fab.flatMap {
f -> map(f) }
```

We already cover map(transform: (B) -> C): (A) -> C and we know that it behaves as a forward function composition. If you pay close attention to flatMap and ap, you'll see that the parameter is kind of backwards (and that ap is implemented as all the other ap functions for other types).

But, what can we do with the function's ap? Let's look at the following code:

```
fun main(args: Array<String>) {
    val add3AndMultiplyBy2: (Int) -> Int = { i: Int -> i + 3 }.ap { { j:
Int -> j * 2 } }
    println(add3AndMultiplyBy2(0)) //6
    println(add3AndMultiplyBy2(1)) //8
    println(add3AndMultiplyBy2(2)) //10
}
```

Well, we can compose functions, which is not exciting at all because we already did that with map. But there is a little trick with function's ap. We can access the original parameter:

```
fun main(args: Array<String>) {
    val add3AndMultiplyBy2: (Int) -> Pair<Int, Int> = { i:Int -> i + 3 }.ap
{ original -> { j:Int -> original to (j * 2) } }
    println(add3AndMultiplyBy2(0)) //(0, 6)
    println(add3AndMultiplyBy2(1)) //(1, 8)
    println(add3AndMultiplyBy2(2)) //(2, 10)
}
```

Accessing the original parameter in a function composition is useful in several scenarios, such as debugging and auditing.

Summary

We've covered a lot of cool concepts with scary names but with simple ideas behind them. The functor, applicative, and monad types open the door for several abstractions and more powerful functional concepts that we'll cover in the following chapters. We learned about some of the limitations of Kotlin and how we can overcome them as we create functions to mimic functor, applicative, and monad for different types. We also explored the hierarchical relationship between functors, applicatives, and monads.

In the next chapter, we'll cover how to work effectively with Streams of data.

11

Working with Streams in Kotlin

So, we are gradually moving towards completing this book. In this chapter, we are going to cover Streams in Kotlin and how to work with them.

Streams were first introduced in Java from Java 8. The Streams API in Kotlin is almost identical to the Java API, but contains a few little additions and extension functions.

This is the contents that we will be covering in this chapter:

- Introduction to Streams
- Collections versus Streams
- Streams versus Observable (ReactiveX-RxKotlin/RxJava)
- Working with Streams
- Different ways to create Streams
- Collecting Streams

So, let's get started.

Introduction to Streams

As we mentioned earlier, Streams were first introduced from Java 8. Starting from Java 8, Java started to give more focus to functional programming and started to add functional features gradually.

Kotlin, on the other hand, started to add functional features from day one. Kotlin added functional features and interfaces. While working with Java, you can use Streams only if you use Java 8 and later versions, but with Kotlin you can still use Streams, even when working with JDK 6.

So, what are Streams? You can think of Streams as an abstract layer over a sequence of elements to perform aggregate operations. Confused? Let's take a code example and then try to understand:

```
fun main(args: Array<String>) {
    val stream = 1.rangeTo(10).asSequence().asStream()
    val resultantList = stream.skip(5).collect(Collectors.toList())
    println(resultantList)
}
```

The output is as follows:

```
"C:\Program Files\Java\jdk1.8.0_131\bin\java" ...
[6, 7, 8, 9, 10]
```

In the preceding program, what we did was create an `IntRange` value, create a `Sequence` value from it, and then get the `stream` value from it. We then skipped the first five items and then collected it back to a `List` instance. We will have a detailed look at all the functions used in the preceding code later in this chapter.

The preceding program utilized the functional interfaces of the Stream API.

 Stream API has a rich set of functional interfaces like we saw in the Collections.

Collections versus Streams

Reading up till here, you're probably thinking that all operations we performed in that program is possible with Collections itself in Kotlin, so why should we use Streams? To answer that, we should first learn the differences between Streams and Collections. So, let's have a look at the following list consisting of differences between Collections and Streams:

- As the definition of Collections says, a **Collection** is a data structure which stores and lets you work with a group of data. **Streams**, on the other hand, aren't data structures and don't store anything; they work like a pipeline or IO channel, which fetches data from its source on demand.

- Every data structure must have a finite size limit, and the same applies to Collections as well. But, as Streams are not data structures, they don't need to have any specific size limit.
- While accessing elements of a Collection directly, you can do it any time, even for the same position, without the requirement of recreating the Collection. But when working with Streams, elements of a Stream are only visited once during the life of a Stream. Like an iterator, a new Stream must be generated to revisit the same elements of the source.
- The Collection API constructs objects in an eager manner, always ready to be consumed. The Stream API creates objects in a lazy, on-demand basis.
- The Collection API is used for storing data in different kinds of data structures. The Stream API is used for the computation of data on a large set of objects.

So, these were very basic differences between the Collection API and the Stream API. At a glance, the Streams seem like RxKotlin, Observables which provide a way to consume the data, but there are a lot of significant differences between Streams and Observables. These are the differences between Streams and Observables:

- The first notable difference is that Streams are pull-based, and Observables are push-based. This may sound too abstract, but it has significant consequences that are very concrete.
- With Observables, it's easy to change threads or specify thread pools for a chain with ease, thanks to Schedulers. But, with Streams, it's a bit tricky.
- Observables are synchronized all the way through. This spares you from checking all the time whether these basic operations are thread safe.
- One more significant difference is that Observables have a lot more functional interfaces than the Streams API, which makes Observables easy to use with a lot of options to accomplish a certain task.

So, we learned that Streams are not a data structure but are like an abstract layer on top of the data source (which may be Collections or anything else), and even though Streams construct objects in a lazy, on-demand basis, they are still pull-based and use loops inside them.

To know more about push-based architecture and Observables, you can have a read of the book, *Reactive Programming in Kotlin*, by Rivu Chakraborty.

Working with Streams

So, we learned a lot of theories regarding Streams, and we also learned that Streams have a set of functional interfaces to work with (actually, the functional interfaces is the only way to work with Streams), but as I mentioned before, they work in a slightly different way than the Collections API.

To make things clearer, have a look back at the following example:

```
fun main(args: Array<String>) {
    val stream = 1.rangeTo(10).asSequence().asStream()
     val resultantList = stream.filter{
         it%2==0
    }.collect(Collectors.toList())
    println(resultantList)
}
```

The preceding program is a simple one; we just grabbed a stream of numbers 1 through 10 and filtered out the odd numbers from that stream, and then collected the results inside a new List.

But let's try to understand the mechanism of how it works. We are already familiar with functional interfaces and with the filter function, as we got introduced to them in the previous chapters, but the thing that's different here is the collect function and the Collectors value, which help collect the resultant data in a new List. We will have a closer look at the collect method and the Collectors value later in this chapter, but for now, let's have a look at the functional interfaces Streams offers, and types of Streams.

So, the following is the list of operations/functional interfaces from the Stream API and their descriptions:

- filter(): Works in the same way like Collection.filter in Kotlin. It returns a stream values consisting of the elements of this stream that match the given predicate.
- map(): Works in the same way as Collection.map in Kotlin. It returns a stream value consisting of the results of applying the given function to each element of this stream.
- mapToInt()/mapToLong()/mapToDouble(): Works the same way as map, but instead of returning a stream value, they return IntStream, LongStream and IntStream values, respectively. We are covering IntStream, LongStream, and IntStream in detail later in this chapter.

- `flatMap()`: Works the same way as `Collection.flatMap` in Kotlin.
- `flatMapToInt()`/`flatMapToLong()`/`flatMapToDouble()`: Works the same way as `flatMap`, but instead of returning a `stream` value, they return the `IntStream`, `LongStream`, and `IntStream` values, respectively.
- `distinct()`: Works in the same way as `Collection.distinct`. It returns a `stream` value of distinct elements.
- `peek()`: This function doesn't have any Kotlin Collection counterpart, however, it has a counterpart in RxKotlin/RxJava. This function returns the `stream` value consisting of the elements of this `stream`, additionally performing the provided action on each element, as elements are consumed from the resulting `stream`, much like the `doOnNext` operator of RxJava.
- `anyMatch()`: Similar to `Collection.any()`, it returns whether any elements of this `stream` match the provided predicate. It may not evaluate the predicate on all elements, if not necessary for determining the result. If the `stream` value is empty, then the `false` value is returned and the predicate is not evaluated.
- `allMatch()`: Similar to `Collection.all`, it returns whether all elements of this `stream` match the provided predicate. It may not evaluate the predicate on all elements, if not necessary for determining the result. If the `stream` value is empty, then the `true` value is returned and the predicate is not evaluated.
- `noneMatch()`: Similar to `Collection.none`, it returns whether no elements of this `stream` match the provided predicate. It may not evaluate the predicate on all elements, if not necessary for determining the result. If the `stream` is empty, then the `false` value is returned and the predicate is not evaluated.

We are skipping examples of these functions, as they are similar to the `Collection` functions and RxJava/RxKotlin operators.

If you're wondering about it then yes, if your project is purely in Kotlin (without any Java or any other language code), you can safely ditch Streams in favor of Collections and coroutines altogether.

So, let's now take a look at the `IntStream`, `DoubleStream`, and `LongStream` values we mentioned earlier and explore what purpose they serve.

Primitive streams

Primitive streams were introduced in Java 8, to take advantage of primitive data types in Java while using Streams (again, Streams are basically from Java, and Kotlin just adds a few extension functions to the Streams API). `IntStream`, `LongStream`, and `DoubleStream` are part of those primitive Streams.

These primitive streams work similarly to the normal Stream with some added features of the primitive data types.

So, let's take an example; have a look at the following program:

```
fun main(args: Array<String>) {
    val intStream = IntStream.range(1,10)
    val result = intStream.sum()
    println("The sum of elements is $result")
}
```

So, we created an `IntStream` value with the `IntStream.range()` function, the `range` function takes two integers as the starting and ending point and creates a Stream ranging from the specified integers, with both included. We then calculated the sum and printed it. The program seems quite easy, and credit goes to `IntStream` obviously, why? Think of calculating the sum of elements with that ease; without `IntStream`, we would have to loop through all the elements to calculate the sum.

The following is another example of primitive streams:

```
fun main(args: Array<String>) {
    val doubleStream = DoubleStream.iterate(1.5,{item ->
item*1.3})//(1)
    val avg = doubleStream
            .limit(10)//(2)
            .peek {
                println("Item $it")
            }.average()//(3)
    println("Average of 10 Items $avg")
}
```

Have a look at the following output before we explain the program:

```
"C:\Program Files\Java\jdk1.8.0_131\bin\java" ...
Item 1.5
Item 1.9500000000000002
Item 2.535
Item 3.2955
Item 4.28415
Item 5.569395000000001
Item 7.240213500000001
Item 9.412277550000002
Item 12.235960815000004
Item 15.906749059500006
Average of 10 Items OptionalDouble[6.392924592450002]


Process finished with exit code 0
```

So, let's explain the program:

- On comment (1), we created a `DoubleStream` value with the factory method `iterate()`. The iterate method takes a `double` as the seed of the Stream, and an operand, which will be iteratively applied to generate the elements of the Stream, for example if you pass *x* as the seed and *f* as the operator, the Stream will return *x* as the first element, *f(x)* as the second element, *f(f(x))* as the third element, and so on. This function creates a Stream of infinite size.
- We used the `limit` operator at comment (2), as we wanted only 10 elements from that stream, not all the elements till infinity. On comment (3), we calculated `average`.

So, let's have a look at the different ways to create a Stream.

Stream factory methods

The Streams API provides numerous ways to get a `Stream` instance. The following is the list of ways to create Streams that we are covering:

- `Stream Builder`
- `Stream.empty()`
- `Stream.of()`
- `Stream.generate()`
- `Stream.iterate()`
- Kotlin extension—`asStream()`

Among the preceding list, we've already seen how the Kotlin extension—`asStream` and the `Stream.iterate` function works (it'll work in the same way as the `DoubleStream.iterate` value, covered in the previous example). We will have a look at the rest.

Stream Builder

The `Stream Builder` interface makes it really easy to create an instance of Stream with ease. Have a look at the following example:

```kotlin
fun main(args: Array<String>) {
    val stream = Stream.builder<String>()
            .add("Item 1")
            .add("Item 2")
            .add("Item 3")
            .add("Item 4")
            .add("Item 5")
            .add("Item 6")
            .add("Item 7")
            .add("Item 8")
            .add("Item 9")
            .add("Item 10")
            .build()
    println("The Stream is ${stream.collect(Collectors.toList())}")
}
```

The output is as follows:

```
"C:\Program Files\Java\jdk1.8.0_131\bin\java" ...
The Stream is [Item 1, Item 2, Item 3, Item 4, Item 5, Item 6, Item 7, Item 8, Item 9, Item 10]

Process finished with exit code 0
```

The `Stream.builder()` method returns an instance of `Streams.Builder`. Then, we used the `Builder.add` function; the `add` function accepts an item for the `stream` value to be built, and returns the same instance of `Stream.Builder`. The `build` function then created the `stream` instance with the items provided to the builder.

Creating empty Streams – Stream.empty()

Creating empty Streams is really easy with the `Streams.empty()` factory method. Consider the following example:

```
fun main(args: Array<String>) {
    val emptyStream = Stream.empty<String>()
    val item = emptyStream.findAny()
    println("Item is $item")
}
```

In the preceding example, we created an `emptyStream` value with `Stream.empty()`, we then used the `findAny()` function to get hold of any element randomly selected from that Stream. The `findAny()` method returns an `Optional` value with a randomly selected item from the Stream, or an empty `Optional`, if the Stream is empty.

The following is the output of the preceding program:

```
"C:\Program Files\Java\jdk1.8.0_131\bin\java" ...
Item is Optional.empty

Process finished with exit code 0
```

Creating a Stream by passing elements – Stream.of()

We can also get an instance of Stream by providing its elements to the `of` function. The `of` function works in a similar way to the `Observable.just` method from RxJava/RxKotlin.

Have a look at the following example:

```
fun main(args: Array<String>) {
    val stream = Stream.of("Item 1",2,"Item 3",4,5.0,"Item 6")
    println("Items in Stream =
${stream.collect(Collectors.toList())}")
}
```

The output is as follows:

```
"C:\Program Files\Java\jdk1.8.0_131\bin\java" ...
Items in Stream = [Item 1, 2, Item 3, 4, 5.0, Item 6]


Process finished with exit code 0
```

Straightforward and easy, isn't it?

Generating Streams – Stream.generate()

We can also create a Stream by using the `Stream.generate()` factory method. It accepts a lambda/supplier instance as a parameter, and will use it to generate the item for each time the item is demanded. This method also creates an infinite Stream.

Consider the following example:

```
fun main(args: Array<String>) {
    val stream = Stream.generate {
        //return a random number
        (1..20).random()
    }
    val resultantList = stream
            .limit(10)
            .collect(Collectors.toList())
    println("resultantList = $resultantList")
}
```

The output is as follows:

```
"C:\Program Files\Java\jdk1.8.0_131\bin\java" ...
resultantList = [10, 2, 10, 9, 8, 17, 14, 2, 7, 13]

Process finished with exit code 0
```

So, the Stream API called the lambda to get each of the elements of the Stream—awesome.

So, now as we are quite familiar with how to use Streams and we know about primitive Streams, let's move forward and see how to work with `Collectors`.

Collector and Stream.collect – collecting Streams

We can perform numerous operations with Stream, but we may come into a situation where we need to repack the elements from the Stream into a data structure. The `Stream.collect()` method helps us achieve the same. It's one of the terminal methods of the Streams API. It allows you to perform mutable `fold` operations (repackaging elements to some data structures and applying some additional logic, concatenating them, and many more) on data elements held in a Stream instance.

The `collect()` method takes a `Collector` interface implementation as a parameter, for the strategy (whether to repackage them to a data structure, concatenate them, or anything else) of collecting.

So, do we need to write our own implementation of the `Collector` interface for repackaging the Stream into a `List/Set` values? Of course not, the Streams API provides you with some of the predefined `Collector` implementations for some of the most common use cases.

The `Collectors` class holds the predefined `Collector` implementations. All of them can be imported with the following line:

```
import java.util.stream.Collectors
```

The following list contains the predefined `Collector` implementations:

- `Collectors.toList()`
- `Collectors.toSet()`
- `Collectors.toMap()`
- `Collectors.toCollection()`
- `Collectors.joining()`
- `Collectors.groupingBy()`

So, let's have a brief look at each of them.

The Collectors.toList(), Collectors.toSet(), and Collectors.toCollection() methods

We've already seen the implementations of `Collectors.toList()`. The `Collectors.toList()` method helps collect the elements of a Stream into a `List`. The important thing to note here is that you can't specify which `List` implementation to use; instead, it'll always use the default one.

`Collectors.toSet()` is similar to the `Collectors.toList()` method, just instead of `List`, it repackages the elements into a set. Again, with `Collectors.toSet()`, you won't be able to specify which set implementation to use.

The `Collectors.toCollection()` method is a complementing version of the `toList()` and `toSet()`; it lets you provide a custom Collection to accumulate the list into.

Consider the following example to explain it:

```
fun main(args: Array<String>) {
    val resultantSet = (0..10).asSequence().asStream()
            .collect(Collectors.toCollection{LinkedHashSet<Int>()})
    println("resultantSet $resultantSet")
}
```

The output is as follows:

```
"C:\Program Files\Java\jdk1.8.0_131\bin\java" ...
resultantSet [0, 1, 2, 3, 4, 5, 6, 7, 8, 9, 10]


Process finished with exit code 0
```

Collecting into Map – Collectors.toMap()

The `Collectors.toMap()` function helps us repackage the Stream into `Map` implementation. This function offers a lot of customizations. The simplest version accepts two lambdas; the first one is to determine the key of Map Entry, and the second lambda is to determine the value of Map Entry. Please note, each element in the Stream will be represented in an entry in the `Map`.

Those two lambdas will get each element of the Stream in separate iterations and are expected to generate a key/value based on them.

Have a look at the following example:

```
fun main(args: Array<String>) {
    val resultantMap = (0..10).asSequence().asStream()
            .collect(Collectors.toMap<Int,Int,Int>({
                it
            },{
                it*it
            }))
    println("resultantMap = $resultantMap")
}
```

In this program, we have used the simplest version of the `Collectors.toMap()` function. We passed two lambdas to it, the first one, determining the key for the entry will return the same value passed to it, the second one, on the other hand, computing and returning the square of the value passed. The important thing to note here is that both the lambdas will have the same parameter.

The output is shown as follows:

```
"C:\Program Files\Java\jdk1.8.0_131\bin\java" ...
resultantMap = {0=0, 1=1, 2=4, 3=9, 4=16, 5=25, 6=36, 7=49, 8=64, 9=81, 10=100}

Process finished with exit code 0
```

Joining Stream of strings – Collectors.joining()

The `Collectors.joining()` function helps you join elements of a Stream, containing strings. It has three optional parameters, namely—`delimiter`, `prefix`, and `postfix`.

Consider the following example of the program:

```
fun main(args: Array<String>) {
    val resultantString = Stream.builder<String>()
            .add("Item 1")
            .add("Item 2")
            .add("Item 3")
            .add("Item 4")
            .add("Item 5")
            .add("Item 6")
            .build()
            .collect(Collectors.joining(" - ","Starts Here=>","<=Ends
Here"))

        println("resultantString $resultantString")
    }
```

The output is as follows:

```
"C:\Program Files\Java\jdk1.8.0_131\bin\java" ...
resultantString Starts Here=>Item 1 - Item 2 - Item 3 - Item 4 - Item 5 - Item 6<=Ends Here

Process finished with exit code 0
```

Grouping elements of Stream – Collectors.groupingBy()

This function lets us collect the elements of a Stream into a `Map` function while grouping them. The basic difference of this function with `Collectors.toMap` is that this function lets you create a `Map<K, List<T>>` function, that is, it lets you create a `Map` function that will hold a `List` value as its value for each of the groups.

Consider the following example:

```
fun main(args: Array<String>) {
    val resultantSet = (1..20).asSequence().asStream()
                .collect(Collectors.groupingBy<Int,Int> { it%5 })
    println("resultantSet $resultantSet")
}
```

The output is as follows:

```
"C:\Program Files\Java\jdk1.8.0_131\bi
resultantSet {0=[5, 10, 15, 20],
  1=[1, 6, 11, 16], 2=[2, 7, 12, 17],
  3=[3, 8, 13, 18], 4=[4, 9, 14, 19]}

Process finished with exit code 0
```

Summary

So, in this chapter, we learned about Streams. We learned how to create Streams, learned how to work with Streams, and how to repackage a Stream into Collections.

In the next chapter, we will get started with the Arrow library, which makes it easy to implement functional programming in Kotlin. So, don't just wait, turn the page and get started with Arrow.

12
Getting Started with Arrow

Arrow (`http://arrow-kt.io/`) is a Kotlin library that provides functional constructs, datatypes, and other abstractions. Kotlin syntax is powerful and flexible, and Arrow takes advantage of it to offer features that don't come as standard.

Arrow is the result of combining the two most successful and popular functional libraries, `funKTionale` and `Kategory`, into one. In late 2017, both developer groups, fearing a split that would damage the whole Kotlin community, decided to join forces and create a single, unified functional library.

In this chapter, we'll cover how to use existing functions to build new and richer functions. Some of the topics that we'll cover are as follows:

- Function composition
- Partial application
- Currying
- Memoization
- Pipes
- Optics

Function composition

One big part of functional programming as a concept is to use functions in the same way that we use any other type—as values, parameters, returns, and so on. One thing that we can do with other types is to take them as construction blocks to build other types; the same concept can be applied to functions.

Function composition is a technique to build functions using existing functions; similar to Unix pipes or channel pipelines, the result value of a function is used as a parameter for the next one.

In Arrow, function composition comes as a set of the `infix` extension functions:

Function	Description
compose	Takes the result of invoking the right-hand function as the parameter for the left-hand function.
forwardCompose	Takes the result of invoking the left-hand function as the parameter for the right-hand function.
andThen	Is an alias for forwardCompose.

Let's compose some functions:

```
import arrow.syntax.function.andThen
import arrow.syntax.function.compose
import arrow.syntax.function.forwardCompose
import java.util.*

val p: (String) -> String = { body -> "<p>$body</p>" }

val span: (String) -> String = { body -> "<span>$body</span>" }

val div: (String) -> String = { body -> "<div>$body</div>" }

val randomNames: () -> String = {
    if (Random().nextInt() % 2 == 0) {
        "foo"
    } else {
        "bar"
    }
}

fun main(args: Array<String>) {
    val divStrong: (String) -> String = div compose strong

    val spanP: (String) -> String = p forwardCompose span

    val randomStrong: () -> String = randomNames andThen strong

    println(divStrong("Hello composition world!"))
    println(spanP("Hello composition world!"))
```

```
        println(randomStrong())
}
```

To build the `div Strong: (String) -> String` function, we compose `div: (String)` `-> String` and `strong: (String) -> String`. In other words, `divStrong` is equivalent to the following code snippet:

```
val divStrong: (String) -> String = { body ->
"<div><strong>$body</div></strong>"}
```

For `spanP: (String) -> String`, we compose `span: (String) -> (String)` and `p: (String) -> String` as follows:

```
val spanP: (String) -> String = { body -> "<span><p>$body</p></span>"}
```

Notice that we are using the same type `(String) -> String`, but any function can be composed if it has the right return type that the other functions need.

Let's rewrite our `Channel` pipeline example with function composition:

```
data class Quote(val value: Double, val client: String, val item: String,
val quantity: Int)

data class Bill(val value: Double, val client: String)

data class PickingOrder(val item: String, val quantity: Int)

fun calculatePrice(quote: Quote) = Bill(quote.value * quote.quantity,
quote.client) to PickingOrder(quote.item, quote.quantity)

fun filterBills(billAndOrder: Pair<Bill, PickingOrder>): Pair<Bill,
PickingOrder>? {
    val (bill, _) = billAndOrder
    return if (bill.value >= 100) {
       billAndOrder
    } else {
       null
    }
}

fun warehouse(order: PickingOrder) {
    println("Processing order = $order")
}

fun accounting(bill: Bill) {
    println("processing = $bill")
}
```

```
fun splitter(billAndOrder: Pair<Bill, PickingOrder>?) {
    if (billAndOrder != null) {
        warehouse(billAndOrder.second)
        accounting(billAndOrder.first)
    }
}

fun main(args: Array<String>) {
    val salesSystem:(Quote) -> Unit = ::calculatePrice andThen ::filterBills
forwardCompose ::splitter
    salesSystem(Quote(20.0, "Foo", "Shoes", 1))
    salesSystem(Quote(20.0, "Bar", "Shoes", 200))
    salesSystem(Quote(2000.0, "Foo", "Motorbike", 1))
}
```

The `salesSystem: (Quote) -> Unit` function is very complex in its behavior, but was built using other functions as building blocks.

Partial application

With function composition, we take two functions to create the third function; with partial application, we create a new function by passing a parameter to an existing function.

Arrow comes with two flavours of partial application—explicit and implicit.

The explicit style uses a series of extension functions called `partially1`, `partially2`, all the way up to `partially22`. The implicit style takes a series of extensions, overloading the `invoke` operator:

```
package com.packtpub.functionalkotlin.chapter11

import arrow.syntax.function.invoke
import arrow.syntax.function.partially3

fun main(args: Array<String>) {
    val strong: (String, String, String) -> String = { body, id, style ->
"<strong id=\"$id\" style=\"$style\">$body</strong>" }

    val redStrong: (String, String) -> String = strong.partially3("font:
red") //Explicit

    val blueStrong: (String, String) -> String = strong(p3 = "font: blue")
//Implicit

    println(redStrong("Red Sonja", "movie1"))
```

```
    println(blueStrong("Deep Blue Sea", "movie2"))
}
```

Both styles can be chained as follows:

```
fun partialSplitter(billAndOrder: Pair<Bill, PickingOrder>?, warehouse:
(PickingOrder) -> Unit, accounting: (Bill) -> Unit) {
    if (billAndOrder != null) {
        warehouse(billAndOrder.second)
        accounting(billAndOrder.first)
    }
}

fun main(args: Array<String>) {
    val splitter: (billAndOrder: Pair<Bill, PickingOrder>?) -> Unit =
::partialSplitter.partially2 { order -> println("TESTING $order") }(p2 =
::accounting)

    val salesSystem: (quote: Quote) -> Unit = ::calculatePrice andThen
::filterBills forwardCompose splitter
    salesSystem(Quote(20.0, "Foo", "Shoes", 1))
    salesSystem(Quote(20.0, "Bar", "Shoes", 200))
    salesSystem(Quote(2000.0, "Foo", "Motorbike", 1))
}
```

Our original `splitter` function was not very flexible as it directly invoked warehouse and
accounting functions. The `partialSplitter` function resolves this problem by taking
`warehouse` and `accounting` as parameters; however a `(Pair<Bill, PickingOrder>?,
(PickingOrder) -> Unit, (Bill) -> Unit)` function can't be used in composition.
Then, we partially apply two functions—a lambda and a reference.

Binding

A special case of partial application is **binding**. With binding, you pass a T parameter to
the `(T) -> R` function but without executing it, effectively returning an `() -> R` function:

```
fun main(args: Array<String>) {

    val footer:(String) -> String = {content ->
"<footer&gt;$content</footer>"}
    val fixFooter: () -> String = footer.bind("Functional Kotlin - 2018")
//alias for partially1
    println(fixFooter())
}
```

The function bind is just an alias for `partially1`, but it makes sense to have a separate name for it and make it more semantically correct.

Reverse

Reverse takes any function and returns it with its parameter in the reverse order (in other languages, this function is known as **flip**). Let's look at the following code:

```
import arrow.syntax.function.partially3
import arrow.syntax.function.reverse

fun main(args: Array<String>) {
    val strong: (String, String, String) -> String = { body, id, style ->
"<strong id=\"$id\" style=\"$style\">$body</strong>" }

    val redStrong: (String, String) -> String = strong.partially3("font:
red") //Explicit

    println(redStrong("Red Sonja", "movie1"))

    println(redStrong.reverse()("movie2", "The Hunt for Red October"))

}
```

Our `redStrong` function is awkward to use, as we'll expect to have `id` first and then `body`, but, is easily fixable with the `reverse` extension function. The `reverse` function can be applied to functions from parameters 1 to 22.

Pipes

A `pipe` function takes a `T` value and invokes a `(T) -> R` function with it:

```
import arrow.syntax.function.pipe

fun main(args: Array<String>) {
    val strong: (String) -> String = { body -> "<strong>$body</strong>" }

    "From a pipe".pipe(strong).pipe(::println)
}
```

A **pipe** is similar to function composition, but instead of generating new functions, we can chain function invocations to produce new values, reducing nesting calls. Pipes are known in other languages, such as **Elm** and **Ocaml**, as the operator |>:

```
fun main(args: Array<String>) {
    splitter(filterBills(calculatePrice(Quote(20.0, "Foo", "Shoes", 1))))
//Nested

    Quote(20.0, "Foo", "Shoes", 1) pipe ::calculatePrice pipe ::filterBills
pipe ::splitter //Pipe
}
```

Both lines are equivalent, but the first one must be understood backwards and the second one should read from left to right:

```
import arrow.syntax.function.pipe
import arrow.syntax.function.pipe3
import arrow.syntax.function.reverse

fun main(args: Array<String>) {
    val strong: (String, String, String) -> String = { body, id, style ->
"<strong id=\"$id\" style=\"$style\">$body</strong>" }

    val redStrong: (String, String) -> String = "color: red" pipe3
strong.reverse()
    redStrong("movie3", "Three colors: Red") pipe ::println
}
```

When `pipe` is applied to a multi-parameter function, using its variants `pipe2` to `pipe22`, it behaves as `partially1`.

Currying

Applying curried to a function of *n* parameters, for example, (A, B) -> R, transforms it into a chain of the n function calls, (A) -> (B) -> R:

```
import arrow.syntax.function.curried
import arrow.syntax.function.pipe
import arrow.syntax.function.reverse
import arrow.syntax.function.uncurried


fun main(args: Array<String>) {

    val strong: (String, String, String) -> String = { body, id, style ->
```

```
"<strong id=\"$id\" style=\"$style\">$body</strong>" }

    val curriedStrong: (style: String) -> (id: String) -> (body: String) ->
String = strong.reverse().curried()

    val greenStrong: (id: String) -> (body: String) -> String =
curriedStrong("color:green")

    val uncurriedGreenStrong: (id: String, body: String) -> String =
greenStrong.uncurried()

    println(greenStrong("movie5")("Green Inferno"))

    println(uncurriedGreenStrong("movie6", "Green Hornet"))

    "Fried Green Tomatoes" pipe ("movie7" pipe greenStrong) pipe ::println
}
```

Functions on curried forms can be transformed into a normal, multi-parameter form with
`uncurried()`.

Differences between the currying and partial application

There is some confusion between currying and partial application. Some authors treat them
as synonymous, but they are different:

```
import arrow.syntax.function.curried
import arrow.syntax.function.invoke

fun main(args: Array<String>) {
    val strong: (String, String, String) -> String = { body, id, style ->
"<strong id=\"$id\" style=\"$style\">$body</strong>" }

    println(strong.curried()("Batman Begins")("trilogy1")("color:black")) //
Curried

    println(strong("The Dark Knight")("trilogy2")("color:black")) // Fake
curried, just partial application

    println(strong(p2 = "trilogy3")(p2 = "color:black")("The Dark Knight
rises")) // partial application
}
```

The differences are significant and they can help us to decide when to use one or the other:

	Currying	Partial application
Return value	When a function of arity *N* gets curried, it returns a chain of functions of *N* size, (curried form).	When a function or arity *N* gets partially applied, it returns a function of arity *N - 1*.
Parameter application	After curried, only the first parameter of the chain can be applied.	Any parameter can be applied in any order.
Reverting	It is possible to take a function on the curried form and revert it to a multi-parameter function.	As partial application doesn't change the function form, reverting is not applicable.

Partial application can be more flexible, but some functional styles tend to favor currying. The important thing to grasp is that both styles are different and both are supported by Arrow.

Logical complement

A **logical complement** takes any predicate (a function with a return `Boolean` type) and negates it. Let's look at the following code:

```
import arrow.core.Predicate
import arrow.syntax.function.complement


fun main(args: Array<String>) {
    val evenPredicate: Predicate<Int> = { i: Int -> i % 2 == 0 }
    val oddPredicate: (Int) -> Boolean = evenPredicate.complement()

    val numbers: IntRange = 1..10
    val evenNumbers: List<Int> = numbers.filter(evenPredicate)
    val oddNumbers: List<Int> = numbers.filter(oddPredicate)

    println(evenNumbers)
    println(oddNumbers)
}
```

Notice that we use a `Predicate<T>` type, but it is just an alias for `(T) -> Boolean`. There are complement extension functions for predicates from 0 to 22 parameters.

Memoization

Memoization is a technique to cache results of pure functions. A memoized function behaves as a normal function, but stores the result of previous computations associated with the parameters supplied to produce that result.

The classic example of memoization is Fibonacci:

```
import arrow.syntax.function.memoize
import kotlin.system.measureNanoTime

fun recursiveFib(n: Long): Long = if (n < 2) {
    n
} else {
    recursiveFib(n - 1) + recursiveFib(n - 2)
}

fun imperativeFib(n: Long): Long {
    return when (n) {
        0L -> 0
        1L -> 1
        else -> {
            var a = 0L
            var b = 1L
            var c = 0L
            for (i in 2..n) {
                c = a + b
                a = b
                b = c
            }
            c
        }
    }
}

fun main(args: Array<String>) {

    var lambdaFib: (Long) -> Long = { it } //Declared ahead to be used
inside recursively

    lambdaFib = { n: Long ->
        if (n < 2) n else lambdaFib(n - 1) + lambdaFib(n - 2)
    }

    var memoizedFib: (Long) -> Long = { it }

    memoizedFib = { n: Long ->
```

```
        if (n < 2) n else memoizedFib(n - 1) + memoizedFib(n - 2)
    }.memoize()

    println(milliseconds("imperative fib") { imperativeFib(40) }) //0.006
    println(milliseconds("recursive fib") { recursiveFib(40) }) //1143.167
    println(milliseconds("lambda fib") { lambdaFib(40) }) //4324.890
    println(milliseconds("memoized fib") { memoizedFib(40) }) //1.588
}

inline fun milliseconds(description: String, body: () -> Unit): String {
    return "$description:${measureNanoTime(body) / 1_000_000.00} ms"
}
```

Our memoized version is more than 700 times faster than a recursive function version (which is almost four times faster than the lambda version). The imperative version is unbeatable, as it is heavily optimized by the compiler:

```
fun main(args: Array<String>) = runBlocking {

    var lambdaFib: (Long) -> Long = { it } //Declared ahead to be used
inside recursively

    lambdaFib = { n: Long ->
        if (n < 2) n else lambdaFib(n - 1) + lambdaFib(n - 2)
    }

    var memoizedFib: (Long) -> Long = { it }

    memoizedFib = { n: Long ->
        println("from memoized fib n = $n")
        if (n < 2) n else memoizedFib(n - 1) + memoizedFib(n - 2)
    }.memoize()
    val job = launch {
        repeat(10) { i ->
            launch(coroutineContext) { println(milliseconds("On coroutine $i -
imperative fib") { imperativeFib(40) }) }
            launch(coroutineContext) { println(milliseconds("On coroutine $i -
recursive fib") { recursiveFib(40) }) }
            launch(coroutineContext) { println(milliseconds("On coroutine $i -
lambda fib") { lambdaFib(40) }) }
            launch(coroutineContext) { println(milliseconds("On coroutine $i -
memoized fib") { memoizedFib(40) }) }
        }
    }

    job.join()
```

```
    }
```

Memoized functions, internally, use a thread-safe structure to store their results, and are therefore safe to use on coroutines or any other concurrent code.

There are potential downsides of using memoized functions. The first is that the process of reading the internal cache is higher than the actual computation or memory consumption, as right now, memoized functions don't expose any behavior to control their internal storage.

Partial functions

A **partial function** (not to be confused with partial applied function) is a function that is not defined for every possible value of its parameter type. In contrast, a **total function** is a function that is defined for every possible value.

Let's have a look at the following example:

```
fun main(args: Array<String>) {
    val upper: (String?) -> String = { s:String? -> s!!.toUpperCase()}
//Partial function, it can't transform null
    listOf("one", "two", null, "four").map(upper).forEach(::println) //NPE
}
```

The `upper` function is a partial function; it can't process a null value despite the fact that `null` is a valid `String?` value. If you try to run this code, it will throw a `NullPointerException` (**NPE**).

Arrow provides an explicit type `PartialFunction<T, R>` for partial functions of type `(T) -> R`:

```
import arrow.core.PartialFunction

fun main(args: Array<String>) {
 val upper: (String?) -> String = { s: String? -> s!!.toUpperCase() }
//Partial function, it can't transform null

 val partialUpper: PartialFunction<String?, String> =
PartialFunction(definetAt = { s -> s != null }, f = upper)

 listOf("one", "two", null, "four").map(partialUpper).forEach(::println)
//IAE: Value: (null) isn't supported by this function
}
```

`PartialFunction<T, R>` receives a predicate `(T) -> Boolean` as the first parameter which must return `true` if the function is defined for that particular value. A `PartialFunction<T, R>` function extends from `(T) -> R`, therefore it can be used as a normal function.

In this example, the code still throws an exception but now of type `IllegalArgumentException` (**IAE**), with an informative message.

To avoid getting exceptions, we must transform our partial function into a total one:

```
fun main(args: Array<String>) {

    val upper: (String?) -> String = { s: String? -> s!!.toUpperCase() }
//Partial function, it can't transform null

    val partialUpper: PartialFunction<String?, String> =
PartialFunction(definetAt = { s -> s != null }, f = upper)

    listOf("one", "two", null, "four").map{ s ->
partialUpper.invokeOrElse(s, "NULL")}.forEach(::println)
    }
```

One option is to use the `invokeOrElse` function that returns a default value in case the value `s` isn't defined for this function:

```
fun main(args: Array<String>) {

    val upper: (String?) -> String = { s: String? -> s!!.toUpperCase() }
//Partial function, it can't transform null

    val partialUpper: PartialFunction<String?, String> =
PartialFunction(definetAt = { s -> s != null }, f = upper)

    val upperForNull: PartialFunction<String?, String> = PartialFunction({ s
-> s == null }) { "NULL" }

    val totalUpper: PartialFunction<String?, String> = partialUpper orElse
upperForNull

    listOf("one", "two", null, "four").map(totalUpper).forEach(::println)
    }
```

The second option is to create a total function using several partial functions with the function `orElse`:

```
fun main(args: Array<String>) {
    val fizz = PartialFunction({ n: Int -> n % 3 == 0 }) { "FIZZ" }
    val buzz = PartialFunction({ n: Int -> n % 5 == 0 }) { "BUZZ" }
    val fizzBuzz = PartialFunction({ n: Int -> fizz.isDefinedAt(n) &&
buzz.isDefinedAt(n) }) { "FIZZBUZZ" }
    val pass = PartialFunction({ true }) { n: Int -> n.toString() }

    (1..50).map(fizzBuzz orElse buzz orElse fizz orElse
pass).forEach(::println)
}
```

Through the `isDefinedAt(T)` function we can reuse the internal predicate, in this case, to build the condition for `fizzBuzz`. When used in a chain of `orElse`, the declaration order takes precedence, the first partial function that is defined for a value will be executed, and the other functions down the chain will be ignored.

Identity and constant

Identity and constant are straightforward functions. The `identity` function returns the same value provided as parameter; similar to additive and multiplicative identity property, adding 0 to any number is still the same number.

The `constant<T, R>(t: T)` function returns a new function that will always return the `t` value:

```
fun main(args: Array<String>) {

    val oneToFour = 1..4

    println("With identity: ${oneToFour.map(::identity).joinToString()}")
//1, 2, 3, 4

    println("With constant: ${oneToFour.map(constant(1)).joinToString()}")
//1, 1, 1, 1
}
```

We can rewrite our `fizzBuzz` value using `constant`:

```
fun main(args: Array<String>) {
    val fizz = PartialFunction({ n: Int -> n % 3 == 0 }, constant("FIZZ"))
    val buzz = PartialFunction({ n: Int -> n % 5 == 0 }, constant("BUZZ"))
    val fizzBuzz = PartialFunction({ n: Int -> fizz.isDefinedAt(n) &&
buzz.isDefinedAt(n) }, constant("FIZZBUZZ"))
    val pass = PartialFunction<Int, String>(constant(true)) { n ->
n.toString() }

    (1..50).map(fizzBuzz orElse buzz orElse fizz orElse
pass).forEach(::println)
}
```

Identity and constant functions are useful in functional programming or in
implementations of math algorithms, for example, constant is K in SKI combinator calculus.

Optics

Optics are abstractions to update immutable data structures elegantly. One form of optics
is `Lens` (or lenses, depending on the library implementation). A `Lens` is a functional
reference that can focus (hence the name) into a structure and read, write, or modify its
target:

```
typealias GB = Int

data class Memory(val size: GB)
data class MotherBoard(val brand: String, val memory: Memory)
data class Laptop(val price: Double, val motherBoard: MotherBoard)

fun main(args: Array<String>) {
    val laptopX8 = Laptop(500.0, MotherBoard("X", Memory(8)))

    val laptopX16 = laptopX8.copy(
        price = 780.0,
        motherBoard = laptopX8.motherBoard.copy(
            memory = laptopX8.motherBoard.memory.copy(
                size = laptopX8.motherBoard.memory.size * 2
            )
        )
    )

    println("laptopX16 = $laptopX16")
}
```

To create a new `Laptop` value from an existing one, we need to use several nested copy methods and references. In this example, it isn't as bad but you can imagine that in a more complex data structure, things can overgrow into madness.

Let's write our very first `Lens` values:

```
val laptopPrice: Lens<Laptop, Double> = Lens(
    get = { laptop -> laptop.price },
    set = { price -> { laptop -> laptop.copy(price = price) } }
)
```

The `laptopPrice` value is a `Lens<Laptop, Double>` that we initialize using the function `Lens<S, T, A, B>` (actually `Lens.invoke`). `Lens` takes two functions as parameters, as `get: (S) -> A` and `set: (B) -> (S) -> T`.

As you can see, `set` is a curried function so that you can write your set like this:

```
import arrow.optics.Lens

val laptopPrice: Lens<Laptop, Double> = Lens(
    get = { laptop -> laptop.price },
    set = { price: Double, laptop: Laptop -> laptop.copy(price = price)
}.curried()
)
```

Which, depending on your preferences, can be easier to read and write.

Now that you have your first lens, it can be used to set, read, and modify a laptop's price. Not too impressive, but the magic of lenses is combining them:

```
import arrow.optics.modify

val laptopMotherBoard: Lens<Laptop, MotherBoard> = Lens(
    get = { laptop -> laptop.motherBoard },
    set = { mb -> { laptop -> laptop.copy(motherBoard = mb) } }
)

val motherBoardMemory: Lens<MotherBoard, Memory> = Lens(
    get = { mb -> mb.memory },
    set = { memory -> { mb -> mb.copy(memory = memory) } }
)

val memorySize: Lens<Memory, GB> = Lens(
    get = { memory -> memory.size },
    set = { size -> { memory -> memory.copy(size = size) } }
)
```

```
fun main(args: Array<String>) {
    val laptopX8 = Laptop(500.0, MotherBoard("X", Memory(8)))

    val laptopMemorySize: Lens<Laptop, GB> = laptopMotherBoard compose
motherBoardMemory compose memorySize

    val laptopX16 = laptopMemorySize.modify(laptopPrice.set(laptopX8,
780.0)) { size ->
        size * 2
    }

    println("laptopX16 = $laptopX16")
}
```

We created `laptopMemorySize` combining lenses from `Laptop` all the way to `memorySize`; then, we can set laptop's price and modify its memory.

Despite how cool lenses are, it looks like a lot of boilerplate code. Fear not, Arrow can generate those lenses for you.

Configuring Arrows code generation

On a Gradle project, add a file called `generated-kotlin-sources.gradle`:

```
apply plugin: 'idea'

idea {
    module {
        sourceDirs += files(
            'build/generated/source/kapt/main',
            'build/generated/source/kaptKotlin/main',
            'build/tmp/kapt/main/kotlinGenerated')
        generatedSourceDirs += files(
            'build/generated/source/kapt/main',
            'build/generated/source/kaptKotlin/main',
            'build/tmp/kapt/main/kotlinGenerated')
    }
}
```

Then, in the `build.gradle` file, add the following content:

```
apply plugin: 'kotlin-kapt'
apply from: rootProject.file('gradle/generated-kotlin-sources.gradle')
```

Add a new dependency in the `build.gradle` file:

```
dependencies {
    ...
    kapt      'io.arrow-kt:arrow-annotations-processor:0.5.2'
    ...
}
```

Once configured, you can generate Arrow code with a normal build command, `./gradlew build`.

Generating lenses

Once Arrow's code generation is configured, you can add the `@lenses` annotation to the data classes that you want to have lenses generated for:

```kotlin
import arrow.lenses
import arrow.optics.Lens
import arrow.optics.modify

typealias GB = Int

@lenses data class Memory(val size: GB)
@lenses data class MotherBoard(val brand: String, val memory: Memory)
@lenses data class Laptop(val price: Double, val motherBoard: MotherBoard)

fun main(args: Array<String>) {
    val laptopX8 = Laptop(500.0, MotherBoard("X", Memory(8)))

    val laptopMemorySize: Lens<Laptop, GB> = laptopMotherBoard() compose
motherBoardMemory() compose memorySize()

    val laptopX16 = laptopMemorySize.modify(laptopPrice().set(laptopX8,
780.0)) { size ->
        size * 2
    }

    println("laptopX16 = $laptopX16")
}
```

Arrow generates as many lenses as constructor parameters our data classes have, with the name convention `classProperty` and in the same package, so no extra imports are needed.

Summary

In this chapter, we covered many features of Arrow that give us tools to create, generate, and enrich existing functions. We composed new functions using existing ones; we included partial application and currying. We also cached results of pure functions with memoization and modified data structures using lenses.

Arrow's features open up the possibility of creating rich and maintainable applications, using basic functional principles.

In the next chapter, we'll cover more Arrow features, including datatypes such as `Option`, `Either,` and `Try`.

13
Arrow Types

Arrow contains many implementations of conventional functional types such as `Option`, `Either`, and `Try`, as well many other types classes, such as functor and monad.

In this chapter, we'll cover the following topics:

- Using `Option` to manage null
- `Either` and `Try` to manage errors
- Combinations and transformers
- `State` to manage application state

Option

The `Option<T>` datatype is the representation of a presence or absence of a value `T`. In Arrow, `Option<T>` is a sealed class with two sub-types, `Some<T>`, a data class that represents the presence of value `T` and `None`, and an object that represents the absence of value. Defined as a sealed class, `Option<T>` can't have any other sub-types; therefore the compiler can check clauses exhaustively, if both cases, `Some<T>` and `None` are covered.

I know (or I pretend to know) what you're thinking at this very moment—why do I need `Option<T>` to represent the presence or absence of `T`, if in Kotlin we already have `T` for presence and `T?` for absence?

And you are right. But `Option` provides a lot more value than nullable types, let's jump directly to an example:

```
fun divide(num: Int, den: Int): Int? {
    return if (num % den != 0) {
```

```
            null
    } else {
        num / den
    }
}

fun division(a: Int, b: Int, den: Int): Pair<Int, Int>? {
    val aDiv = divide(a, den)
    return when (aDiv) {
        is Int -> {
            val bDiv = divide(b, den)
            when (bDiv) {
                is Int -> aDiv to bDiv
                else -> null
            }
        }
        else -> null
    }
}
```

The `division` function takes three parameters—two integers (a, b) and a denominator (den) and returns a `Pair<Int, Int>`, if both numbers are divisible by `den` or `null` otherwise.

We can express the same algorithm with `Option`:

```
import arrow.core.*
import arrow.syntax.option.toOption

fun optionDivide(num: Int, den: Int): Option<Int> = divide(num,
den).toOption()

fun optionDivision(a: Int, b: Int, den: Int): Option<Pair<Int, Int>> {
    val aDiv = optionDivide(a, den)
    return when (aDiv) {
        is Some -> {
            val bDiv = optionDivide(b, den)
            when (bDiv) {
                is Some -> Some(aDiv.t to bDiv.t)
                else -> None
            }
        }
        else -> None
    }
}
```

The function, `optionDivide` takes the nullable result from divide and returns it as an `Option`, using the `toOption()` extension function.

There are no major changes on `optionDivision` compared to `division`, it is the same algorithm expressed with different types. If we stop here, then `Option<T>` doesn't provide extra value on top of nullables. Luckily, that isn't the case; there are more ways to use `Option`:

```
fun flatMapDivision(a: Int, b: Int, den: Int): Option<Pair<Int, Int>> {
    return optionDivide(a, den).flatMap { aDiv: Int ->
        optionDivide(b, den).flatMap { bDiv: Int ->
            Some(aDiv to bDiv)
        }
    }
}
```

`Option` provides several functions to process its internal value, in this case, `flatMap` (as a monad) and now our code looks a lot shorter.

Take a look at the following short list with some of the `Option<T>` functions:

Function	Description
`exists(p :Predicate<T>): Boolean`	Returns predicate p result if value T exists, otherwise null.
`filter(p: Predicate<T>): Option<T>`	Returns Some<T> if the value T exists and fulfills the predicate p, otherwise None.
`flatMap(f: (T) -> Option<T>): Option<T>`	A flatMap transform function (like monad).
`<R> fold(ifEmpty: () -> R, some: (T) -> R): R<R>`	Returns value transformed as R, invoking ifEmpty for None and some for Some<T>.
`getOrElse(default: () -> T): T`	Returns value T if exists, otherwise returns default result.
`<R> map(f: (T) -> R):Option<T>`	A transform function (like functor).
`orNull(): T?`	Returns the value T as a nullable T?.

The last implementation of division will use comprehensions:

```
import arrow.typeclasses.binding

fun comprehensionDivision(a: Int, b: Int, den: Int): Option<Pair<Int, Int>>
{
    return Option.monad().binding {
        val aDiv: Int = optionDivide(a, den).bind()
        val bDiv: Int = optionDivide(b, den).bind()
        aDiv to bDiv
    }.ev()
}
```

Comprehension is a technique to compute sequentially over any type (such as `Option`, `List`, and others) that contains a `flatMap` function and can provide an instance of monad (more on this later).

In Arrow, comprehensions use coroutines. Yes, coroutines are useful outside the asynchronous execution domain.

If we outline the continuations from our previous example it will look like this (which is a helpful mental model to understand coroutines)

```
fun comprehensionDivision(a: Int, b: Int, den: Int): Option<Pair<Int, Int>>
{
    return Option.monad().binding {
        val aDiv: Int = optionDivide(a, den).bind()
        // start continuation 1
            val bDiv: Int = optionDivide(b, den).bind()
            //start continuation 2
                aDiv to bDiv
            //end continuation 2
        // end continuation 1
    }.ev()
}
```

`Option.monad().binding` is a coroutine builder and the `bind()` function is a suspended function. If you recall correctly from our coroutines chapter, a continuation is a representation of any code after a suspension point (that is, when a suspended function is invoked). In our example, we have two suspension points and two continuations, when we return (in the last block line) we are in the second continuation, and we have access to both values, `aDiv` and `bDiv`.

Reading this algorithm as continuations is very similar to our `flatMapDivision` function. Behind the scenes, `Option.monad().binding` uses `Option.flatMap` with continuations to create the comprehension; once compiled, both `comprehensionDivision` and `flatMapDivision` are equivalent, roughly speaking.

The `ev()` method will be explained in the next section.

Arrow's type hierarchy

There is a limitation in Kotlin's types system—it doesn't support **Higher-Kinded Types (HKT)**. Without getting too much into type theory, an HKT is a type that declares other generic values as type parameters:

```
class MyClass<T>() //Valid Kotlin code

class MyHigherKindedClass<K<T>>() //Not valid kotlin code
```

Lacking HKT is not great for Kotlin concerning functional programming, as many advanced functional constructs and patterns use them.

 The Arrow team is working on **Kotlin Evolution and Enhancement Process (KEEP)**—the community process for adding new language features, called Type Classes as extensions in Kotlin (`https://github.com/Kotlin/KEEP/pull/87`) to support HKT and other features. At this very moment, it isn't clear if this KEEP (coded as *KEEP-87*) will be included anytime soon in Kotlin, but right now is the most commented proposal and has attracted a lot of attention. Details aren't clear now as it is still a work in progress, but there is a glimpse of hope.

Arrow's solution to this problem is to simulate HKT through a technique called evidence-based HKTs.

Let's have a look at an `Option<T>` declaration:

```
package arrow.core

import arrow.higherkind
import java.util.*

/**
 * Represents optional values. Instances of `Option`
 * are either an instance of $some or the object $none.
 */
```

```
@higherkind
sealed class Option<out A> : OptionKind<A> {
  //more code goes here
```

Option<A> is annotated with @higherkind which is similar to @lenses from our previous chapter; this annotation is used to generate code to support evidence-based HKTs. Option<A> extends from OptionKind<A>:

```
package arrow.core

class OptionHK private constructor()
typealias OptionKind<A> = arrow.HK<OptionHK, A>

@Suppress("UNCHECKED_CAST", "NOTHING_TO_INLINE")
inline fun <A> OptionKind<A>.ev(): Option<A> =
  this as Option<A>
```

OptionKind<A> is a type alias for HK<OptionHK, A>, all this code is generated using the @higherkind annotation processor. OptionHK is an uninstanciable class that is used as a unique tag name for HK and OptionKind is a kind of intermediate representation of HKT. Option.monad().binding returns OptionKind<T>, that is why we need to call ev() at the end to return a proper Option<T>:

```
package arrow

interface HK<out F, out A>

typealias HK2<F, A, B> = HK<HK<F, A>, B>

typealias HK3<F, A, B, C> = HK<HK2<F, A, B>, C>

typealias HK4<F, A, B, C, D> = HK<HK3<F, A, B, C>, D>

typealias HK5<F, A, B, C, D, E> = HK<HK4<F, A, B, C, D>, E>
```

HK interface (short-hand for **higher-kinded**) is used to represent an HKT of arity one up to HK5 for arity 5. On HK<F, A>, F represents the type and A the generic parameter, so Option<Int> is OptionKind<Int> value which is HK<OptionHK, Int>.

Let's have a look now at Functor<F>:

```
package arrow.typeclasses

import arrow.*

@typeclass
```

```
interface Functor<F> : TC {

    fun <A, B> map(fa: HK<F, A>, f: (A) -> B): HK<F, B>

}
```

Functor<F> extends TC, a marker interface and, as you can guess, it has a map function. The map function receives HK<F, A> as the first parameter and a lambda (A) -> B to transform the value of A into B and transform it into HK<F, B>.

Let's create our basic datatype Mappable that can provide instances for the Functor type class:

```
import arrow.higherkind

@higherkind
class Mappable<T>(val t: T) : MappableKind<T> {
    fun <R> map(f: (T) -> R): Mappable<R> = Mappable(f(t))

    override fun toString(): String = "Mappable(t=$t)"

    companion object
}
```

Our class, Mappable<T> is annotated with @higherkind and extends MappableKind<T> and must have a companion object, it doesn't matter if is empty or not.

Now, we need to create our implementation of Functor<F>:

```
import arrow.instance
import arrow.typeclasses.Functor

@instance(Mappable::class)
interface MappableFunctorInstance : Functor<MappableHK> {
    override fun <A, B> map(fa: MappableKind<A>, f: (A) -> B): Mappable<B> {
        return fa.ev().map(f)
    }
}
```

Our MappableFunctorInstance interface extends Functor<MappableHK> and is annotated with @instance(Mappable::class). Inside the map function, we use the first parameter, MappableKind<A> and use its map function.

The `@instance` annotation will generate an object extending the interface, `MappableFunctorInstance`. It will create an `Mappable.Companion.functor()` extension function to get the object implementing `MappableFunctorInstance` using `Mappable.functor()` (which is how we can use `Option.monad()`).

Another alternative is to let Arrow-derived instances automatically provided that your datatypes have the right functions:

```
import arrow.deriving

@higherkind
@deriving(Functor::class)
class DerivedMappable<T>(val t: T) : DerivedMappableKind<T> {
    fun <R> map(f: (T) -> R): DerivedMappable<R> = DerivedMappable(f(t))

    override fun toString(): String = "DerivedMappable(t=$t)"

    companion object
}
```

The `@deriving` annotation will generate `DerivedMappableFunctorInstance` that normally you will write manually.

Now, we can create a generic function to use our `Mappable` functor:

```
import arrow.typeclasses.functor

inline fun <reified F> buildBicycle(mapper: HK<F, Int>,
                    noinline f: (Int) -> Bicycle,
                    FR: Functor<F> = functor()): HK<F, Bicycle> =
FR.map(mapper, f)
```

The `buildBicycle` function will take as parameter any `HK<F, Int>` and apply the function `f` using its `Functor` implementation, returned by the function `arrow.typeclasses.functor` and returns `HK<F, Bicycle>`.

The function `arrow.typeclass.functor` resolves at runtime, instances that adhere to the `Functor<MappableHK>` requirement:

```
fun main(args: Array<String>) {

    val mappable: Mappable<Bicycle> = buildBicycle(Mappable(3),
::Bicycle).ev()
    println("mappable = $mappable") //Mappable(t=Bicycle(gears=3))
```

```
val option: Option<Bicycle> = buildBicycle(Some(2), ::Bicycle).ev()
println("option = $option") //Some(Bicycle(gears=2))

val none: Option<Bicycle> = buildBicycle(None, ::Bicycle).ev()
println("none = $none") //None

}
```

We can use buildBicycle with Mappeable<Int>, or any other HKT class such as Option<T>.

One problem with the Arrows approach to HKTs is that it must resolve its instances at runtime. This is because Kotlin does not have support for implicits or can solve type class instances at compile time, leaving Arrow with this only alternative until *KEEP-87* is approved and included in the language:

```
@higherkind
class NotAFunctor<T>(val t: T) : NotAFunctorKind<T> {
    fun <R> map(f: (T) -> R): NotAFunctor<R> = NotAFunctor(f(t))

    override fun toString(): String = "NotAFunctor(t=$t)"
}
```

So, you can have an HKT that has a map function but without an instance of Functor can't be used, yet isn't a compilation error:

```
fun main(args: Array<String>) {

    val not: NotAFunctor<Bicycle> = buildBicycle(NotAFunctor(4),
::Bicycle).ev()
    println("not = $not")

}
```

Calling buildBicycle with a NotAFunctor<T> function compiles, but it will throw a ClassNotFoundException exception at runtime.

Now that we understand how Arrow's hierarchy works, we can cover other classes.

Either

Either<L, R> is a representation of one of two possible values L or R, but not both at the same time. Either is a sealed class (similar to Option) with two subtypes Left<L> and Right<R>. Usually Either is used to represent results that can fail, using the left side to represent the error and the right side to represent a successful result. Because representing operations that can fail is a common scenario, Arrow's Either is right biased, in other words, unless it is documented otherwise all operations run on the right side.

Let's translate our division example from Option to Either:

```
import arrow.core.Either
import arrow.core.Either.Right
import arrow.core.Either.Left

fun eitherDivide(num: Int, den: Int): Either<String, Int> {
    val option = optionDivide(num, den)
    return when (option) {
        is Some -> Right(option.t)
        None -> Left("$num isn't divisible by $den")
    }
}
```

Now instead of returning a None value, we're returning valuable information to our user:

```
import arrow.core.Tuple2

fun eitherDivision(a: Int, b: Int, den: Int): Either<String, Tuple2<Int,
Int>> {
    val aDiv = eitherDivide(a, den)
    return when (aDiv) {
        is Right -> {
            val bDiv = eitherDivide(b, den)
            when (bDiv) {
                is Right -> Right(aDiv.getOrElse { 0 } toT bDiv.getOrElse { 0
})
                is Left -> bDiv as Either<String, Nothing>
            }
        }
        is Left -> aDiv as Either<String, Nothing>
    }
}
```

In eitherDivision, we're using Arrow's Tuple<A, B> instead of Kotlin's Pair<A, B>. Tuples provide more features than Pair/Triple, and from now on we'll use it. To create a Tuple2, you can use the extension infix function, toT.

Next, a short list of the `Either<L, R>` functions:

Function	Description
`bimap(fa:(L) -> T, fb:(R) -> X): Either<T, X>`	Transform using `fa` on `Left` and `fb` on `Right` to return `Either<T, X>`.
`contains(elem:R): Boolean`	Returns `true` if the `Right` value is the same as `elem` parameter, `false` for `Left`.
`exists(p:Predicate<R>):Boolean`	If `Right`, returns Predicate `p` result, always `false` for `Left`.
`flatMap(f: (R) -> Either<L, T>): Either<L, T>`	A `flatMap` function as in Monad, using the value of `Right`.
`fold(fa: (L) -> T, fb: (R) -> T): T`	Returns a `T` value executing `fa` for `Left` and `fb` for `Right`.
`getOrElse(default:(L) -> R): R`	Returns `Right` value, or results from the `default` function.
`isLeft(): Boolean`	Returns `true` if is an instance of `Left` and `false` for `Right`.
`isRight(): Boolean`	Returns `true` if is an instance of `Right` and `false` for `Left`.
`map(f: (R) -> T): Either<L, T>`	A `map` function as in `Functor`, if `Right`, uses function `f` to transform it to `Right<T>`, if `Left`, returns same value without transformation.
`mapLeft(f: (L) -> T): Either<T, R>`	A `map` function as in `Functor`, if `Left`, uses function `f` to transform it to `Left<T>`, if `Right`, returns same value without transformation.
`swap(): Either<R, L>`	Returns `Either` with its types and value swapped.
`toOption(): Option<R>`	`Some<T>` for `Right` and `None` for `Left`.

The `flatMap` version looks as expected:

```
fun flatMapEitherDivision(a: Int, b: Int, den: Int): Either<String,
Tuple2<Int, Int>> {
    return eitherDivide(a, den).flatMap { aDiv ->
        eitherDivide(b, den).flatMap { bDiv ->
            Right(aDiv toT bDiv)
        }
    }
}
```

`Either` has a monad implementation, so we can invoke the binding function:

```
fun comprehensionEitherDivision(a: Int, b: Int, den: Int): Either<String,
Tuple2<Int, Int>> {
    return Either.monad<String>().binding {
        val aDiv = eitherDivide(a, den).bind()
        val bDiv = eitherDivide(b, den).bind()

        aDiv toT bDiv
    }.ev()
```

Pay attention to `Either.monad<L>();` for `Either<L, R>` it must define the L type:

```
fun main(args: Array<String>) {
    eitherDivision(3, 2, 4).fold(::println, ::println) //3 isn't divisible
by 4
}
```

In our next section, we'll learn about monad transformers.

Monad transformers

`Either` and `Option` are simple to use, but what happens if we combine both?

```
object UserService {
    fun findAge(user: String): Either<String, Option<Int>> {
        //Magic
    }
}
```

`UserService.findAge` returns `Either<String, Option<Int>>`; `Left<String>` for errors accessing the database or any other infrastructure, `Right<None>` for no value found on the database, and `Right<Some<Int>>` for a value found:

```
import arrow.core.*
import arrow.syntax.function.pipe

fun main(args: Array<String>) {
 val anakinAge: Either<String, Option<Int>> = UserService.findAge("Anakin")

 anakinAge.fold(::identity, { op ->
        op.fold({ "Not found" }, Int::toString)
    }) pipe ::println
}
```

To print an age, we need two nested folds, nothing too complicated. Problems arrive when we need to do operations accessing multiple values:

```
import arrow.core.*
import arrow.syntax.function.pipe
import kotlin.math.absoluteValue

fun main(args: Array<String>) {
    val anakinAge: Either<String, Option<Int>> =
UserService.findAge("Anakin")
    val padmeAge: Either<String, Option<Int>> = UserService.findAge("Padme")

    val difference: Either<String, Option<Either<String, Option<Int>>>> =
anakinAge.map { aOp ->
        aOp.map { a ->
           padmeAge.map { pOp ->
              pOp.map { p ->
                 (a - p).absoluteValue
              }
           }
        }
    }

    difference.fold(::identity, { op1 ->
       op1.fold({ "Not Found" }, { either ->
          either.fold(::identity, { op2 ->
             op2.fold({ "Not Found" }, Int::toString) })
       })
    }) pipe ::println
}
```

Monads don't compose, making these operations grow in complexity, very quickly. But, we can always count on comprehensions, can't we? Now, let's look at the following codes:

```
import arrow.core.*
import arrow.syntax.function.pipe
import arrow.typeclasses.binding
import kotlin.math.absoluteValue


fun main(args: Array<String>) {
    val anakinAge: Either<String, Option<Int>> =
UserService.findAge("Anakin")
    val padmeAge: Either<String, Option<Int>> = UserService.findAge("Padme")

    val difference: Either<String, Option<Option<Int>>> =
Either.monad<String>().binding {
        val aOp: Option<Int> = anakinAge.bind()
        val pOp: Option<Int> = padmeAge.bind()
        aOp.map { a ->
           pOp.map { p ->
              (a - p).absoluteValue
           }
        }
    }.ev()

    difference.fold(::identity, { op1 ->
        op1.fold({ "Not found" }, { op2 ->
           op2.fold({ "Not found" }, Int::toString) }) }) pipe ::println
}
```

This is better, the returning type is not that long, and `fold` is more manageable. Let's take a look at the nested comprehensions in the following code snippet:

```
fun main(args: Array<String>) {
    val anakinAge: Either<String, Option<Int>> =
UserService.findAge("Anakin")
    val padmeAge: Either<String, Option<Int>> =
UserService.findAge("Padme")

    val difference: Either<String, Option<Int>> =
Either.monad<String>().binding {
        val aOp: Option<Int> = anakinAge.bind()
        val pOp: Option<Int> = padmeAge.bind()
        Option.monad().binding {
           val a: Int = aOp.bind()
           val p: Int = pOp.bind()
           (a - p).absoluteValue
```

```
        }.ev()
    }.ev()

    difference.fold(::identity, { op ->
        op.fold({ "Not found" }, Int::toString)
    }) pipe ::println
}
```

Now, we have the same type of both values and result. But we still have another option, monad transformers.

A **monad transformer** is a combination of two monads that can be executed as one. For our example, we will use `OptionT`, (shorthand for **Option Transformer**) as `Option` is the monad type that is nested inside `Either`:

```
import arrow.core.*
import arrow.data.OptionT
import arrow.data.monad
import arrow.data.value
import arrow.syntax.function.pipe
import arrow.typeclasses.binding
import kotlin.math.absoluteValue


fun main(args: Array<String>) {
    val anakinAge: Either<String, Option<Int>> =
UserService.findAge("Anakin")
    val padmeAge: Either<String, Option<Int>> = UserService.findAge("Padme")

    val difference: Either<String, Option<Int>> =
OptionT.monad<EitherKindPartial<String>>().binding {
        val a: Int = OptionT(anakinAge).bind()
        val p: Int = OptionT(padmeAge).bind()
        (a - p).absoluteValue
    }.value().ev()

    difference.fold(::identity, { op ->
        op.fold({ "Not found" }, Int::toString)
    }) pipe ::println
}
```

We use `OptionT.monad<EitherKindPartial<String>>().binding`.
The `EitherKindPartial<String>` monad means that the wrapper type is an
`Either<String, Option<T>>`.

Inside the `binding` block, we use `OptionT` on values of type `Either<String,` `Option<T>>` (technically on values of type `HK<HK<EitherHK, String>, Option<T>>`) to call `bind()`: `T`, in our case `T`, is `Int`.

Previously we used just the `ev()` method, but now we need to use the `value()` method to extract the `OptionT` internal value.

In our next section, we'll learn about the `Try` type.

Try

Try is a representation of a computation that may or may not fail. `Try<A>` is a sealed class with two possibles sub-classes—`Failure<A>`, representing a fail and `Success<T>` representing a successful operation.

Let's write our division example with `Try`:

```
import arrow.data.Try

fun tryDivide(num: Int, den: Int): Try<Int> = Try { divide(num, den)!! }
```

The easiest way to create a `Try` instance is to use the `Try.invoke` operator. If the block inside throws an exception, it will return `Failure`; if everything goes well, `Success<Int>`, for example, the `!!` operator will throw `NPE` if divide returns a null:

```
fun tryDivision(a: Int, b: Int, den: Int): Try<Tuple2<Int, Int>> {
    val aDiv = tryDivide(a, den)
    return when (aDiv) {
        is Success -> {
            val bDiv = tryDivide(b, den)
            when (bDiv) {
                is Success -> {
                    Try { aDiv.value toT bDiv.value }
                }
                is Failure -> Failure(bDiv.exception)
            }
        }
        is Failure -> Failure(aDiv.exception)
    }
}
```

Let's take a look at a short list of the `Try<T>` functions:

Function	Description
`exists(p: Predicate<T>): Boolean`	If `Success<T>` returns p result, on `Failure` always return `false`.
`filter(p: Predicate<T>): Try<T>`	Returns `Success<T>` if operation is successful and pass predicate p, otherwise `Failure`.
`<R> flatMap(f: (T) -> Try<R>): Try<R>`	`flatMap` function as in monad.
`<R> fold(fa: (Throwable) -> R, fb:(T) -> R): R`	Returns value transformed as R, invoking fa if `Failure`.
`getOrDefault(default: () -> T): T`	Returns value T, invoking default if `Failure`.
`getOrElse(default: (Throwable) -> T): T`	Returns value T, invoking default if `Failure`.
`isFailure(): Boolean`	Returns `true` if `Failure`, otherwise `false`.
`isSuccess(): Boolean`	Returns `true` if `Success`, otherwise `false`.
`<R> map(f: (T) -> R): Try<R>`	Transforming function as in functor.
`onFailure(f: (Throwable) -> Unit): Try<T>`	Act on `Failure`.
`onSuccess(f: (T) -> Unit): Try<T>`	Act on `Success`.
`orElse(f: () -> Try<T>): Try<T>`	Returns itself on `Success` or f result on `Failure`.
`recover(f: (Throwable) -> T): Try<T>`	Transform `map` function for `Failure`.
`recoverWith(f: (Throwable) -> Try<T>): Try<T>`	Transform `flatMap` function for `Failure`.
`toEither() : Either<Throwable, T>`	Transform into `Either`—`Failure` to `Left<Throwable>` and `Success<T>` to `Right<T>`.

`toOption(): Option<T>`	Transform into `Option`—`Failure` to `None` and `Success<T>` to `Some<T>`.

The `flatMap` implementation is very similar to `Either` and `Option` and shows the value of having a common set of name and behavior conventions:

```
fun flatMapTryDivision(a: Int, b: Int, den: Int): Try<Tuple2<Int, Int>> {
    return tryDivide(a, den).flatMap { aDiv ->
        tryDivide(b, den).flatMap { bDiv ->
            Try { aDiv toT bDiv }
        }
    }
}
```

Monadic comprehensions are available for `Try` too:

```
fun comprehensionTryDivision(a: Int, b: Int, den: Int): Try<Tuple2<Int, Int>> {
    return Try.monad().binding {
        val aDiv = tryDivide(a, den).bind()
        val bDiv = tryDivide(b, den).bind()
        aDiv toT bDiv
    }.ev()
}
```

There is another kind of monadic comprehension using an instance of `MonadError`:

```
fun monadErrorTryDivision(a: Int, b: Int, den: Int): Try<Tuple2<Int, Int>>
{
    return Try.monadError().bindingCatch {
        val aDiv = divide(a, den)!!
        val bDiv = divide(b, den)!!
        aDiv toT bDiv
    }.ev()
}
```

With `monadError.bindingCatch` any operation that throws an exception is lifted to `Failure`, at the end the returns is wrapped into `Try<T>`. `MonadError` is also available for `Option` and `Either`.

State

State is a structure that provides a functional approach for handling application state. `State<S, A>` is an abstraction over `S -> Tuple2<S, A>`. **S** represents the state type, and `Tuple2<S, A>` is the result, with `S` for the newly updated state and `A` for the function return.

We can start with a simple example, a function that returns two things, a price and the steps to calculate it. To calculate a price, we need to add `VAT` of 20% and apply a discount if the `price` value goes above some threshold:

```
import arrow.core.Tuple2
import arrow.core.toT
import arrow.data.State

typealias PriceLog = MutableList<Tuple2<String, Double>>

fun addVat(): State<PriceLog, Unit> = State { log: PriceLog ->
    val (_, price) = log.last()
    val vat = price * 0.2
    log.add("Add VAT: $vat" toT price + vat)
    log toT Unit
}
```

We have a type alias `PriceLog` for `MutableList<Tuple2<String, Double>>`. `PriceLog` will be our `State` representation; each step represented with `Tuple2<String, Double>`.

Our first function, `addVat(): State<PriceLog, Unit>` represents the first step. We write the function using a `State` builder that receives `PriceLog`, the state before applying any step and must return a `Tuple2<PriceLog, Unit>`, we use `Unit` because we don't need the price at this point:

```
fun applyDiscount(threshold: Double, discount: Double): State<PriceLog,
Unit> = State { log ->
    val (_, price) = log.last()
    if (price > threshold) {
        log.add("Applying -$discount" toT price - discount)
    } else {
        log.add("No discount applied" toT price)
    }
    log toT Unit
}
```

The `applyDiscount` function is our second step. The only new element that we introduce here are two parameters, one for `threshold` and the other for `discount`:

```
fun finalPrice(): State<PriceLog, Double> = State { log ->
    val (_, price) = log.last()
    log.add("Final Price" toT price)
    log toT price
}
```

The last step is represented by the function `finalPrice()`, and now we return `Double` instead of `Unit`:

```
import arrow.data.ev
import arrow.instances.monad
import arrow.typeclasses.binding

fun calculatePrice(threshold: Double, discount: Double) =
State().monad<PriceLog>().binding {
    addVat().bind() //Unit
    applyDiscount(threshold, discount).bind() //Unit
    val price: Double = finalPrice().bind()
    price
}.ev()
```

To represent the sequence of steps, we use a monad comprehension and use the `State` functions sequentially. From one function to the next one, the `PriceLog` state is flowing implicitly (is just some coroutine continuations magic). At the end, we yield the final price. Adding new steps or switching existing ones is as easy as adding or moving lines:

```
import arrow.data.run
import arrow.data.runA

fun main(args: Array<String>) {
    val (history: PriceLog, price: Double) = calculatePrice(100.0,
2.0).run(mutableListOf("Init" toT 15.0))
    println("Price: $price")
    println("::History::")
    history
            .map { (text, value) -> "$text\t|\t$value" }
            .forEach(::println)

    val bigPrice: Double = calculatePrice(100.0,
2.0).runA(mutableListOf("Init" toT 1000.0))
    println("bigPrice = $bigPrice")
}
```

To use the `calculatePrice` function, you must provide the threshold and discount values and then invoke the extension function `run` with an initial state. If you're interested just in the price, you can use `runA` or for just the history, `runS`.

> Avoid problems using `State`. Don't confuse the extension function `arrow.data.run` with the extension function, `kotlin.run` (imported by default).

Corecursion with State

`State` is beneficial on corecursion; we can rewrite our old examples with `State`:

```
fun <T, S> unfold(s: S, f: (S) -> Pair<T, S>?): Sequence<T> {
    val result = f(s)
    return if (result != null) {
        sequenceOf(result.first) + unfold(result.second, f)
    } else {
        sequenceOf()
    }
}
```

Our original `unfold` function use a function, `f: (S) -> Pair<T,S>?` which is very similar to `State<S, T>`:

```
fun <T, S> unfold(s: S, state: State<S, Option<T>>): Sequence<T> {
    val (actualState: S, value: Option<T>) = state.run(s)
    return value.fold(
            { sequenceOf() },
            { t ->
                sequenceOf(t) + unfold(actualState, state)
            })
}
```

Instead of having a lambda `(S) -> Pair<T, S>?`, we use `State<S, Option<T>>` and we use the function fold from `Option`, with an empty `Sequence` for `None` or a recursive call for `Some<T>`:

```
fun factorial(size: Int): Sequence<Long> {
    return sequenceOf(1L) + unfold(1L to 1) { (acc, n) ->
        if (size > n) {
            val x = n * acc
            (x) to (x to n + 1)
        } else
```

```
            null
    }
}
```

Our old factorial function uses `unfold` with `Pair<Long, Int>` and a
lambda—`(Pair<Long, Int>) -> Pair<Long, Pair<Long, Int>>?`:

```
import arrow.syntax.option.some

fun factorial(size: Int): Sequence<Long> {
    return sequenceOf(1L) + unfold(1L toT 1, State { (acc, n) ->
        if (size > n) {
            val x = n * acc
            (x toT n + 1) toT x.some()
        } else {
            (0L toT 0) toT None
        }
    })
}
```

The refactored factorial uses `State<Tuple<Long, Int>, Option<Long>>` but internal
logic is almost the same, although our new factorial doesn't use null, which is a significant
improvement:

```
fun fib(size: Int): Sequence<Long> {
    return sequenceOf(1L) + unfold(Triple(0L, 1L, 1)) { (cur, next, n) ->
        if (size > n) {
            val x = cur + next
            (x) to Triple(next, x, n + 1)
        }
        else
            null
    }
}
```

Similarly, `fib` uses unfold with `Triple<Long, Long, Int>` and a lambda
`(Triple<Long, Long. Int>) -> Pair<Long, Triple<Long, Long, Int>>?`:

```
import arrow.syntax.tuples.plus

fun fib(size: Int): Sequence<Long> {
    return sequenceOf(1L) + unfold((0L toT 1L) + 1, State { (cur, next, n)
->
        if (size > n) {
            val x = cur + next
            ((next toT x) + (n + 1)) toT x.some()
        } else {
```

```
            ((0L toT 0L) + 0) toT None
        }
    })
}
```

And the refactored `fib` uses `State<Tuple3<Long, Long, Int>, Option<Long>>`. Pay close attention to the extension operator function `plus`, used with `Tuple2<A, B>` and `C` will return `Tuple3<A, B, C>`:

```
fun main(args: Array<String>) {
    factorial(10).forEach(::println)
    fib(10).forEach(::println)
}
```

And now, we can use our corecursive functions to generate sequences. There are many other uses for `State` that we can't cover here, such as *Message History* from *Enterprise Integration Patterns* (`http://www.enterpriseintegrationpatterns.com/patterns/messaging/MessageHistory.html`) or navigation on forms with multiple steps such as plane checking or long registration forms.

Summary

Arrow provides many datatypes and type classes that reduce significantly complex tasks and provide a standard set of idioms and expressions. In this chapter, we learned how to abstract over null values with `Option` and to express computations with `Either` and `Try`. We created a datatype class, and we also learned about monadic comprehensions and transformations. Last but not least, we used `State` to represent the application state.

And with this chapter, we reach the final of this journey, but rest assured, this isn't the end of your journey learning functional programming. As we learned in the first chapters, functional programming is all about using functions as building blocks to create complex programs. In the same way, with all the concepts that you learn here, now you can understand and master new, exciting and more powerful ideas.

Now a new learning journey begins for you.

Kotlin's Quick Start

This book is intended for people that are already familiar with the way Kotlin works. But if you are completely new to the language, worry not, we have you covered with everything that you need to read, understand, and take full advantage of this book.

In this appendix, we'll cover the following topics:

- Different ways to use Kotlin
- Basic Kotlin control structures
- Other resources

Writing and running Kotlin

We'll cover a comprehensive set of options to write and run Kotlin, from the easiest to the most professional.

Kotlin online

Nothing to install, just open Kotlin (`https://try.kotlinlang.org/`). Kotlin online includes everything that you need to write and run simple Koltin programs, including JVM and JavaScript compilation options. You can even create and save your programs if you have an account:

On your console

For anything serious and destined to be in production code, the online option isn't optimal. Let's explore how to install it on your machine.

Installing SDKMAN

The most accessible option to install Kotlin is to use SDKMAN, a tool used to install and update JVM tools.

Use the following command to install SDKMAN (if you don't have it installed):

```
$ curl -s "https://get.sdkman.io" | bash
```

Once SDKMAN is installed, we can use it to install Kotlin and keep it updated, among other tools such as Gradle and Maven.

Installing Kotlin through SDKMAN

To install Kotlin through SDKMAN, you just need to type the following:

```
$ sdk install kotlin
```

Now we have Kotlin commands in our console.

Kotlin's REPL

To play with Kotlin's REPL, you can type the following:

```
$ kotlinc
```

Now you can type and execute Kotlin expressions:

```
$ kotlinc
Welcome to Kotlin version 1.2.21 (JRE 1.8.0_111-b14)
Type :help for help, :quit for quit
>>> println("Hello, World!")
Hello, World!
>>>
```

To exit Kotlin's REPL, you can type `:quit`

Compiling and executing Kotlin files

There are several editors that support Kotlin—Micro, Vim, NeoVim, Atom, and VS Code.

My go-to-use editor is Micro, (`https://micro-editor.github.io/index.html`). It is a fast and easy-to-use editor (sort of an over-powered Nano):

In your favourite editor, create a file named `hello.kt` and type the following code:

```
fun main(args: Array<String>) {
    println("Hello, World!")
}
```

Now in your console, compile your program with this:

```
$ kotlinc hello.kt
```

To execute it, type this in your console:

```
$ kotlin HelloKt
```

Using Gradle

For any project that goes beyond a couple of files, a build tool becomes a necessity. A build tool offers you a pragmatic way to compile, manage libraries, and package and execute applications. Gradle (`https://docs.gradle.org/current/release-notes.html`) is a build tool that supports many languages, including Kotlin.

Install Gradle through SDKMAN

To install Gradle through SDKMAN, you just need type the following:

```
sdk install gradle
```

Now we have the `gradle` command available in our console.

Creating a distributable Gradle command

Although Gradle is a great tool, it isn't easy to share code that depends on Gradle to be built. The potential users of our open source project may not have installed Gradle or even the same Gradle version as we have. Luckily for us, Gradle provides a way to create a distributable Gradle utility or command.

In a new, clean directory, type this in your console:

```
$ gradle wrapper
```

This command creates a `gradlew` script that can be executed. The first time that you run the command, it downloads all the necessary Gradle files and then it becomes a repeatable command.

Creating a Gradle project file

For Gradle to work, we must have a `build.gradle` file. In this file, we'll set different options and settings for Gradle to use and run.

For our basic `Hello World` program, our file must look like this:

```
group 'com.packtpub'
version '1.0'

buildscript {
    ext.kotlin_version = '1.2.21'

    repositories {
        mavenCentral()
    }
    dependencies {
        classpath "org.jetbrains.kotlin:kotlin-gradle-
plugin:$kotlin_version"
    }
}

apply plugin: 'kotlin'
apply plugin: 'application'

mainClassName = 'com.packtpub.appendix.HelloKt'

defaultTasks 'run'

repositories {
    mavenCentral()
}

dependencies {
    compile "org.jetbrains.kotlin:kotlin-stdlib-jdk8:$kotlin_version"
}

compileKotlin {
    kotlinOptions.jvmTarget = "1.8"
}

compileTestKotlin {
    kotlinOptions.jvmTarget = "1.8"
}
```

Typically, in a `build.gradle` file we define some plugins (Gradle plugins define support for languages and frameworks), repositories to download dependencies, the dependencies themselves, and other options.

In this file we define two plugins—one for Kotlin and other to define our project as an application with a starter point or main class.

Creating our Hello World code

The default position where Gradle searches for Kotlin files is in the `src/main/kotlin` directory. We'll place our `hello.kt` file in the `src/main/kotlin/com/packtpub/appendix` directory:

```
package com.packtpub.appendix

fun main(args: Array<String>) {
    println("Hello, World!")
}
```

And now we can compile and run in one go with the following command:

```
$ ./gradlew
```

As we defined that our default task is `run` and our main class is `com.packtpub.appendix.HelloKt`, just by running `./gradlew` we can build and run our peogram.

Using IntelliJ IDEA or Android Studio

IntelliJ IDEA and Android Studio (which is based on the open source version of IntelliJ IDEA) are fantastic IDEs for Kotlin (and other languages, such as Java, Scala, Groovy, and others). Both offer autocomplete, formatting and support for Gradle and Maven.

Both IDEs are very well documented, and you can read more about Kotlin support on their websites:

- IntelliJ IDEA (`http://kotlinlang.org/docs/tutorials/getting-started.html`)
- Android Studio (`https://developer.android.com/kotlin/get-started.html`)

Importing Gradle files with IntelliJ IDEA

We can import our Gradle project inside IntelliJ IDEA. Once we start IDEA, we can open our `build.gradle` file:

A dialog will appear that will ask whether you want to open it as a file or as a project. Click on **Open As Project**:

If you have a JDK installed and set it on IntelliJ IDEA, you just need to click **OK**. If you don't have a JDK configured, then do it (IntelliJ IDEA will guide you through) and then continue with **OK**:

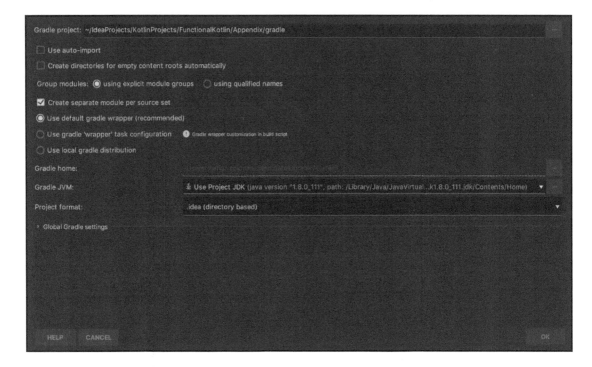

Now we can edit and work on our project using all the IntelliJ IDEA features:

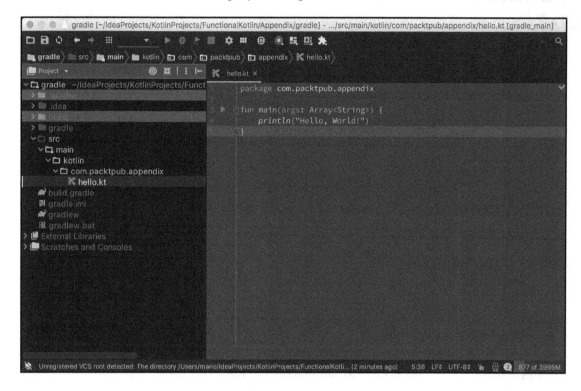

You can open all the example code from this book in the same way.

Basic Kotlin syntax

Kotlin syntax will look familiar to developers with experience of other languages based on C style syntax, such as C, Java, Scala, Groovy, and TypeScript.

General features

Various Kotlin features are common among other JVM Languages. If you have experience of Java, you'll feel at home with Kotlin.

Packages

Packages are sets of files (usually defined in the same directory) that define logic units, for example, controllers, and repositories.

To set a file in a particular package, use the `package` keyword in the first line:

```
package com.packt.functionalkotlin
```

Ideally, a file inside the package `com.packt.functionalkotlin` should be in the directory `com/packt/functionalkotlin`. It makes files easier to find but isn't mandatory in Kotlin.

String concatenation and interpolation

String concatenation in Kotlin uses the plus (+) operator:

```
val temperature = 12

println("Current temperature: " + temperature + " Celsius degrees")
```

String interpolation is an easy way to do complex concatenations:

```
val temperature = 12

println("Current temperature: $temperature Celsius degrees")
```

Using the symbol dollar ($) lets you use simple values inside a string:

```
val temperature = 12

println("Temperature for tonight: ${temperature - 4} Celsius degrees")
```

For anything more complex than just using values, you can use a dollar symbol with braces (`${... }`):

Comments

Single-line comments use a double slash (//):

```
// This is a single line comment

println("Hello, World!") // This is a single line comment too, after valid
code
```

Block comments use a slash and asterisk to open the block (/*) and an asterisk and slash to close (*/):

```
/*
This is a multi-line comment,
Roses are red
... and I forgot the rest

*/

println(/*block comments can be inside valid code*/ "Hello, World!")
```

Control structures

There are four basic control structures in Kotlin—if, when, for, and while.

if expression

if in Kotlin looks exactly like any other C-style language:

```
if (2 > 1) { //Boolean expression
    println("2 is greater than 1")
} else {
    println("This never gonna happen")
}
```

In Kotlin, if (and when) is an expression. It means that the if statement returns a value:

```
val message = if (2 > 1) {
    "2 is greater than 1"
} else {
    "This never gonna happen"
}

println(message)
```

Kotlin doesn't have ternary expressions, but an if expression can be written in a single line:

```
println(if(2 > 1) "2 is greater than 1" else "This never gonna happen")
```

when expression

Unlike other C-style languages, Kotlin doesn't have a `switch` statement, but a `when` expression that is a lot more flexible:

```
val x: Int = /*Some unknown value here*/

when (x) {
    0 -> println("x is zero")
    1, 2 -> println("x is 1 or 2")
    in 3..5 -> println("x is between 3 and 5")
    else -> println("x is bigger than 5... or maybe is negative...")
}
```

`when` are expressions:

```
val message = when {
    2 > 1 -> "2 is greater than 1"
    else -> "This never gonna happen"
}

println(message)
```

And they also can be used to replace `if` expression:

for loop

`for` loops can iterate over anything that provides an iterator (for example, collections and ranges):

```
for(i in 1..10) { // range
    println("i = $i")
}
```

while and do loops

`while` and `do` loops are standard C-style loops:

```
var i = 1

while (i <= 10) {
    println("i = $i")
    i++
}
```

```
do {
    i--
    println("i = $i")
} while (i > 0)
```

Now that you have all the basic pieces you have everything that you need to read and understand the contents of this book.

Going further

If you want to advance your Kotlin knowledge and understanding, the best way to go forward is to try the Kotlin Koans.

Kotlin Koans is a tutorial that will lead you step by step from a rookie to a very competent Kotlin programmer in a few days, and even better, it's free.

You can try Kotlin Koans at `https://try.kotlinlang.org/#/Kotlin%20Koans/ Introduction/Hello,%20world!/Task.kt`:

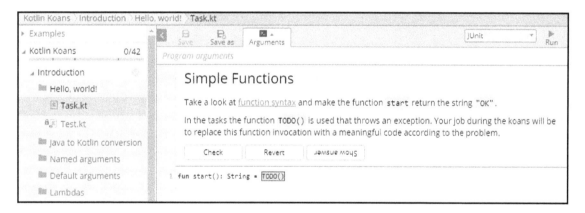

Other Books You May Enjoy

If you enjoyed this book, you may be interested in these other books by Packt:

Mastering Android Development with Kotlin
Milos Vasic

ISBN: 978-1-78847-369-9

- Understand the basics of Android development with Kotlin
- Get to know the key concepts in Android development
- See how to create modern mobile applications for the Android platform
- Adjust your application's look and feel
- Know how to persist and share application database
- Work with Services and other concurrency mechanisms
- Write effective tests
- Migrate an existing Java-based project to Kotlin

Reactive Programming in Kotlin
Rivu Chakraborty

ISBN: 978-1-78847-302-6

- Learn about reactive programming paradigms and how reactive programming can improve your existing projects
- Gain in-depth knowledge in RxKotlin 2.0 and the ReactiveX Framework
- Use RxKotlin with Android
- Create your own custom operators in RxKotlin
- Use Spring Framework 5.0 with Kotlin
- Use the reactor-kotlin extension
- Build Rest APIs with Spring,Hibernate, and RxKotlin
- Use testSubscriber to test RxKotlin applications
- Use backpressure management and Flowables

Leave a review - let other readers know what you think

Please share your thoughts on this book with others by leaving a review on the site that you bought it from. If you purchased the book from Amazon, please leave us an honest review on this book's Amazon page. This is vital so that other potential readers can see and use your unbiased opinion to make purchasing decisions, we can understand what our customers think about our products, and our authors can see your feedback on the title that they have worked with Packt to create. It will only take a few minutes of your time, but is valuable to other potential customers, our authors, and Packt. Thank you!

Index

www.ingramcontent.com/pod-product-compliance
Lightning Source LLC
Chambersburg PA
CBHW080617060326
40690CB00021B/4731